T0248159

Bring Judgment Day

Known worldwide as Lead Belly, Huddie Ledbetter (1889–1949) is an American icon whose influence on modern music was tremendous – as was, according to legend, the temper that landed him in two of the South's most brutal prisons, while his immense talent twice won him pardons. But, as this deeply researched book shows, these stories were shaped by the white folklorists who "discovered" Lead Belly and, along with reporters, recording executives, and radio and film producers, introduced him to audiences beyond the South. Through a revelatory examination of arrest, trial, and prison records; sharecropping reports; oral histories; newspaper articles; and more, author Sheila Curran Bernard replaces myth with fact, offering a stunning indictment of systemic racism in the Jim Crow era of the United States and the power of narrative to erase and distort the past.

SHEILA CURRAN BERNARD is an Emmy and Peabody Award-winning filmmaker, author, and educator. The recipient of an NEH Public Scholars award, Bernard is an associate professor in the Department of History at the University at Albany, State University of New York.

BRING JUDGMENT DAY
RECLAIMING LEAD BELLY'S TRUTHS FROM JIM CROW'S LIES

Sheila Curran Bernard

CAMBRIDGE
UNIVERSITY PRESS

Shaftesbury Road, Cambridge CB2 8EA, United Kingdom

One Liberty Plaza, 20th Floor, New York, NY 10006, USA

477 Williamstown Road, Port Melbourne, VIC 3207, Australia

314–321, 3rd Floor, Plot 3, Splendor Forum, Jasola District Centre,
New Delhi – 110025, India

103 Penang Road, #05–06/07, Visioncrest Commercial, Singapore 238467

Cambridge University Press is part of Cambridge University Press & Assessment,
a department of the University of Cambridge.

We share the University's mission to contribute to society through the pursuit of
education, learning and research at the highest international levels of excellence.

www.cambridge.org
Information on this title: www.cambridge.org/9781009098120

DOI: 10.1017/9781009103619

First published 2024

Printed in the United Kingdom by TJ Books Limited, Padstow Cornwall

A catalogue record for this publication is available from the British Library

Library of Congress Cataloging-in-Publication Data
Names: Bernard, Sheila Curran, author.
Title: Bring judgment day : reclaiming Lead Belly's truths from Jim Crow's lies /
Sheila Curran Bernard.
Description: [First edition]. | New York : Cambridge University Press, 2024. |
Includes bibliographical references and index.
Identifiers: LCCN 2023051800 | ISBN 9781009098120 (hardback) | ISBN
9781009107990 (paperback) | ISBN 9781009103619 (ebook)
Subjects: LCSH: Leadbelly, 1885–1949. | Leadbelly, 1885–1949 – Trials, litigation,
etc. | Blues musicians – United States – Biography. | Lomax, John A. (John Avery),
1867–1948. | Lomax, Alan, 1915–2002. | African Americans – Legal status, laws, etc.
| Racism in criminal justice administration – United States.
Classification: LCC ML420.L277 B4 2024 | DDC 782.421643092 [B]–dc23/eng/
20231201
LC record available at https://lccn.loc.gov/2023051800

ISBN 978-1-009-09812-0 Hardback

Cambridge University Press & Assessment has no responsibility for the persistence
or accuracy of URLs for external or third-party internet websites referred to in this
publication and does not guarantee that any content on such websites is, or will remain,
accurate or appropriate.

Go down, ol' Hannah,
Don't you rise no more,
And if you rise in the morning,
Bring Judgment Day.

Huddie Ledbetter

For librarians, archivists, and others who preserve and make accessible the records of the past,

and in memory of Judge Joni Tidwell Haldeman of DeKalb, Texas.

Contents

Figures

Note on the Text

Throughout his life, Huddie Ledbetter (with Huddie pronounced somewhere between "muddy" and "hoody") signed his personal letters and referred to himself with his given name, Huddie Ledbetter, rather than what was almost certainly a prison moniker, "Lead Belly." His wife, family members, and friends called him "Huddie"; in interviews, some of his New York City musician friends referred to him as "Led." To Ledbetter, "Lead Belly" was a stage name, and he spelled it with two words. That is the convention used in this book, except when quoting print sources that merged the two as "Leadbelly."

I have chosen not to spell out the N-word even when it is included in historical documents. The harmful intent is clear; there is no need to replicate it. I left intact, for historical purposes, the offensive dialect and stereotypes used at times by the Lomaxes and others, and I regret any distress this may cause. In addition, there may be misspellings, typos, or inconsistent capitalization in these sources, which I have generally chosen not to point out. In quoting from unpublished oral histories conducted in the 1950s and after, I've modified the transcriber's attempts to convey accented speech. Except as quoted in published material, Black is capitalized, but not white, in line with current guidelines of the *Columbia Journalism Review*.

I acknowledge that much of this history, and the ways in which sources describe it, is shocking and difficult to read. It is not my intent to cause further harm, but to illuminate a past that remains deeply relevant to the present.

Chronology

1863   President Lincoln issues Emancipation Proclamation, declaring as free the enslaved people in states still in rebellion.

1865   January: Congress passes the 13th Amendment to the US Constitution.

        April: Confederate general Robert E. Lee surrenders to Union general Ulysses S. Grant, beginning the process of ending the US Civil War.

1867   John A. Lomax is born in Goodman, Mississippi. Two years later, the family relocates to Texas, purchasing 183 acres of land in Bosque County.

1877   The era of post-war Reconstruction ends as federal troops are withdrawn from the South.

1889   Huddie Ledbetter is born near Mooringsport, Louisiana. Within five years, his family relocates to Texas, purchasing 68.5 acres of land in Harrison County.

1915   Alan Lomax is born.

        Ledbetter is arrested in Harrison County and sentenced to a county chain gang.

1917   Using the alias "Walter Boyd," Ledbetter is arrested in Bowie County, Texas and convicted of murder and attempted murder. He serves time at Shaw State Prison Farm outside DeKalb, Texas, and at the Imperial State Prison Farm in Sugar Land, Texas.

1925   January: Ledbetter is pardoned by outgoing Texas governor Pat M. Neff.

1930	Ledbetter is arrested in Mooringsport and convicted of assault with attempt to murder. He is sent to the Louisiana State Penitentiary at Angola.
1933	July: John and Alan Lomax meet Ledbetter while recording at Angola.
1934	July: The Lomaxes return to Angola and record again with Ledbetter.
	August 1: Ledbetter is released.
	September 26: Lomax "hires" Ledbetter as an assistant.
	December 28: Lomax introduces Ledbetter at the Modern Language Association gathering in Philadelphia.
1935	The Lomaxes and Ledbetter arrive in New York to a storm of publicity. They settle in Wilton, Connecticut to work on *Negro Folk Songs as Sung by Lead Belly* and launch a northern performing tour. Martha Promise marries Huddie Ledbetter.
	March 26: Martha and Huddie Ledbetter return to Shreveport, Louisiana.
1936	February: The Ledbetters return to New York City and remain there.
	November: *Negro Folk Songs as Sung by Lead Belly* is published by Macmillan.
1948	John A. Lomax dies, age eighty.
1949	Huddie Ledbetter dies, age sixty.
1968	Martha Ledbetter dies, age sixty-eight. The Ledbetter estate passes to Martha's niece, Queen ("Tiny") Robinson.
2002	Alan Lomax dies, age eighty-seven.

Introduction

Many years ago, I spent some time helping to develop a documentary film about the life and legend of Huddie Ledbetter, better known as Lead Belly (1889–1949). An African American musician born in Louisiana, Ledbetter found fame but not fortune among New York City's folk music and labor movements in the 1930s and 1940s. Among some 200 songs he recorded, he is perhaps best known for "Goodnight, Irene," "In the Pines," "Midnight Special," and "Rock Island Line," music popularized in the years after his death by a wide range of artists including Frank Sinatra, Odetta, Robert Plant, and Kurt Cobain. As sometimes happens, that documentary did not end up being produced. More recently, in 2010, I was hired to write a feature documentary for PBS based on Douglas A. Blackmon's Pulitzer Prize-winning *Slavery by Another Name* (Anchor Books, 2008). Immersing myself in this history of convict leasing and other forms of forced labor in the US South in the decades between the end of the Civil War and World War II, I kept thinking back to Huddie Ledbetter, incarcerated in both Texas and Louisiana in the years between 1915 and 1934. His first conviction, I remembered, was for "carrying a pistol," a charge that I now understood might be one of the vague charges levied against African Americans, and rarely against whites, as a means of asserting white dominance while also securing a tightly controlled and virtually cost-free labor force in the industrializing South.[1]

Bring Judgment Day is structured around Ledbetter's interaction with two white men, folklorist John Lomax and his son, Alan Lomax, who met the performer in 1933 and later spent six months with him, from late September 1934 through late March 1935. The Lomaxes introduced Ledbetter to national audiences, and they were the first to publish an account of his life, *Negro Folk Songs as Sung by Lead Belly* (The Macmillan Company,

1936). The Lomax book, despite considerable inaccuracies, remains the main source of information about Ledbetter's early life, and it sets the tone for the portrait of "Lead Belly" that continues to the present day, emphasizing a career of violence and incarceration. Subtitled "KING OF THE TWELVE-STRING GUITAR PLAYERS OF THE WORLD, LONG-TIME CONVICT IN THE PENITENTIARIES OF TEXAS AND LOUISIANA," the Lomaxes' book is divided into two parts: Part I: The "Worldly N[–]" and Part II: The Sinful Songs. Part I, which runs to sixty-three pages, begins with a one-page chronology, followed by:

- "Lead Belly Tells His Story" (pages 3–28), which purports to tell the story of Ledbetter before he met the Lomaxes, primarily in Ledbetter's own words;
- "Finding Lead Belly" (pages 29–33), about their meeting in prison;
- "Traveling with Lead Belly" (pages 34–46), featuring Lead Belly's work with the Lomaxes from late September 1934 to the end of the year, as they toured southern prisons and Black communities in search of music; and
- "New York City and Wilton" (pages 47–64), about the events that followed after John Lomax arranged for Ledbetter to perform at the annual meeting of the Modern Language Association in Philadelphia, in December 1934, and the trio began to seek out academic and general audiences in the Northeast. The section drives to a split between John Lomax and Ledbetter, who returned to Louisiana in late March 1935.

Part II is a compilation of songs, with explanations from the Lomaxes and Ledbetter, with an emphasis on his prison repertoire.

The credibility accorded the early biography stems from the ways in which the authors, especially in the section titled "Lead Belly Tells His Story," presented Ledbetter's words as if they were a transcript of spoken, recorded speech, and therefore a reliable primary source. They used quotation marks and stereotyped dialect, such as "Yassuh, my papa he was a wuckah. I reckon I got it from him to be such a good wuckah in de penitenshuh," even as they acknowledged that "[s]ometimes Lead Belly spoke in dialect, sometimes he didn't."[2] They repeatedly emphasized the authenticity of this account. "In this book we present his life's story and some of our novel experiences with him," they wrote. "We print the story of his life before he met us, **told in his own words**, and we offer forty-nine of the songs he sang for us, together with the background of these songs, again, in many instances, in Lead Belly's vernacular."[3] (Emphasis added.) Reviewers and scholars, when the book was published, and in the decades since, have therefore relied upon the Lomax book as a credible primary source. This includes Kip Lornell and Charles Wolfe (*The Life and Legend of Leadbelly*, Da Capo Press, 1992), who noted that the Lomaxes had "a chance to do something hardly anybody else in folk music research in that day had done: record a singer's total repertoire. Along the way, they would also record the singer's autobiography, and comment about his songs."[4] It also includes John Lomax's principal biographer, Nolan Porterfield (*Last Cavalier: The Life and Times of John A. Lomax*, University of Illinois Press, 1996), who credited the Lomaxes as the source of information for his own brief discussion of Ledbetter's early years.[5] More recently, Alan Lomax's biographer, John Szwed (*Alan Lomax: The Man Who Recorded the World*, Penguin Books, 2010), wrote: "[Ledbetter] was also interviewed while he was being recorded to create an oral auto-biography to be deposited in the Library of Congress."[6] Even the website for the Association for Cultural Equity, founded by Alan Lomax in 1983, suggests transcription.[7]

In fact, there is no transcript because there was no recording of an autobiography. In the first months of 1935, as they compiled the book, the Lomaxes recorded Ledbetter singing and at times speaking as he introduced or interrupted his songs to explain them, but the twelve-inch aluminum discs on which they recorded were expensive and scarce. In unpublished drafts of *Negro Folk Songs as Sung by Lead Belly*, part of a collection donated to the Library of Congress in 2004, the Lomaxes made this clear as they explained how they documented Ledbetter's story. (The "XXX" and crossed-out lines are in the original, and, although the excerpt ends mid-sentence, a follow-up page was not found in the archive.)

And here follows the story of the XXX "worldly n[-]" so far as we have been able to reconstruct it from his own reluctant, contradictory and intentionally confusing statements, from prison records, from a few scattering, brief and uninterested letters written by white men who have known him, and from the ~~statement~~ recollections of two of his women – Margaret, his childhood sweetheart, ~~by whom he had his only child, who lives now in Dallas~~ – and

Martha, his present wife. ~~whom we brought East and saw him legally marry~~. Some of the most interesting and significant stories we have had to omit because of ~~the bad impression they would make all around~~ their complete unprintableness. Some of the tales are told in his own idiom with as close an approximation to his narrative style as we could reconstruct.* There is certainly an over-emphasis of the violent and criminal side of Lead Belly's life, and that because we had some basis (in his criminal record) for our questions. [*inserted* Therefore] we present this loosely woven texture of reconstructed stories and letters, not as accurate biographical material, but as a set of dramatic ~~and exciting stories~~ tales through which the

The asterisk leads to:

*Since neither of us could write shorthand, we soon despaired of taking notes on his stories as he told them. In writing long-hand we lost some ~~portions~~ of ~~his~~ each tale in ~~being accurate in the~~ attempting accuracy of idiom. ~~of others~~. Besides, Lead Belly soon become embarrassed and unnatural *when he saw us taking notes* [italics is a handwritten insert from Alan]. We, therefore, wrote down the stories complete directly after he told them.

In the draft, the Lomaxes wrote that they had reconstructed these stories, "not as accurate biographical material but as a set of dramatic tales." They acknowledged an "overemphasis" on Ledbetter's "violent and criminal side," because that is what they asked him about.[8] However, in the book as published, this explanation is absent, and instead the biography's authenticity is emphasized. As a result, the book became a source for other "biographical" accounts. This included Edmond Addeo and Richard Garvin's self-described "historical novel," *The Midnight Special: The Legend of Leadbelly*, published by Bernard Geis Associates in 1971. In their preface, the authors stated that the book was "the truth, so far as we can ever know it,"[9] although in a 1990 interview with Kip Lornell, Addeo noted that they had taken "some literary liberties, dramatic liberties" and included "scenes we made up ... out of whole cloth, just for dramatic continuity."[10] A few years later, screenwriter Ernest Kinoy seems to have been influenced both by the Lomax book and by *The Midnight Special* as he wrote the screenplay for *Leadbelly* (Paramount Pictures, 1976), directed by Gordon Parks. Although the film is a fictionalized account of Ledbetter's life, reviewers often saw it as biography.[11]

What is especially troubling about the Lomaxes' framing of Huddie Ledbetter is that by casting one man as the violent center of the narrative, they erased the context of racial terror that marked the economic and political dominance of white southerners in the decades following the Civil War. It was Ledbetter's personal traits and actions, the Lomaxes argued – and most audiences accepted this as fact – that led to his repeated incarceration. Conversely, it was the Lomaxes' personal traits and actions, and not any sort of privilege or the exclusion of others, that made them deserving of the opportunities and advancement that they and millions of other white southerners enjoyed in education, housing, and employment. This erasure can be found in liner notes, articles, books, and websites, up to the present day, even those intended to celebrate the performer. "Unfortunately, Ledbetter had a violent temper and was in and out of prison several times in the course of his life," reports the Bullock Museum in Austin.[12] The website of the Louisiana Music Hall of Fame, into which Ledbetter was inducted in 2008, reads: "Possessing a legendary quick temper, he was arrested and convicted of murder in Texas in 1917 and sentenced to 20 years imprisonment."[13] Until it was changed in 2019, Ledbetter's biography on the website of the Rock and Roll Hall of Fame, into which he was inducted in 1988, read, "A man possessed with a hot temper and enormous strength, Lead Belly spent his share of time in Southern prisons."[14]

It is true that Huddie Ledbetter spent several years in captivity. He served on a county chain gang in 1915 and was incarcerated in state penitentiaries in Texas (1918–1925) and Louisiana (1930–1934) and in jail at Rikers Island in New York (1939). Yet, without historical context, even those who celebrate Ledbetter's ability to survive his time in these institutions are robbed of an opportunity to understand not only the performer but also the nation in which he came of age. At the same time, to write a biography of Ledbetter's early life without acknowledging the Lomaxes and their engagement with him, including their writing of *Negro Folk Songs as Sung by Lead Belly*, would be a mistake. First and foremost, it is the Lomax narrative that has defined Ledbetter for the better part of a century. Exploring the choices that they made as they created a persona for Ledbetter, and the ease with which their version of him was accepted and augmented by others, often in highly negative ways, is an important part of *Bring Judgment Day*. Reporters, radio producers, motion picture executives, academics, and the general public willingly went along with what historian Hazel Carby described as "[t]he political project of the Lomaxes," which was "to cast the black male body into the shape of an outlaw. John Lomax intended to recover an unadulterated form of black music, and in the process actually invented a particular version of black authenticity."[15]

Additionally, there are elements of the Lomaxes' writings that can be verified and prove useful, including both the description of their travels with Huddie Ledbetter and even some discussion of his early life. Notably, where their book seems most aligned with Ledbetter's past, it is when he talked about music, storytelling, and good times with family and friends. Where it is often demonstrably false is when he is quoted as describing terrible acts of violence, always "against his own people," as the Lomaxes put it, as if to reassure themselves and their white readers. Certainly, some of this was Ledbetter himself being selective about what he shared, understanding, as did the Lomaxes, that any reported charge that he had been violent toward white people would end the possibility of a national career. Some of Ledbetter's songs contain elements of autobiography; some also contain lyrics of violence, notably against women, but the extent to which they should be trusted as character-based is unclear. Much of his repertoire was drawn and adapted from material that had been performed by others he'd encountered, and the choices of which songs he would perform, which he would record, and which he would release to the public were generally made by white gatekeepers, whether prison officials, the Lomaxes, or northern record producers. Further confusing the narrative, Ledbetter himself liked to share what he called "tall tales," as they were known "down home."[16] The Lomaxes, too, could be selective and at times deceptive when describing their own actions. John Lomax, in particular, is an unreliable narrator, often presenting himself as being drawn into events rather than orchestrating them, even when evidence shows otherwise. In addition, throughout the time he spent "interpreting" Ledbetter for the benefit of audiences and the press and in *Negro Folks Songs as Sung by Lead Belly*, Lomax emphasized his knowledge and expertise while continually minimizing the achievements, talent, and expertise of Ledbetter. At times, though, he paints such a negative portrait of himself in the book that the results gain credibility.

Bring Judgment Day is structured around the relationship of Huddie Ledbetter and John Lomax, primarily between 1933 and 1935, while also drawing on the historical record of Ledbetter's life from 1889, when he was born, to the mid-1930s, when he and his wife, Martha Promise Ledbetter, by then independent of John Lomax, permanently relocated to New York City. Ultimately, though, this book is Ledbetter's. The Lomaxes, for better and worse, played an important role in bringing his music to new audiences, but it was Ledbetter himself who rose to this opportunity and challenge, as he had so often in the past, and then moved beyond it. As a performer, he was a link between the past and the future, a collector and promoter of America's tremendously diverse musical heritage and an innovator whose creative drive played a vital role in shaping the foundation not only of modern American culture but also of world culture. To truly understand that culture, a fresh look at the early history of this important American musician is essential – today more than ever. As political pressure is building to limit and even criminalize efforts to teach evidence-based history of the nation's past, a book that re-examines the life and legacy of Huddie Ledbetter in the broader context of the United States' social, political, and legal systems is especially timely.

CHAPTER 1

Encounter at Angola

In June 1933, Huddie Ledbetter, prisoner #19469 at the Louisiana State Penitentiary at Angola, received welcome news. Pending the governor's signature, the Louisiana Board of Pardons had agreed to commute his minimum sentence from six years to three, making him eligible to apply for parole. Ledbetter, forty-four years old, had been fighting for his freedom since he arrived at Angola on February 26, 1930. His intake papers described him as 5′ 7.5″ tall, 171 pounds, with black hair streaked with gray. He had "[g]ood teeth, medium ears, medium nose, black burn scar back of right hand, long cut scar right side of neck, cut scar left shoulder, sore scar right thigh."[1] His full sentence, if served, would run until February 6, 1940. For the first time since his incarceration, freedom seemed to be in sight.

A month later, John Lomax and his eighteen-year-old son, Alan, gathering material for an anthology of American folk music for Macmillan and the Library of Congress (eventually titled *American Ballads and Folk Songs*), arrived at Angola. The pair had recorded at three prisons in Texas before traveling east to Louisiana. They arrived on Sunday, July 16, 1933 and stayed for four days in hot, muggy weather; it rained both Sunday and Monday. Lomax, a portly, white sixty-five-year-old with a graduate degree from Harvard and a cigar frequently between his teeth, complained that they "found the fountains drier than they are in Texas" because at Angola, "Negro prisoners [were] not allowed to sing as they work," thus limiting the Lomaxes' ability to gather material. Yet "[o]ne man ... almost made up for the deficiency."[2] At Camp A, they were introduced to "Huddie Ledbetter – called by his companions Lead Belly" who "was unique in knowing a very large number of tunes, all of which he sang effectively while he twanged his twelve-string guitar." As an added bonus for the

Lomaxes, Ledbetter, a seasoned performer, was well-versed in the type of songs they wanted to hear. "Alan and I were looking particularly for the song of the Negro laborer, the words of which sometimes reflect the tragedies of imprisonment, cold, hunger, heat, the injustice of the white man," John Lomax wrote. "Fortunately for us and, as it turned out, fortunately for him, Lead Belly had been fond of this type of songs."[3] Ledbetter performed seven songs, some of them multiple times, as the Lomaxes recorded. These included "The Western Cowboy," with a refrain of "cow cow yippie yippie yay"; "Frankie and Albert," a ballad of love gone wrong; and "Goodnight, Irene," an edgy waltz with a captivating tune:

> Irene, goodnight;
> Irene, goodnight;
> Goodnight, Irene; goodnight, Irene –
> I'll kiss you in my dreams.[4]

Other songs included the up-tempo "Take a Whiff on Me," a risqué song about cocaine that he said he learned from his father's brother, Terrell; "You Can't Lose-a-Me, Cholly," which the Lomaxes described as a "ragtime strut" for dancing; and "Ella Speed," another ballad of doomed love. Equipment problems meant that they caught only bits of some songs, including "Angola Blues," which Ledbetter said he wrote while at the prison. It's a lament about incarceration and being forced out of bed at 3:30 a.m. to work; about the woman he loved in Shreveport; and about the possibility of release.

> If I leave here walkin', hang crape on de do',
> If I leave here walkin', hang crape on de do',
> I may not be dead, but I ain't comin' back here no mo'.

The Lomaxes would later claim that the song was "a mélange of stanzas from many different 'blues.'" But it spoke powerfully to Ledbetter's situation and frustration, especially the final stanza:

> I wouldn' min' rollin' no two, three years,
> I wouldn' min' rollin' no two, three years,
> But I'll tell de gov'nor, can't go ten or twelve.[5]

As evidenced by audio archives in the Library of Congress, the recording quality in 1933 was poor.[6] Lomax had been working with sound engineers to design and build a machine that would improve the quality of field recording, but it was not yet ready when he and Alan set out that summer. "The whole idea of using a phonograph to preserve authentic folk music was, in 1933 . . . radically different from the popular notion of recording," wrote scholars Charles Wolfe and Kip Lornell. "Field recordings are not intended as commercial products, but as attempts at cultural preservation."[7] Setting out in June, the Lomaxes settled for a "cylinder model" dictating machine, "equipped with a spring motor," from the Dictaphone Corporation.[8] A year later, in 1934, they returned to Angola with the new machine, and the fidelity of these recordings makes it easy to imagine the astonishment the Lomaxes must have felt when they first heard Ledbetter's powerful twelve-string guitar as it drove through the fast-paced tunes, accompanied by a voice that could caress with sweetness, howl in lament, and force the listener to pay attention. When Ledbetter played, he was in total charge, sometimes slapping his guitar in rhythm, sometimes contrasting the rhythmic movement of his feet and hands. In an age before amplifiers, his sound could – and eventually would – fill a concert hall.

In *Negro Folk Songs as Sung by Lead Belly*, the Lomaxes claimed that after each song Ledbetter performed, "when Captain Reaux was not about," he told them that he was eligible for parole and begged them to see if he could be paroled to work for them. Their book, published after the Lomaxes had begun to face criticism for their working arrangement with Ledbetter, alleged that it was Ledbetter who proposed the terms of employment: He would drive their car, cook their meals, wash their clothes, and be their man "as long as I live," they quoted him as saying. Once he started his "old twelve-string to twanging" in any town in the United States, people would come running. "I'll make you a lot of money," they said he told them. "You needn't give me none, 'cept a few nickels to send my woman."[9] Whether the passage is factual or not, the Lomaxes do seem to have investigated the possibility of getting Ledbetter released to them. In his 1947 autobiography, *Adventures of a Ballad Hunter*, John Lomax wrote, "He knew so many songs which he sang with restraint and sympathy that, accepting his story in full, I quite resolved to get him out of prison and take him along as a third member of our party."[10] After finishing their work at Angola, father and son drove to Baton Rouge to check the penitentiary records. "Often he had been in trouble with the law," John Lomax reported in *Negro Folk Songs as Sung by Lead Belly.* "Once he had been convicted for murder in Texas and given a thirty-year sentence; also he had been whipped twice in Angola for misconduct."[11] He couldn't take Ledbetter with him, he told readers. "The picture kept coming to my mind of Alan and myself asleep by the roadside in the swamps of Louisiana and Mississippi with this particular black man on his cot near by, and the prospect did not look attractive."[12] Still, Lomax was intrigued by the performer and especially a song he recorded three times, "Goodnight, Irene." On July 21, 1933, as he and Alan left Baton Rouge, Lomax wrote about it to his future wife, Ruby Terrill, Dean of Women at the University of Texas in Austin. "He sung us one song which I shall copyright as soon as I get to Washington," he said, "and try to market in sheet music form."[13]

Known as "The Farm," the Louisiana State Penitentiary at Angola was then, and remains, the largest maximum-security prison in the United States. It reached its current size by the early 1920s: 18,000 acres (28 square miles) of land, a bit larger than Manhattan, and surrounded on three sides by the Mississippi River.[14] Then, as now, Louisiana's prison population was the racial inverse of the state's population overall.[15] According to the US census, in 1930 Louisiana had a total population of about 2.1 million people. Of these, 63 percent were identified as white, and 37 percent as Black.[16] That year, 35 percent of those in Louisiana's state and federal prisons were white, while 65 percent were Black.[17] There were roughly 2,200 people incarcerated at the state penitentiary at Angola at the time of Ledbetter's arrival, including 80 women. That total grew yearly,[18] leading to overcrowding in the segregated, open-plan dormitories. "Beds have grown from one story – so to speak – to two story, and now three story beds are common," the prison's general manager reported to the state legislature in 1932.[19]

The penitentiary was built on the grounds of multiple plantations in West Feliciana Parish, including one named Angola, that had been owned by Isaac Franklin, a notorious domestic slave trafficker.[20] His death in 1846 was "national news," reported historian Joshua Rothman, whose 2021 book estimated Franklin's worth to be "the modern equivalent of more than $435 million." Nearly 70 percent of that value "was embodied in 636 people he enslaved. His obituaries never mentioned that fact, framing Franklin's life as that of a self-made man."[21] With the abolition of slavery in 1865, farmers and plantation[22] owners in Louisiana and throughout the South, including Franklin's widow, Adelicia, found other ways to exploit Black labor. One involved a system known as sharecropping. "Sharecropping was the system of tenure designed for (and partly by) Negro freedmen in the aftermath of the Civil War," wrote historian Jack Temple Kirby. It was a form of labor that bound entire families to landowners – nearly all of them white – through a form of rental in which the workers owned nothing, and instead were dependent on landowners for everything needed to farm, including "mules, horses, equipment or other capital," he wrote. The landlord might provide "cabins, water, firewood, and other tangibles," and in exchange supervised every aspect of the labor, often brutally. "Landlords' control included extension of vital credit during much of the crop year," and many "charged usurious interest rates." Year after year, families might find themselves even farther behind than they had been the previous year, because "at settlement time," sharecroppers, "especially" Black sharecroppers, "were generally obliged to accept without a question white bosses' calculations both of commissary charges and cotton and other production," Kirby wrote. "Share cropping was both a racial and a class system."[23] While itinerant workers could and did move from crop to crop, sharecropping families often became bound to a property because of debt: Attempting to leave without paying would result in criminal charges.[24]

Southern landowners as well as leaders in a range of non-agricultural industries also relied on the unpaid or low-paid labor of convicted prisoners. After emancipation, this was possible because of a clause in the Thirteenth Amendment to the US Constitution, ratified in 1865, that prohibited slavery and involuntary servitude "except as punishment for a crime whereof the party shall have been duly convicted."[25] Prisoners – a majority of whom, after the war's end, were Black – were forced to do the most dangerous and undesirable work, putting their lives at risk to extract coal, turpentine, lumber, iron ore, and other materials; clear fetid, snake-infested swampland; and labor in sawmills, brickyards, and endless fields of cotton, sugar cane, and corn. A flagrant disregard for the prisoners' well-being led to extraordinarily high rates of death, disease, and disfigurement. If the work itself didn't kill them, the absence of safe housing, nutritious food, clean water, or medical care, and the extreme brutality of white overseers might. If more laborers were needed for a particular task, more could be rounded up. As historian Matthew Mancini reported, quoting a gloating southern delegate to the National Prison Association's 1883 meeting: "Before the war, we owned the negroes . . . . But these convicts, we don't own 'em. One dies, get another."[26]

This post-war exploitation of southern Black labor was not inevitable. For a period of roughly a decade, from 1867 to 1877, Congress intervened to stop the effort of white southerners to effectively reinstate slavery by imposing draconian laws known as "Black Codes," and enforcing them through escalating white violence and terror. Congress passed the Reconstruction Act of 1867, which "divided the eleven Confederate states, except Tennessee, into five military districts under commanders empowered to employ the army to protect life and property," wrote historian Eric Foner. The act "laid out the steps by which new state governments could be created and recognized by Congress – essentially the writing of new constitutions providing for manhood suffrage, their approval by a majority of registered voters, and ratification of the Fourteenth Amendment."[27] In 1868, with southern states now under federal control, the Fourteenth Amendment was ratified, acknowledging the full citizenship of "all persons born or naturalized in the United States" and their right to "due process of law" and "equal protection of the laws." In 1870, the Fifteenth Amendment was ratified, acknowledging the right of all male citizens to vote, "regardless of race, color, or previous condition of servitude."[28] Black electoral involvement led to Black political leadership. "Sixteen African Americans served in Congress during Reconstruction," wrote Foner. "[M]ore than 600 [served] in state legislatures, and hundreds more in local offices from sheriff to justice of the peace scattered across the South." He noted, "Reconstruction governments established the South's first state-funded public school systems, sought to strengthen the bargaining power of plantation labourers, made taxation more equitable, and outlawed racial discrimination in public transportation and accommodations. They also offered lavish aid to railroads and other enterprises in the hope of creating a 'New South' whose economic expansion would benefit Blacks and whites alike."[29]

But whites in southern states fought hard to end this era of reform and "redeem" the South from shared governance. By 1877 – when John

Lomax was about ten years old, and Wesley Ledbetter (Huddie's father) was about seventeen – they succeeded, and the last federal troops were withdrawn following a political compromise that put a Republican president in the White House. Southern Democrats quickly moved to regain dominance, revising state constitutions to dismantle the economic, political, and social gains that had been made by Black southerners. By the 1890s, "the full imposition of the new system of white supremacy known as Jim Crow" had taken root.[30] Virtually all of the 2,000 Black men who had "served in some kind of elective office" during the Reconstruction era were out of office by 1900, a point by which "Southern states disenfranchised black voters." The term of the last Black congressman of this era ended in 1901.[31] In Louisiana, the president of the 1898 state constitutional convention bragged about its ability to now "protect the purity of the ballot box, and to perpetuate the supremacy of the Anglo-Saxon race in Louisiana." Another speaker crowed, "We met here to establish the supremacy of the white race, and the white race constitutes the Democratic party of this State."[32] (Over the course of the twentieth century, notably, the platforms of the two major parties would significantly shift. As historian David Blight wrote in 2019, "the Republicans have not been the party of Lincoln on race relations for at least 60 years."[33])

The history of Reconstruction and its aftermath is important for two reasons. The first is that it establishes the legal systems that Huddie Ledbetter faced in both Texas and Louisiana. The second is that the South's prison farms were built on the former plantations. These sites had exploited Black laborers first through enslavement and then through various forms of forced, coercive, and exploitive labor practices. This was the case with the Louisiana State Penitentiary, which took its name from one of those plantations. In 1880, three years after the federal troops left Louisiana, the widow of Isaac Franklin sold properties including Angola to a partnership headed by Tennessean Samuel L. James. Since 1869, James and his associates had enjoyed the exclusive right to manage Louisiana's state prison system, meaning that they could exploit convict labor for their own benefit and also lease individuals out, for profit, to work on farms, plantations, levees, and other public and private interests. With their purchase of Franklin's property, and in the absence, now, of federal oversight, they expanded these operations, launching what historian Mark Carleton described as "the most cynical, profit-oriented, and brutal prison regime."[34] Between 1870 and 1901, an estimated 3,000 prisoners leased under the system died.[35]

By the time Huddie Ledbetter was sentenced to Angola in 1930, convict leasing had been officially outlawed throughout the South, including Louisiana, although not eradicated,[36] but the conditions under which the labor of Black men, women, and even children were exploited persisted. In 1901, Louisiana ended its contract with the James estate and resumed control over state prisoners, buying 8,000 acres of land from the family, including Angola and other plantations.[37] Gradually, as the state built up its penitentiary's infrastructure, it acquired additional land. The "profit motive" that had characterized the land's use under convict leasing endured, noted Mark Carleton, "surviving for many years as the dominant principle in the state's philosophy of prison management."[38] Over time, more land was purchased, and penitentiary structures were built on the site. In 1917, as a cost-cutting measure, "most of the professional guards" at Angola were fired, and their jobs were given "to 'trusty' convicts," who enjoyed special privileges and carried weapons.[39] In 1928, two years before Ledbetter's incarceration, Louisiana's prisons came under the authority of Huey P. Long, Jr., Louisiana's governor from May 1928 to January 1932 (and US Senator from then until he was assassinated in 1935), who "looked upon the penitentiary simply as a state-operated business enterprise" that would, at minimum, be "self-supporting" – although it was not. Frequent flooding at the site and the onset of the Great Depression exacerbated problems.[40]

In June 1930, just four months after Ledbetter's arrival, a state senate committee investigated Governor Long's claim that Angola was "on a paying basis" – in other words, self-supporting. The committee's report, released in July, found that the penitentiary's financial affairs were in "a deplorable condition." Further, the committee found evidence that forms of convict leasing were still operating. They charged that the current general manager, a Long appointee, had "entered into an illegal contract with John P. Burgin, Inc.," a Pointe Coupee rice plantation operator, "for the cultivation of some twelve hundred acres of land" despite the prohibition against convict leasing.[41] On August 25, 1930, a month after the report's release, prisoners overseen by a man named Wallace W. Pecue staged an uprising at the rice farm. They locked themselves in a temporary wooden barracks to protest "brutal conditions, bad food, bad housing, long hours, and being obliged to work when ill without medical care."[42] Violence ensued, and, at Pecue's order, a trusty shot and killed a nineteen-year-old prisoner. Pecue told the press that he found no grounds for the complaints; the men, he said, were just "too lazy to work."[43]

The following spring, in April 1931, Governor Long appointed sixty-two-year-old Robert L. Himes, known as "Tighty,"[44] to serve as general manager. The governor told the Baton Rouge *Morning Advocate* that he had "directed Mr. Himes to operate the penitentiary 100 per cent on the basis of efficiency."[45] Under this new leadership, the death rates escalated; between 1931 and 1935 they "were the highest since the days of the old convict-lease system," according to historian Anthony J. Badger.[46] In 1941, reporter Bernard Lewis "B.L." Krebs investigated Angola on behalf of *The Times-Picayune*. The article is damning: "The machine politicians promised the taxpayers they would take the penitentiary 'out of the red' – and they did," Krebs wrote. "But they didn't tell the people of Louisiana that money they were making at the penitentiary . . . was coming from the blood and sweat and agony of 10,000 officially recorded floggings." Krebs described thirty convicts whose official cause of death was "sunstroke," when in fact they were "beaten in cane, rice and vegetable fields with five-foot clubs, redoubled grass ropes, blacksnake whips and in later years with the lashes of the captains." He wrote of forty more prisoners shot dead, allegedly for trying to escape,[47] and of many others who endured as many as sixty strikes of a whip at a time.[48]

Huddie Ledbetter, as the Lomaxes saw in the files, was among those disciplined. In their book, they were dismissive of what he had endured: "He was whipped twice for impudence," they wrote, "but on the whole had as easy a time as a man can have at Angola."[49] A closer look at the records shows that it was Captain W.W. Pecue, who had overseen operations at the Burgin rice farm, who conducted both of the whippings. On November 21, 1931, he lashed Ledbetter ten times for "laziness." On June 27, 1932, it was fifteen lashes for "impudence." Pecue, born in 1875, was in his late fifties at the time of Ledbetter's imprisonment. He attended school up to the eighth grade and had worked at Angola at least as far back as 1914.[50] The instrument he likely used consisted of two belts of leather, each as thick as the sole of a shoe, roughly four inches wide and five feet long. At times, these straps would be dampened and dragged through sand, to increase the pain. Other prisoners would be ordered to hold the victim down, and his clothing would be pulled to expose a bare back or buttocks. "Three or four blows ... could and generally did break the skin," wrote Krebs. "Few prisoners failed to start screaming at the fifth or sixth blow."[51]

That it was Pecue who did the beating offers some insight into Ledbetter's placement within the prison. Ledbetter's records state that on May 1, 1930, shortly after his arrival, he was made a "waiter" at Camp F. (Data from the previous year showed that Angola had nine camps, or quarters, labeled A to I. All but Camp D, the women's camp, were segregated, and each housed between 140 and 225 people. There was also a receiving station and hospital, as well as road crews.)[52] It seems likely that sometime after the uprising at the Burgin farm, Ledbetter was assigned to a road-building crew – a chain gang – overseen by Pecue. The 1932 penitentiary report listed four road camps: Pines, in Washington Parish (159 prisoners); Pine Grove, in St. Helena Parish (249 prisoners); Norwood, in East Feliciana Parish (159 prisoners); and Star Hill, in West Feliciana Parish (125 prisoners). "The Star Hill camp was organized in October [1931], after the Pointe Coupee rice crop had been harvested, the old rice camp being transformed and revamped into a road camp," general manager Himes reported to the state legislature.[53] As noted, in November 1931, Ledbetter was whipped for the first time by Pecue, although his change of assignment wasn't noted in his record until February 8, 1932, when he was reported to be working on "R/C 5" (road crew 5) as a tailor.[54] Pecue was overseeing this crew, 127 prisoners, as of April 1932.[55] There were three deaths on this road crew in May: On May 14, Allen Julius died of typhoid fever; on May 23, Jeff Burns died of peritonitis, likely from an untreated injury; on May 25, W.O. Barney was shot and killed "while escaping."[56] Ledbetter was likely still with this crew on June 27, 1932, when he was again whipped by Pecue. Less than a month later, July 19, he was reassigned as a "Freemen's waiter" at Camp A, serving the white camp personnel.

Captain James N. Reaux, the guard at Camp A where the Lomaxes first encountered Ledbetter in 1933 and again in 1934, and in whose presence Ledbetter did not dare speak freely, does not seem to have whipped him, although as Mark Carleton noted, "only 'official punishments' were recorded."[57] Reaux was, in fact, particularly brutal. Between 1930 and

1938 he was personally responsible for administering the greatest number of floggings at Angola: a total of 26,500 lashes. On sixty-two occasions, he whipped prisoners thirty-five times or more in a single session, according to Krebs' analysis of the punishment records.[58] The federal census of 1930 lists James N. Reaux as white and fifty-six years old, living with his wife and six children in a home on the penitentiary grounds.[59] In 1933 alone, the year the Lomaxes first visited Angola, Captain Reaux's record of flogging included 184 prisoners, according to Krebs. "They included one flogging of 50 lashes, two of 45 lashes, and one of 40 lashes for escaping; 25 lashes for 'faking a telegram'; 25 for 'refusing to go to work,' and 15 for 'sleeping after [w]rap-up.'"[60]

In the summer of 1934, John Lomax wrote to General Manager R.L. Himes: "Will you kindly let me know if Ledbetter, the 12 string Negro guitar player, is still in Angola?" A year had passed since his and Alan's first visit, and Lomax had a "greatly improved machine"[61] and wished to record more songs for the Library of Congress. Himes replied in the affirmative.[62]

The previous summer's collecting, while not without its frustrations, had proven successful for Alan and John Lomax. Shortly after leaving Angola, they finally acquired the new recording machine. "The rear of the car was now stuffed with a 315-pound disc-cutting recorder, a vacuum tube amplifier, two 75-pound Edison batteries to power them, a generator for recharging the batteries, piles of aluminum and celluloid blank discs, a mixing board, a loudspeaker, a microphone, and boxes of replacement parts," Alan Lomax's biographer, John Szwed, wrote.[63] The discs themselves were "twelve inches in diameter" and "hard to find anywhere in the United States."[64]

The Lomaxes traveled to New Orleans, where John was briefly hospitalized for what Alan described as "a rather bad attack of malarial fever, which he contracted at the Louisiana state farm about two weeks ago."[65] After his release, Lomax looked up "Bertrand Cohn, a university classmate, who gave us cards to the New Orleans Athletic Club."[66] Cohn, an attorney whose wife's family owned a lumber mill in the state,[67] also "assigned" to the Lomaxes "a plainclothes man who will go with us tomorrow night into the jungles of Negroland where we hope to find some ballads and ballad music devoted to the seamy side of Negro life in

1.1 Camp A, Angola, July 1934. Huddie Ledbetter is in the foreground (no hat, striped shirt, at left and behind man with open shirt). Alan Lomax, photographer. Library of Congress, Prints & Photographs Division, Lomax Collection, reproduction number LC-DIG-ppmsc-00346. Courtesy of the Lead Belly Estate, Murfreesboro, Tennessee.

the city," John Lomax wrote.[68] He was too ill to go, though, and, not surprisingly, the arrival of a white teenager and a posse of white detectives into the "dives and joints of New Orleans" led to a "constrained silence." Invariably, Alan Lomax and the others, along with the bartender, "would be the only ones left in the hall."[69]

An inability to gain trust from communities in which they wanted to record was part of the reason the Lomaxes were intrigued by the idea of working with Huddie Ledbetter. Some of the people they encountered were well aware that commercial record companies had been recruiting southern blues performers for roughly a decade. In New Orleans, for example, Alan Lomax encountered a "Billy Williams," whom he described as "calculating" because Williams' response, when asked to sing secular songs, was to wonder aloud what was in it for him.[70] Others were uncomfortable or offended at being asked to sing material they considered "gutbucket" or, in the Lomaxes' words, "sinful." Some feared, for good reason, that cooperation with these white men from Washington would put themselves and their families at risk. A few, like "Blue," a sharecropper they encountered on a plantation in Texas in 1933, bravely stepped forward to record a request for help from the newly inaugurated president, Franklin D. Roosevelt. In an article published the following year, Alan described the song, "Po' Farmer," which Blue claimed to have written and insisted that they record before he would agree to sing the song they requested, "Stagolee," about a murderer. Alan noted Blue's heightened awareness of the white plantation manager, keeping a close eye on the sharecroppers he'd gathered to sing, at night, for the Lomaxes. He reported "nervous merriment" among those listening, as Blue "sang of the tribulations of the Negro renter in the South, living and working under a system which is sometimes not far different from the peonage of Old Mexico."[71] The reference was to a form of debt bondage outlawed by Congress in 1867 but persistent throughout the South. As historian Pete Daniel noted, "the federal government acknowledged that the labyrinth of local customs and laws which bound men in debt" in the decades that followed "was peonage," but federal efforts to address the injustice were slow.[72] Blue's song decried conditions that kept workers in rags, hunched over as they picked cotton, and in debt to the landowner's commissary. Forty years later, in the 1970s, Alan wrote that recording Blue singing "Po' Farmer" had "totally changed" his life,[73] yet its import was minimized in his 1935 article, and the song was not included in *American Ballads and Folk Songs*. It did receive mention in the book's introduction: "Only this summer [1933] a Negro on a large cotton plantation we visited, misunderstanding our request for 'made-up' songs, composed a satire on the overseer," the Lomaxes wrote. "This song, 'Po' Farmer,' was greeted with shouts of approval when the author sang it that night at the plantation schoolhouse. It is the type of song that may grow into a genuine ballad."[74]

Research for *American Ballads and Folk Songs*, submitted in manuscript form to Macmillan in October 1933,[75] meant that John and Alan Lomax had journeyed "in a Ford car more than 15,000 miles"[76] through Texas, Louisiana, Mississippi, Tennessee, and Kentucky. Two months later, eager to continue field recording, they submitted a proposal to the Carnegie Corporation, arguing that further collection of African American musical traditions had to be done before it was too late. "The Negro in the South is the target for such complex influences that it is hard to find genuine folk singing," they wrote. They blamed Black political leadership, religious leaders, "prosperous members of the community," and "the radio with its flood of jazz, created in tearooms for the benefit of city-dwelling whites" for "killing the best and most genuine Negro folk songs."[77] Their proposal was successful, as was another, more modest request to the Rockefeller Foundation. "In the end," wrote Lomax biographer Nolan Porterfield, "the Carnegie grant … paid for a substantial part of Lomax's travel expenses, while the Rockefeller money went for recording accessories and rebuilding the back of a brand-new blue Ford sedan."[78] And so, in July 1934, they were ready to return to Angola.

Despite all of his efforts, Huddie Ledbetter was still incarcerated in July 1934. More than a year had passed since the Board of Pardons approved the commutation of his sentence, but the governor's signature was still pending. Learning that the Lomaxes would be returning, Ledbetter began to update an appeal he had mailed to Louisiana's previous governor, Huey Long, in the fall of 1931. Long had apparently found the missive amusing, because it reached the press: "Prisoner Asks His Freedom in Poetic Epistle."

> New Orleans, Oct. 9. – Huddie Ledbetter, serving a sentence of from 6 to 10 years for shooting Dick Ellet at Shreveport, sought his freedom in the following epistle to Gov. Huey P. Long:
>
> > "In 1923 the jury took my liberty away from me;
> > I left my wife, ring in hand, and crying,
> > Lord, have mercy on that man of mine.
> > I am your servant that composed this song,
> > Have mercy on me, Governor Long."[79]

The following day, an article about the poem also appeared in *The Times-Picayune*. It quoted Lawrence A. Sauer, Secretary of the Board of Pardons, who explained that Ledbetter's poetic appeal "could not be considered because it was not advertised and was irregular in other respects."[80] It is not clear why it took so long, but in May 1933, about two months before the Lomaxes' first visit, Huddie Ledbetter successfully submitted a formal application, number 6633, for "commutation of sentence." It was this request that reached the Board of Pardons and was approved.[81] By then, it was the signature of fifty-year-old Oscar Kelly "O.K." Allen, Louisiana's latest governor, that Ledbetter needed. In the meantime, Ledbetter, as required and in anticipation of the governor's signature, posted a public notice in *The Shreveport Times*. It ran on July 18 and July 28, 1933: "I am applying for parole. HUDDIE LEDBETTER."[82]

By November 1933, when there was no further action, Ledbetter wrote a note to Governor Allen, enclosing a version of the poem he'd sent to Governor Long. Whether Allen received the letter or not is unclear, because it was the penitentiary's general manager, R.L. Himes, who responded, noting that, because Ledbetter was a "second termer," he could "not be reprieved." Unless his sentence was reduced (commuted), he would not be eligible "to parole" until February 1936, Himes wrote, reminding Ledbetter – as he already knew – that "[t]he only other relief than this is through the Board of Pardons."[83]

On December 8, Ledbetter, or someone assisting him, typed a response to Himes, arguing that he was *not* a second timer. "I am certain you have been misinformed or an error was made in looking up my record. I have never been in prison before anywhere. I have never served a jail sentence anywhere. I have been arrested for fighting once but only got a fine of thirty dollars for it." He asked Himes to "straighten this up" for him, and then pointed out, correctly, that he had "already made a time cut on the June [Parole] Board but up until this date it hasn't been signed by the Governor." Did Himes "think it advisable to try the board again?"[84]

Ledbetter may have hoped that Louisiana prison officials did not know about his incarceration in Texas under the alias "Walter Boyd," but they did. Three months after he arrived at Angola, a fellow prisoner informed on him. Following up, an Angola prison captain wrote to the warden in Texas for details. "There is a prisoner in this La. State pen. Angola, La., under an assume name," the captain typed. "This man is known by another prisoner here to be Walter Boyd. Escaped from Texas Pen. Between 1919 and 1921, But he thinks it was in 1920." The Louisiana captain asked if Texas had "any record on a party by this name. If so you may come out and look this man over. This prisoner states that Boyte has about 40 or 50 years to do in Texas." By hand, the captain added: "PS. This man is a Negro, Walter Boyd. He is a great dancer and guitar picker."[85] Texas responded on May 12, 1930: "You are respectfully advised that our prisoner #42738, Walter Boyd is possibly the man that you have. He was received into the Texas Prison System in 1918 with a thirty (30) year sentence for Murder, but was pardoned on Jan. 16, 1925."[86] The letter noted that "Boyd" was not wanted by the Texas institution.

Now, more than three years later, Himes responded to Ledbetter's note from December 8, 1933: "Dear Huddie: It's unusual for these finger prints to make a mistake. I wish you would try real hard to remember and see if you remember being an inmate of the Texas State Penitentiary in 1918. Let me know about that. You were under the name Walter Boyd at that time."[87] Still Ledbetter persisted, handwriting a note to Himes dated March 2, 1934, "pleading for freedom." He said his fingerprints had only been taken once, and added, truthfully, that "Governor Pat M Neff pardon me with a full pardon." He had already been at Angola for four years, he wrote. He asked if Himes would please clear up his record and let him go back to his "happy home."[88] On March 13, Himes sent a brief response: "Last June the Board of Pardons recommended a change in your sentence from 6 to 10 years to 3 to 10 years. The Governor has not signed." In what must have been a frustrating addition, because this was where the correspondence began, Himes closed by suggesting that Ledbetter "write your letters to the Governor."[89]

Huddie Ledbetter was growing desperate. On April 2, 1934, he sent another typed note to Himes, reminding him that the governor "had not signed the recommendation of the Board of Pardons." He said that he would "appreciate very much" if Himes would let him know "what has been done toward giving me my freedom." Ledbetter seems to have also been calculating how much of his sentence would be left even without the pardon, if good time credits were awarded. "I have only four months to serve before my time is up," he told Himes, "and will appreciate anything you can do to help me gain my freedom." But Himes was done corresponding. Instead, he made a note on the letter: "Do not answer. 3/13/34, suggested he write Governor."[90]

Still, Himes decided to investigate Ledbetter's claim that he had been pardoned in Texas, because the information had apparently not made it into his Louisiana State Penitentiary record, and Himes may not have seen the 1930 correspondence. On June 21, 1934, the same day that Himes wrote to John Lomax to let him know that Ledbetter was still at

Camp A, Himes sent an inquiry to the Texas Prison System's Bureau of Records and Identification.[91] In reply, he was informed that "an examination of the records reveals that he [Boyd/Ledbetter] was granted a full pardon on January 21st, 1925 by Governor Pat M. Neff by proclamation #1814 dated January 16th, 1925."[92] Walter Boyd's Texas Prison System "Certificate of Conduct" noted that he received a "FULL PARDON" (capitalized in the original) and, below that, added the words, "CLEAR RECORD."[93] With this information, Himes or an assistant updated Ledbetter's Louisiana penitentiary record. A typed version, dated June 27, 1934, noted the punishments at Angola and Ledbetter's work and camp assignments. It also noted: "He served a term in Texas for murder; was pardoned." Below that is typed, "D.G.T. [double good time] would have released him June 26, 1934. Fact of his pardon has just been ascertained. In the ordinary course, he will come up July 15th for consideration for discharge August 1st."[94]

Ledbetter's advocacy for himself had paid off. By the summer of 1934, with or without the governor's signature, and with or without a second visit by the Lomaxes, Ledbetter was due to be released.

John and Alan Lomax returned to Angola on July 1, 1934. Now forty-five, knowing that his release should be imminent but not leaving anything to chance, Ledbetter was once again "ready to sing in his strong, resonant voice; ready to play marvelously his old twelve-string guitar," the Lomaxes reported in *Negro Folk Songs as Sung by Lead Belly*.[95] Ledbetter began by launching into an astounding performance of "Mister Tom Hughes' Town," after which, clearly satisfied, he shouted, "Lord!" He was then recorded, speaking clearly and with none of the dialect ascribed to him later, that the song "has been sung by Huddie Ledbetter, sometimes known as Lead Belly, on the farm at Angola, Louisiana in Camp A, for the Library of Congress in Washington." Later, following a recording of "The Western Cowboy," Ledbetter announced: "This song was composed by Huddie Lead Belly, Camp A, under Captain Reaux," adding that he was from Mooringsport, Louisiana and was the "Twelve-String King." Twice more during this July visit, Ledbetter made sure that his name accompanied a song, including a lengthy rendition of "Blind Lemon Blues." When he was done playing, he said, "This song was composed by

Huddie Ledbetter in memory of Blind Lemon of Dallas, Texas, with whom he used to work .... The song has been sung by Huddie Ledbetter for the Library of Congress in Washington." Following "Matchbox Blues," he said: "This song was played and sung by Huddie Ledbetter, of camp number one, Angola Farm, the state penitentiary of Louisiana ... otherwise known as Lead Belly, for the Library of Congress in Washington." The next song was a driving, fast-paced performance of "Midnight Special," followed by a few starts and stops on "Goodnight, Irene." In all, he sang and recorded fourteen songs that day.[96]

The energy of Ledbetter's performances is not conveyed by the Lomaxes' description of them in their book. They wrote: "All that Sunday he sang for us in the rain – a pitiful-looking figure in bedraggled, ragged stripes – while the drizzle formed in drops and ran down his face."[97] The book collapsed the two Angola visits, and this is likely an example of it. During the 1933 visit, it rained during two of the four days they recorded, and it seems clear from correspondence that they did not meet Ledbetter on their first day, a Sunday. In 1934, they *did* record on a Sunday, and it wasn't raining. The Lomaxes wrote that "at every pause" during this second visit, Ledbetter was "urging [them] to help him win his freedom." After "Goodnight, Irene," the seventh of the fourteen songs they recorded, they said that Ledbetter "sang a petition – a crude version of his own composition – to Governor O.K. Allen to pardon him, telling us that he had once sung a similar song to Governor Pat Neff of Texas."[98] The lyrics echoed the poem he'd sent to Governor Long in 1931, and then revised and tried to get to Governor Allen in 1933:

> In nineteen hundred and thirty-two
> Honorable Gov'nor O.K. Allen, I'm 'pealing to you.
> I left my wife wringin' her hands an' cryin',
> Sayin' "Governor O.K. Allen, save this man of mine."

In the book, John Lomax took credit for suggesting the recording, saying that the "power of his singing, his earnestly repeated appeals, his plight" finally "moved" him to offer to record the plea. This seems unlikely; it's clear from the lyrics that Ledbetter revised the song in anticipation of the chance to record it. He appealed by name to the white men in charge of his fate – not only the governor, but also the general manager, the warden, and the lieutenant governor. He also made it clear that he had been paying attention to newspaper accounts about Himes releasing prisoners to maintain prison finances and "relieve severe crowding."[99]

> And the Honorable Mr. Hymes looked over de pen,
> Told Governor O.K. Allen, "You've got too many men."
> Governor O.K. Allen began to turn about,
> "Got to make some 'rangements to turn some of them out."

After additional verses, Ledbetter ended the song with a dramatic flourish:

> Had you Governor O.K. Allen, like you got me,

He slowed the pace and stretched out the phrasing:

> I'd wake up in de morning,

He then strummed the guitar a few times, calling the listener to attention before finishing:

> Let you out on reprieve.[100]

The Lomaxes reportedly brought the aluminum disc to the governor's office in Baton Rouge a day later, intent on playing it for him. Governor Allen was in a meeting with Senator Huey Long, John Lomax wrote in the book, and so he left the record with a secretary, "who promised to play it for his chief."[101] Whether this happened or not is unknown; it seems unlikely that the governor's office had the means to play the disc. Undeterred, Lomax implied cause-and-effect as he jumped to the next sentence: "On August 1, Lead Belly was across the Mississippi River and headed for Shreveport. In a bag he carried a carefully folded document. Governor Allen's pardon had come." An asterisk follows this, and small type at the bottom of the page reads, "*General Manager Hymes [*sic*] has since written to me that Lead Belly's pardon was due to his 'good time.'"[102] In fact, Himes made it clear that Ledbetter had not been pardoned at all, although the book repeatedly says he was, referring to "Lead Belly's pardon papers" and the "'Pardon Songs,' successful appeals for freedom addressed to Governor Pat Neff of Texas and Governor O.K. Allen of Louisiana."[103]

The real story is simpler. About three weeks after the Lomaxes' second visit to Angola, on July 1, 1934, the governor finally turned his attention to the commutation recommendations. As historian Marianne Fisher-Giorlando wrote, "Ledbetter's was one of six commutations signed on July 20, 1934, and one of 179 in the whole year, for crimes including murder, manslaughter, shooting at a dwelling, and carnal knowledge – such commutations were common enough to be essentially routine."[104] But thirteen months had passed since the Board of Pardons recommended commutation, and, by the summer of 1934, Ledbetter didn't need to seek parole. Because of his own successful efforts to correct his record, Ledbetter's good time allowance alone, under Louisiana Act 311 of 1926[105] (as Himes noted in his file), could have freed him by June 26, 1934. Ledbetter "was not allowed all of his extra good time, and was [therefore] not discharged until August 1, 1934," Himes clarified.[106] This good time release was provisional, however, a fact that Himes shared with John Lomax in a letter. Should Huddie Ledbetter again be committed to the penitentiary in Louisiana, Himes wrote, Ledbetter "would be required to serve out the balance of 5 years, 6 months, 25 days" before beginning to serve the new sentence.[107]

Yet, throughout their time together, John Lomax would continue to suggest that he had played a role in Ledbetter's "pardon." It made for a good story, one that reflected benevolently on Lomax and, by extension, the judicial system. It also created grounds by which John Lomax could expect gratitude from the performer, and public repetition of the story could assuage criticism that he was exploiting him. In the months to come, however, as John Lomax felt his control over Ledbetter waning, his insistence on taking credit for Ledbetter's freedom would morph into a gnawing sense of responsibility for a man he had come to dislike, and even fear.

For now, though, it was gratitude that Lomax planned to use to his advantage. On September 24, 1934, less than two months after his release from Angola, Huddie Ledbetter met up with John Lomax at the hotel in Marshall, Texas, ready to spend much of the next three months on the road together, gathering folk songs. However much Lomax might previously have played up his concerns about Ledbetter and his knife, he had no such qualms now. "Ledbetter is here and we are off," he wrote to Ruby Terrill, now Mrs. John Lomax. "Don't be uneasy. He thinks I freed him. He will probably be of much help."[108]

CHAPTER 2

Two Men from Texas

Evidence suggests that Huddie Ledbetter did not believe that John Lomax played a role in his release, but perhaps found it advantageous to humor him by playing along. Released from the Louisiana State Penitentiary on August 1, 1934, with ten dollars discharge money and some work clothes,[1] he was a free man for the first time in more than four years. In addition to reconnecting with family and friends, what he most urgently needed was paid work, and John Lomax had offered him a job. The two men corresponded regularly during the summer of 1934. On July 20, not quite three weeks after the Lomaxes' second visit to Angola, Ledbetter wrote to Lomax from Camp A, addressing him as "Mr. John A. Lomax/Dear Boss man." He had received two letters from Lomax, he said, and was looking forward to getting out. He seemed aware that his release date had already passed, but at the same time, may have been confused about whether or not he was still waiting for action from the governor (he wasn't). He hoped "that the record is in the governor's hand" and wanted to know if Lomax could find out "just when is he going to let me go." In any event, Ledbetter wrote, the "warden says he was going to see about my time." He suggested that Lomax could either come back to get him or send him a ticket so they could meet up in Texas.[2]

The correspondence continued after Ledbetter's discharge as the two men kept trying and failing to connect. Ledbetter's letters do not contain expressions of gratitude for his freedom, but instead are focused on arranging employment. His first post-release note, dated August 10, reads (in its entirety): "Kindly sir I am out of the pen in Shreveport on my way to my daughters house in Dallas Texas if you get there before I do I will be in Kildgo [Kilgore] Texas But I am looking for you I am going to work for you."[3] In a September 4 note, Ledbetter sounded impatient, offering "just a few lines" to let Lomax know that he was in Shreveport and "looking for" him. He hoped that Lomax would "get this letter at once and com[e] and get [him]," as he was "ready to work" for him. He added, "Like I told you you can [write] me let me hear from you. Com[e] after me soon as you can I am not got no job waiting on you so I haven['t] got any money."[4]

The September 4 note was written in pencil on a petty cash voucher from the Excelsior Steam Laundry in Shreveport, where Ledbetter's girlfriend, thirty-four-year-old Martha Promise, worked. In the weeks since his release, Ledbetter had reconnected with Martha, whom he'd known and dated, on and off, for years.[5] After his release, "he looked for me everywhere," she told Elizabeth Goodman Lomax, Alan's first wife, in a 1950s interview. One evening, Martha remembered, she was sitting on the porch, "when he rolled up there, him and his cousin in a car." Teasing, they pretended not to recognize her and asked if she'd go in and get Martha. "I had just come from work and had kicked my shoes off," she said. "I was trying to get my shoes on, but he thought I was too slow moving. He got out of the car, and he had his guitar in his hand. Lord, I just grabbed him. Him and me just wrung one another." Martha invited him in, and the next evening he returned. "I've come to stay," he told her. While she went to work every day, "He'd clean the house and everything else he could do around here."[6]

Part of the challenge Ledbetter faced in contacting Lomax was that Lomax, too, was on the move. On July 21, 1934, shortly after recording Ledbetter, sixty-six-year-old John Lomax and forty-eight-year-old Ruby Terrill were married in Texas. They spent their honeymoon driving "nearly eight thousand miles through the West," wrote biographer Nolan Porterfield, "eventually spending most of their time in Lakeview, Idaho, [an] idyllic mountain resort."[7] They were back in Austin on September 5, in time to receive Ledbetter's September 4 note. Lomax replied on September 6, but apparently his letter wasn't received, because Ledbetter wrote again on September 12 from Shreveport, looking to "see or hear" from Lomax "at once." Lomax could come after him or send a ticket, he repeated, asking that Lomax please respond.[8] Finally, Lomax sent a telegram. "Can you meet me at Plaza Hotel Marshall Saturday September twenty-second," it read. "Come prepared to travel. Bring guitar. Wire me collect also write as soon as this telegram comes …. Answer quick."[9]

2.1 John and Ruby Terrill Lomax on their wedding day, 1934. Christianson and Leberman Studio, photographer. John Avery Lomax family papers [e_lfp_0029], The Dolph Briscoe Center for American History, The University of Texas at Austin. Courtesy of the estate of John A. Lomax.

While Lomax would later tell a story in which Ledbetter surprised him by showing up at the Marshall hotel to beg for work, the truth is that he needed Ledbetter as much as Ledbetter needed him. At some point after the pair left Angola in the summer of 1934, Alan Lomax had become seriously ill, and he was recuperating in Lubbock, Texas at the home of his sister Shirley and her husband, a physician. Lomax's new wife was not yet willing to retire from her career at the University of Texas, and his son John, Jr. ("Johnny") was employed elsewhere, so there was no one in his family available to assist with driving and collecting. If Lomax harbored any doubts about not wanting to do field work on his own, he was certain of it by the time he arrived in Marshall after driving hundreds of miles alone in East Texas. On Sunday, September 23, his sixty-seventh birthday, he wrote to Ruby to complain about "rough and hilly" roads, accommodations offering "a hard bed after a cold bath," and the glaring lights of a nighttime football game. Things improved once he was in Marshall, though; in "this comfortable hostelry I have slept and relaxed back to normalcy; have spent some time trying to reach Leadbelly on the phone (and didn't) and am now hungry for lunch," he wrote.[10] Finally, on Monday, September 24, Ledbetter arrived in Marshall, to what must have been Lomax's relief.

Furthermore, as helpful as his teenaged son had been – and Lomax hoped he would be able to join him again soon – Alan could not match Ledbetter's expertise, experience, and perspective. Like Lomax, Huddie Ledbetter was deeply immersed in the American songbook, particularly the musical traditions of Texas and Louisiana. One man was an academic, the other an entertainer, but each, in his own way, was a collector with a deep appreciation for tradition. The key difference was that Ledbetter was also open to the future, eager to embrace new material, reach new audiences, and take advantage of the emerging technologies of mass entertainment. John Lomax viewed popular entertainment and its transmission via records, the radio, and the movies as antithetical to his preservation of the past, a creeping blight that would corrupt the archive before he'd had a chance to fully capture it. Most importantly, while both men had spent most of their lives in Texas, they came from two very different worlds.

Huddie Ledbetter was born on the Jeter plantation near Mooringsport in Caddo Parish, Louisiana on January 20, 1889,[11] a quarter-century after slavery's end and a dozen years after the end of Reconstruction. Now part of the Shreveport–Bossier City metropolitan area, Mooringsport is on the southern shore of Caddo Lake, a 25,400-acre body of water that spans northwest Louisiana, northeast Texas, and southern Arkansas. Both of Ledbetter's parents – his father, Wesley Ledbetter, Jr. (born c. 1858 in North Carolina), and his mother, Sallie Pugh Ledbetter (born c. 1859 in Louisiana)[12] – were children when the Union victory over Confederate forces in 1865 brought an end to the Civil War. Both grew up on the Jeter place, first as enslaved people and later as sharecroppers. Sallie had a son, Alonzo Batts, Jr., born in 1874, with a man named Joseph Batts.[13] In 1877, she married Hence Brown in a ceremony witnessed by Wesley Ledbetter, Jr. (Sallie's future husband), Mose Coleman, and Tom Brown.[14] All of the participants signed the document with a mark, indicating that they had not yet learned to read or write. The marriage between Sallie and Hence

Brown didn't last, and, by 1880, Ledbetter's parents, listed as husband and wife, can be found in census records, living together with young Alonzo in a home next door to Wesley's parents and three of Wesley's siblings.[15] They officially married on February 26, 1888,[16] and in January 1889, Huddie was born. Three years later, in 1892, they adopted an infant daughter, Australia Carr, after her mother died.

Huddie Ledbetter's paternal grandparents – Wesley Ledbetter, Sr. (born 1833) and Ammie Ledbetter (born 1836) – had been enslaved in North Carolina, where they were married in 1854.[17] Sometime within the next three years, they were moved to the Jeter plantation, most likely making the journey of several hundred miles at least in part by foot, chained together with scores of other people in long "coffles." They remained at the Jeter place after the war, and all of their children were born there. Records for Ledbetter's maternal grandparents are less clear. Sallie's parents were not married to each other at the time of her birth.[18] Her mother was named Louise Birch.[19] Her father was Allen Pugh (born 1824), who later married a woman named Barbara (born 1825), and Sallie remained close with the families of both her parents.[20]

By the time Huddie Ledbetter was born, in 1889, his parents were eager to leave the Jeter plantation. It took its name from William Nathan Jeter (born 1821) and James Addison Jeter (born 1832), brothers born into a wealthy, white Virginia family.[21] According to Monty and Marsha Brown, musicians who researched Ledbetter's life from what was then their home in nearby Bossier City, Louisiana, the Jeters were "[a]mong the ante-bellum white settlers in the Shreveport region ... [who] came as part of that southeast migratory pattern that opened up millions of acres of land to the cultivation of cotton in Alabama, Mississippi, Louisiana, and, finally, Texas." In settling their newly acquired land in northwestern Louisiana, the Jeters "brought money and possessions, including some slaves." These enslaved people "cleared the land, planted cotton, [and] built a large house for the owners and small houses for themselves," the Browns wrote.[22] William Jeter arrived first, buying a tract of 320 acres "of wooded land northeast of Caddo Lake" from "Richard T. Noel" in 1849, according to the Browns. After going back to Virginia to marry, he returned to Louisiana, where he was joined by his younger brother, twenty-one-year-old James. In 1853, for "the sum of $1,500, James bought [480] acres from one Randolph Martin," the Browns wrote. "This land was to the west of the village of Blanchard, which is halfway between Shreveport and Mooringsport. James Jeter was a surveyor, and many maps of this area are based on 'Jeter's Country Plat.'" In 1860, William added another 160 acres "south of Caddo Lake." In this, he was helped by the US government's Land Act of 1820, part of federal efforts to encourage white settlement of midwestern and western territories. It provided that "public" land – from which indigenous populations had been removed through violence, disease, and forced relocation – be made available to white settlers for a modest price.[23]

In 1893, as control of the Jeter plantation was transferred from William Jeter to his son Francis ("Frank"), the Ledbetters moved about fifteen miles across the border from Caddo Parish, Louisiana to Harrison County, Texas. They were following in the footsteps of a Black landowner, Henry Sims, born in North Carolina in 1838 and listed on census records as being of partially white racial parentage.[24] Like the Ledbetters, Sims and his children, including Henry Sims, Jr., can be found in the 1870 census living on the Jeter plantation with several family members.[25] Sims also served as a deacon at the Shiloh Baptist Church in Mooringsport, where Wesley and Sallie Ledbetter worshipped. (Others who served there as deacons included Ledbetter's cousin, Edmon Ledbetter, and Martha Promise's brother, Dan Primus.)[26] In time, Sims became an independent farmer, eventually owning about 4,000 acres in Harrison County, Texas; there, he joined Elizabeth Church in Karnack, as did the Ledbetters. It's not clear how Sims managed to acquire so much land. When he died in 1907, he was one of the rare Black residents of the region whose obituary was published in a local paper, *The Marshall Messenger*. "Henry Simms [*sic*], a colored man of high standing, died at his farm on Caddo Lake today and will be buried at Elizabeth Church. 'Uncle Henry,' as he was familiarly called, was known and respected by all in the eastern part of the county as a man of integrity and honor, and by his industry accumulated a competency." The obituary continued with a gratuitously racist note: "His death marks the passing of another of the ante-bellum types of his race now so seldom met with."[27]

The Ledbetters entered into an agreement with Sims to work "for halves" on his property while they built up savings to buy land of their own. On July 1, 1897, when Huddie was eight years old, his parents achieved that dream, entering into an agreement to buy 68.5 acres of land in the area of Leigh, Harrison County, about a mile south of Caddo Lake (part of the John Carroll survey) from white landowners Asbery "Doc" and Sue Swanson Waskom. Unable to buy the land outright, the Ledbetters arranged a payment plan: The total purchase price of $240, about $3.50 per acre, would be paid in installments of $60, plus interest at 10 percent, every year on January 1, from 1898 through 1901. Ultimately, it took them seven years to buy the property outright, working the land on their own property when they weren't tied to their sharecropping schedule for Sims.[28] Ledbetter spoke with pride of his parents and their efforts as they worked to break this new ground, converting wilderness into farmland. They would be out until one or two o'clock in the morning, he said, clearing the land, cutting trees that would be sold as lumber, and burning brush while he and his sister slept in the house. He remembered waking up late at night and watching fires out in the bottomlands.[29] As he grew older, he too worked long hours alongside his parents, leaving school around the eighth grade. Ledbetter's childhood friend Margaret Coleman told the Lomaxes that the Ledbetters "worked hard on the farm to make an honest living. They had a standard record throughout Harrison County and Louisiana as being good honest respectable people."[30] On February 24, 1904, the Ledbetters' balance was paid in full, and they were the independent owners of nearly seventy acres of land.[31]

A trip from the Ledbetters' farm to the nearest town, Leigh, a tiny village about fourteen miles northeast of Marshall, was an occasion. "We was living out in the country," Ledbetter said. "We had to ride five miles to get mail and get it once a week. Read a newspaper once a week."[32] His nieces, Irene and Viola (daughters of Sally's son, Alonzo Batts, and his wife, Queen Victoria Batts), born in 1902 and 1904, grew up next door to the Ledbetters in Leigh, and, in 1913, moved in with Sallie and Wesley after their mother died. "We didn't see a store unless we went to town or something," Irene said. Her sister agreed: "Get the wagon and come to Leigh. Buy something. That wasn't so often, but you would walk to Leigh, five miles." By then, their grandfather, Wesley, Jr., who had been unable to sign his own name on his marriage license, was an avid reader, part of a post-war rush to literacy that was widespread among the formerly enslaved. One of the storekeepers in Leigh used to "save all the papers for him to read," Viola said. "He'd have a stack of them when he'd come in, and he read every one of them." Irene added that Wesley Ledbetter "couldn't read fluently, but what he read, he understood it." In time, Wesley taught Bible classes at Elizabeth Church, where Sallie was "a song leader, in the Amen Corner," Irene said. "They had a place where the ladies sit, where they're going to say 'Amen' and they're going to lead songs."[33] The girls' uncle Huddie would occasionally play the organ at services but was not a regular attendee, although they said this did not indicate an absence of faith. Viola Batts described visiting her uncle in New York City in the 1940s. Some musicians were coming by to pick Ledbetter up for a "gig," she said. "[T]hat's what I call it because that's what the other bunch called it." One of the men began making fun of the church, and Ledbetter stopped him. "You can't low-rate the church," he told the man, adding that Viola's father had baptized him (Ledbetter's half-brother, Alonzo, was an itinerant preacher). "That's my brother and this is my niece, and I can't have that." The other man fell silent.[34]

In Leigh, there was a post office, a railroad station, and a large general store, one of two (the other was in Karnack) owned by Thomas Jefferson "T.J." Taylor, a prominent white businessman and landowner and the father of "Lady Bird," the future wife of President Lyndon B. Johnson.[35] Born into a family of sharecroppers in Alabama in 1874, Taylor moved to Texas in the mid-1890s. He ultimately owned about 15,000 acres of land, which he used primarily to produce cotton, and he was extremely influential in the area. "Taylor amassed considerable wealth by using the profits from his store and other business ventures to advance money to needy farmers at ten percent [interest] and by investing heavily in real estate," biographer Mark Odintz wrote. "Very much a typical successful rural entrepreneur of his times, he was called 'Cap'n Taylor' by his business associates and 'Mister Boss' by black sharecroppers; he was probably the largest landowner in Harrison County by the 1930s."[36] In a frank appraisal of what was the norm among white landowners of the period, Taylor's daughter would later describe his approach to farming and to the tenants who worked his land as "feudal."[37]

The workdays were long and hard, and children often had to miss school to help out. Still, there was always time for adventure, much of it around the shores of Caddo Lake. The road to the lake was "muddy" and "full of holes . . . just through the woods," remembered Viola. They'd go out onto the grounds, and "Papa was a fisherman. He'd go out at night and fish, and we had all kinds of big fish." People would also wade out into the lake, mussel-hunting and hoping to find pearls, Irene said. "Wagonloads" of family and friends would gather along the shore, and their uncle would "furnish the music," she continued. "We'd have guitar-picking and dancing and plays, and of course, we had meals. We always had a picnic lunch," she said. "We called it 'dinner on the ground.' They were good times."[38]

Ledbetter grew up at a time when music was something shared live, with or without the accompaniment of musical instruments. Music was present in the fields to make the work somewhat lighter; in church to celebrate one's faith; at home to mark everything from weddings and funerals to the end of a long, hard week. By all accounts, Ledbetter was a musical prodigy, a child whose talents were encouraged by his immediate and extended family, several of whom were also musicians. Margaret Coleman, who was about six months younger[39] and knew Huddie from when they were children in school together, told the Lomaxes that Ledbetter was "an apt boy in his books," "quiet and respectful," and "always willing to learn. He was smart [and] swift toward any kind of work." He couldn't go far in his studies, though, because his parents were older and needed him on the farm. But "his talent was music," she said. Before the guitar, he played the mouth harp, accordion, and piano. He talked of the things he wanted to do "when he became a man," she wrote, adding that "something about Hudie's [sic] life was quite different from other children." Through his music, he hoped, "he would make lots of money so that he could make his mother and father happy in their old age."[40]

Queen Esther "Queenie" Pugh Davidson, born two years after her cousin Huddie, also remembered him playing a mouth harp as a child. One day, she said, he told her father, his uncle Kemp Pugh (Sallie's half-brother),[41] that he wanted a windjammer, a button accordion. "My daddy said, 'Well, you help me find some of this fat pine and I'll carry it to Shreveport and sell it and I'll get you an accordion,'" Davidson told Monty and Marsha Brown. "Huddie wasn't nothing but a boy, [but he] got the pine and they went on to Shreveport in the wagon, sold the pine, and got the accordion." Ledbetter's niece, Viola, said that a little rocking chair he'd had as a child was passed down to her. "They said before his feet could touch the floor in that little rocker, he was playing the accordion."[42]

Huddie's cousin Edmon Ledbetter was just six months younger than
Huddie, and people often mistook them for brothers. "We went everywhere together," Edmon told an interviewer in 1955. "He would come
over to my house after school and we would play in the yard. He liked the
horseshoes and was the best player around." Edmon said that it was he
who taught Ledbetter to play the guitar. "Huddie used to play the accordion and then I taught him to play the six-string guitar," he said. "He was
a quick learner. He was the [only person] I knew who could just pick up an
instrument and play it like he had lessons . . . He would sit by the fireplace
and keep trying 'til he got it right. We each had our own songs and would
write them down so people in our family could sing them, too. These were
happy times."[43] Margaret Coleman remembered how quickly Ledbetter
learned new songs. She said that the first night he had his new guitar, he
taught himself to play "There Ain't No Corn Bread Here" and soon after
could play "Frankie Was a Good Woman" and "Boll Weevil Blues." Soon,
she said, he was being asked to play at school recitals, and then to play for
"all the big parties and dances. He was noted to be the best dancer and
guitar player around." Ledbetter's niece, Irene Campbell, remembered
"the Saturday night get togethers we used to have." She told an interviewer, "We'd sing songs, then have music, and dance. He did tap dancing. He was the first person that I ever saw do tap dancing." It was
"entertainment, sometimes just for the family," she said. "You know that
we had a large family. Sometimes neighbors in the community would
come by. They would have competitions to see who could 'cut it,' called it,
'Cut the Pigeon Wing.'"[44]

According to authors Charles Wolfe and Kip Lornell, the first "real
models" for Ledbetter's musicianship came from his uncles Bob (Edmon's
father) and Terrell Ledbetter. They "enjoyed local reputations as guitarists
and vocalists of the kind Huddie later referred to as a 'songster.'" From
Terrell, they reported, Ledbetter learned "Looky Yonder Where the Sun
Done Gone," "Take a Whiff on Me," and "De Ballit of De Boll Weevil,"
about a beetle that was devastating cotton production.[45] Additional
musical influences, they wrote, were local performers Bud Coleman, who
played guitar, and Jim Fagin, who played mandolin.[46] According to scholar
John Cowley, Ledbetter also picked up songs, such as "Becky Dean,"
from levee workers and others who occasionally performed day labor on
the Ledbetter farm.[47] Over time, Ledbetter learned several other

instruments, and he enjoyed teaching others to play, including his sister Australia. "They had a way of tuning the guitars so they would have melody," his niece, Irene, remembered.[48] "We had a musical family, we had a togetherness family."

For a time, Edmon and Huddie traveled and performed together. "Sometimes he played a mandolin and I'd second him with a guitar and sometimes we played the guitar together," Edmon told a reporter in 1974. "Used to play all [around] here, up to Mooringsport, over to Leigh and back on the Jeter Plantation."[49] They played at house parties and events, and in addition, according to Margaret Coleman, "the white people with stores and drugstores asked Hudie to play Saturday evening and nights at their places to draw the crowd." This, she said, provided more opportunities to earn money that "enabled him to be lots of help to his parents. They were proud of him."[50] According to Edmon, his cousin Huddie "liked the weekend excitement of being in town and all the glitter that went with him." He added, "The women were crazy about him. He liked all that attention."[51] Edmon decided that he wanted a different life for himself. His daughter Pinkie, born in 1917, told Kip Lornell, "I used to hear my daddy talk about how those parties were pretty rough. That's what caused him to stop going out playing and went to going to church."[52] Edmon Ledbetter devoted his life and talent to the Shiloh Baptist Church in Mooringsport, serving as superintendent for forty years and as deacon for thirty-nine years.[53] When Ledbetter returned to visit in later years, though, Pinkie remembered that he and her father would "get out in the yard, and they'd play and sing."

Ledbetter continued to perform on his own, traveling between gigs on his prized horse, Booker. "He was black as a crow and he had a blaze face and all four of his feet were white stocking feet," Preston Brown, a friend eleven years younger than Ledbetter, remembered. "He used to take that horse down to the creek and wash him, you know. Kept it sleek." Ledbetter would "come down the road, singing on that pony. It was a beautiful pony, with a star on its face," said Mary Patterson, who was a couple of years older than Ledbetter and attended school with him.[54] Ledbetter "had that horse shining all the time," confirmed Viola Batts Daniels, and he had "a robe across his lap keeping his suit from getting hair or whatever on it. And that's how he traveled, with his guitar."[55] Sometimes, Preston Brown would ride with Ledbetter to the train station, bringing Booker back home and taking care of him while the performer was out of town.

Ledbetter especially loved to play for children. His nieces remembered him singing along as they played games like "In and Out the Window," "London Bridge," and "Little Sally Walker." Children took to Ledbetter "like ducks to water," wrote white recording executive Moses "Moe" Asch, years later, describing a performance Ledbetter gave at a children's playground in New York's Greenwich Village. "He had them 'Skipping to My Lou' and dancing and singing 'Little Sally Walker,' and what surprised me most was that they understood (they were 5–7 years old) his directions and colloquialisms," he said. "Nor was this an isolated incident. In fact, the concert that remains most vivid in my memory is the one he gave at Christmas for children at the Metropolitan Museum of Art. It was jam-packed, children all over the place, frantic parents. But the moment Leadbelly started to play and sing, the audience hushed, the children grouped around him as though it was grandfather singing for them, some sang with him, others danced, parents were bewitched."[56]

John Avery Lomax, like Huddie Ledbetter, was raised to believe that he would become a farmer, and he, too, rejected that lifestyle. Born in Goodman, Holmes County, Mississippi in 1867, just after the Civil War ended, Lomax was just two years old when his family moved to Texas. He was the sixth of ten children of James Avery Lomax (1816–1892) and Susan Frances Cooper Lomax (1835–1928); James Lomax also had five children from a previous marriage. His family was not wealthy, Lomax said, but they weren't poor. "My family and I belonged to the upper crust of the 'po' white trash,' traditionally held in contempt by the aristocracy of the Old South and by their Negro slaves," he wrote in his 1947 autobiography. "Father always owned a few acres of land which kept him from being at the bottom of the social scale. However, his brother, whose wife inherited a large cotton plantation and a swarm of slaves, lived closely enough so that Father's family was sneered at as poor kinfolk."[57]

Lomax's great grandson, John Nova Lomax (grandson of John Lomax, Jr.), described James Avery Lomax as "a fairly typical white Southern man of his time." Born in South Carolina in 1816, John Lomax's father worked as a field hand, tanner, and finally "slave overseer, saving enough at that odious occupation to buy a farm of his own."[58] Like the Jeters but to a lesser extent, both James Lomax and his younger brother Tillman benefited from the land grants authorized by Congress. Tillman also achieved wealth and influence through marriage, joining "the 1 percent of antebellum Mississippi society," John Nova Lomax reported, adding that Tillman "was a considerable planter before the Rebellion."[59] In the 1860 census, the real estate held by Tillman Lomax and his family was valued at $8,900, and their personal estate – including the value of the people they enslaved – at $20,190. In contrast, the 1860 census valued the real estate of James Lomax (John's father) at $2,500, and the family's personal estate at $2,140.[60]

Both James and Tillman Lomax, John Lomax's father and uncle, fought for the Confederacy. After the war, Tillman and his family chose to remain in Mississippi, but James and Susan Lomax sold their belongings and, in early November 1869, headed for Texas with their family. Twelve travelers in all, they arrived in Bosque County by wagon at the end of December, a two-month journey that thirty-four-year-old Susan Lomax endured while caring for six children (all under twelve years of age) and heavily pregnant with another, George Lomax, who was born in January 1870. But the Lomaxes were not starting from scratch. Before they moved, Susan Lomax wrote, they sold their "household things, cows, horses, mules, with our land," which netted the family "about four thousand dollars in gold." Using only about a quarter of these savings – roughly $1,100 – they bought 183 acres of Bosque River bottom and built a small home. The family raised horses and cattle, cut and sold timber, and cleared new ground for farming.

John Lomax "complained that his youth had been closed off by 'manual toil and a frontier life,'" biographer Nolan Porterfield wrote.[61] But the Lomax family had a rule that after attending high school, "each child should 'go off to school' for one year; that year would complete his twenty-one years of service for the common good of the family," according to Lomax.[62] He paid for his education with proceeds from wheat he salvaged after floods damaged eleven acres his father had set aside for him, plus the sale of his pony and a loan from his cousin, Alonzo "Lon" Cooper, a son of former enslavers in Mississippi.[63] Lomax finished his year of college and began working in small rural schools as a teacher and principal. In the fall of 1895, nearing his twenty-eighth birthday and again with the financial support of his cousin, Lomax enrolled full time at the University of Texas, which had opened its doors only a dozen years earlier and would remain whites-only until 1956.[64] He took on a double course load, earning a bachelor's degree at the end of his second year. Administrators invited him to stay on as university registrar, which required him to work toward a master's degree, and Lomax accepted.[65] He spent six years as registrar, 1897–1903, and then became an administrator at Texas Agricultural & Mechanical College (Texas A&M). A romance ended tragically when the woman he loved died of tuberculosis, but he then began dating twenty-three-year-old Bess Brown, a student at the University of Texas. She left school and they were married in June 1904, when he was thirty-six. Finally, in the fall of 1906 and with support from Texas A&M, the Lomaxes moved temporarily to Cambridge, Massachusetts, where John – now thirty-nine and the father of one-year-old Shirley – enrolled in a one-year master's program at Harvard University.

At Harvard, for the first time in his life, Lomax found support for his interest in cowboy and other folk songs, according to Nolan Porterfield. He graduated in 1907 and embarked on a song-collecting and lecturing career, interspersed with work as an administrator at the University of Texas and as a bond salesman in Chicago. He published three books, *Cowboy Songs and Other Frontier Ballads* (Sturgis and Walton, 1910), *The Book of Texas* (with co-author H.Y. Benedict, Doubleday, 1916), and *Songs of the Cattle Trail and Cow Camp* (Macmillan, 1919). By 1925, this career had stalled, and he found a more profitable one. Forced out by political tensions between the university and the Texas state government, Lomax used his professional network to secure employment as "Manager of the Bond Department" at Republic Savings and Trust, a Dallas bank. He was "obviously doing well," wrote Porterfield, citing as evidence his purchase and construction of a "sprawling, nine-room bungalow set . . . on several acres of timberland" some "six or seven miles" from downtown Dallas.[66] But Lomax's life began to unravel in the early 1930s. In May 1931, Bess, his wife of more than twenty-five years and mother of their four children, ranging in age from twenty-five to ten,[67] had died at the age of fifty. In the midst of global economic depression, his services were no longer needed at the Republic Bank. He was unemployed, "heavily in debt," still financially responsible for two of his children, and "barely recovering from an exhausting illness."[68]

According to Porterfield, it was Lomax's oldest son, Johny, twenty-five years old and also an out-of-work banker, who convinced Lomax that he might enjoy a return to college touring and lecturing.[69] When it turned out that audiences were no longer interested in his cowboy material,[70] Lomax began to conceive of a new collection of material that would be broader in scope. In June 1932, he met with Harold S. Latham, Macmillan's editor-in-chief, to propose the book that eventually came to be titled *American Ballads and Folk Songs*. He began his pitch by performing a couple of traditional tunes that didn't get much of a response. "Then I fired my third and last shot," Lomax recalled in his autobiography, "a ballad I had found on the Texas Gulf Coast in the district between the Colorado and Brazos Rivers where … Negroes are thicker than mustang grapes." It was "Ida Red," the story of a regretful man held by a ball and chain, waiting for the train to prison. "As Mr. Latham laughed he was also mopping the lower part of his brow," Lomax reported. "'I am very much interested,' he said."[71]

Within a couple of weeks, Lomax had a book contract and an advance of $250. From New York, he and Johnny traveled to Washington, where he met with Herb Putnam, who had been serving as the Librarian of Congress since 1899. In turn, Putnam introduced him to Carl Engel, the chief of the Library of Congress's Music Division, and a fruitful professional relationship was established. Soon after, in July 1932, thanks to some networking from his father, Johnny was offered a job with the newly established Reconstruction Finance Corporation and was no longer available to travel. Instead, Lomax's other son, seventeen-year-old Alan, would join his father on a song-collecting tour the following summer. In the meantime, they spent the fall of 1932 in Austin, where Alan was enrolled as a junior at the University of Texas, and Lomax pored over university archives to ensure that he wouldn't be duplicating songs that had already been gathered and copyrighted. In the summer of 1933, they began recording the material that appeared in *American Ballads and Folk Songs*, and first encountered Huddie Ledbetter. The following summer, funded by Carnegie and Rockefeller, father and son were again on the road, until Alan fell ill.

Waiting alone at the hotel in Marshall, Texas on that hot, overcast Monday in September, 1934, John Lomax was facing several more weeks of collecting, and was almost certainly pleased when Huddie Ledbetter arrived. But rather than admit this, or acknowledge the valuable assistance Ledbetter might provide, or even be forthcoming that they had been corresponding for weeks, John Lomax chose to present the encounter in Marshall, Texas as being a complete surprise to him. In *Negro Folk Songs as Sung by Lead Belly*, Lomax says that he looked up from reading a newspaper in the Marshall hotel lobby "to see a Negro man standing timidly by my chair. He had touched my shoulder to draw my attention as he stood there, his face ashen with uncertainty and fear." Lomax claims that he said, "Why, hello, Lead Belly! What are you doing here?"[72] This is false; not only was Lomax anticipating Ledbetter's arrival, but he had already planned an ambitious itinerary that would take them to prisons he had not yet visited in Arkansas, Alabama, Georgia, South Carolina, North Carolina, and Texas. Yet even two days later, writing to his wife, Lomax portrayed the meeting as a job interview. In his "first talk" with the performer, he wrote, he asked "what weapons he was carrying along." This scene would later be repeated in the Lomaxes' book and – reaching much larger audiences – *The March of Time*, a national news magazine program that in 1935 carried stories about Ledbetter on the radio and in movie theaters. Lomax told Ruby that Ledbetter showed him a "dangerous looking" knife "with a long keen blade."[73] The knife, visible in the newsreel, is a pocketknife, and Lomax opens it to reveal a blade that appears to be about three inches long and less than an inch wide at the base. As Lomax would soon learn, Ledbetter sometimes used the knife in place of a guitar slide, in a style of performance described as "Hawaiian" or "bottleneck." Ledbetter's younger cousin, Queenie Pugh Davidson, described how he'd use the knife to suggest various sound effects: "He said he could make that guitar sound just like that train, that whistle."[74] Despite the fact that Lomax, like many men of his era, probably also carried some kind of utility knife – an especially useful tool for someone like Lomax, who camped by the roadside and often needed to repair jury-rigged recording equipment – he chose to present the knife in Ledbetter's possession as a threat. With bravado that he later included in the book, he told his new wife that he'd warned Ledbetter, "[W]henever you decide that you are going to take my money and car, you won't have to use this knife on me. Just tell me what you want and I'll give it to you without a struggle." He claimed that Ledbetter was almost in tears as he answered, "[P]lease, suh, don't talk that way. You got me out of the pen. I'se your man. You won't ever have to tie yo shoes again if you don't want to. I'll step in front of you if ever anybody tries to shoot you. I'm ready to die for you, Boss."[75]

This account gains some credibility by virtue of it being written so soon after the event, but the full nature of the conversation is elusive. Ledbetter had traveled to Marshall about a job he had watched young Alan Lomax perform. The recording machinery was not complicated, but it was unwieldy, heavy, and prone to breaking down, all of which Ledbetter could handle. Beyond that, Ledbetter understood more about the music being sought, and the men and women who performed it, than Lomax ever could. Lastly, he had been holding out for the promise of this job since his release, which meant that he had not earned any significant money for two months, on top of not having an income during the five years of his incarceration. Now, it seemed, the job he'd traveled to undertake was less than certain. The tone in Ledbetter's letters prior to the meeting in Marshall – self-confident and eager for the work – seems to have shifted once the two men were together. Ledbetter may have assessed, quickly, that this white, patrician south-erner had specific expectations of who he was and how he should behave. For pragmatic reasons, perhaps, he went along, donning what poet Paul Laurence Dunbar described as "the mask."[76] His pledge of loyalty clearly flattered Lomax, because Lomax repeated it often in the weeks and months to come.

It's not clear how or when Lomax made it clear that the "job" he had for Ledbetter was unpaid, offering just an allowance, handed out daily, to cover food and housing as needed. Instead, as he later described the meeting, Lomax presented himself as a benefactor offering hope of redemption to a man who had none. Long after he knew that Ledbetter had a very close extended family and community along the Texas–Louisiana border, Lomax wrote: "I realized that probably no one in the world, except his woman, felt the slightest interest in him, that he might soon be back in the penitentiary for some crime against his own people." The reasons that Ledbetter agreed to the financial terms are also not known, but there are a few possibilities. One is that he was not welcome in the Shreveport–Mooringsport–Oil City area, where he'd worked in the

2.2 Portrait of John A. Lomax, c. 1935–1936. John Avery Lomax family papers, e_lfp_0001, The Dolph Briscoe Center for American History, The University of Texas at Austin. Courtesy of the estate of John A. Lomax.

years prior to his 1930 arrest. Shreveport sheriff Tom Hughes had been notified of his release and was concerned, and possibly Ledbetter had been made aware of this.[77] Additionally, after years of incarceration, the idea of traveling to areas he'd never been, meeting and sharing music with performers along the way, might have intrigued him. Finally, it seems likely that Lomax dangled a tantalizing promise: that if things worked out, he might bring the performer north and introduce him to influential people. This is supported by Lomax's letters in the weeks that followed, and by a statement he made in the book: "Thirty minutes" after the meeting, "with Lead Belly at the wheel, we were on our way headed for the Negro prison camps of the State of Arkansas. Lead Belly's Odyssey had begun. 'I wants to see New Yawk.'"[78]

CHAPTER 3

On the Road

Traveling with Huddie Ledbetter posed a challenge that John Lomax had not faced with his sons: negotiating the highly segregated and often dangerous systems of the Jim Crow South. There was nothing untoward about a white man using the services of a Black driver, but when it came to rest stops, meals, and sleeping accommodation, they had to be very aware of their surroundings. Writing to his wife after they arrived in Little Rock, Arkansas, Lomax said that he was staying in a "tourist cottage three or four miles out of town." It was comfortable – "showers, bath, good bed, cool and not too noisy" – and remote enough to serve as "a place to bring any singing negroes we find." Ledbetter was staying "in town with friends," Lomax reported.[1] As would be the case throughout their travels together, in the North as well as the South, Ledbetter was generally left to fend for himself at night. (*The Negro Motorist Green Book*, by Victor Hugo Green, a guide to navigating where African Americans could safely eat and sleep in the United States under Jim Crow segregation, was not published until 1936.) Lomax turned their separation into an advantage, making it "part of [Ledbetter's] duties to circulate on his own in the black sections and look for possible song sources, demonstrating by his own playing and singing what Lomax wanted," biographer Nolan Porterfield wrote. He added that Ledbetter "took to this with considerable enthusiasm."[2] On his own with his guitar, Ledbetter found fellowship and audiences, as well as an opportunity to earn money beyond the small allowance Lomax gave him each morning for expenses. On the more remote prison farms, when hotels and rooming houses weren't nearby – and because they often recorded long into the night – John Lomax was hosted by prison administrators. This meant that he stayed in comfortable manor homes with running water and good meals, usually prepared and served by Black prisoners who also cleaned and did laundry.[3] Ledbetter, though, had no choice but to eat and sleep with the trusties and other prisoners, and to be forced out of bed with them before dawn.

In Little Rock and elsewhere on the itinerary, Lomax followed a routine he had established the prior summer. After arriving in the capital of each state, he worked his professional and personal networks to secure meetings with governors and other political leaders, who then supplied introductions to senior prison officials, opening the doors to the prisons themselves. He would also let Ruby and others know where to reach him by mail, general delivery, for the next few days. Soon after they arrived in Little Rock, they picked up a package from Ruby. Lomax had told her to "[s]end for [Ledbetter] that old black suit and the worn shirt and some of the old ties; also something, if you have it, that will serve him for a valise."[4] Ledbetter was pleased. He had shown up in Marshall with only his guitar and a "brown-paper sugar bag," Lomax wrote, and subsequent photographs support this. "He wore no coat; only an old hat, a blue shirt, a patched pair of overalls and rusty, yellow shoes."[5] Lomax presumed the outfit was provided to Ledbetter by the Louisiana State Penitentiary, although he had been free for nearly two months by then. Ledbetter had certainly tried to look his best. His niece Viola Batts Daniels remembered her uncle's fastidiousness, even on days when he was headed into the fields to work. "Everything had to be just so," she said. "His overalls were washed, starched, and ironed. Clean one every day."[6] He dressed up even more to perform. His friend Preston Brown remembered that "he had good clothes. His wife used to fix his shirts, looked like they came out of a laundry. White shirt, black tie."[7] Years later in New York City, musician Walter "Brownie" McGhee, a Tennessee performer born, like Alan Lomax, in 1915, decided to cut short a stay at the Ledbetters' apartment because he couldn't live up to Ledbetter's standards. Quoting Ledbetter, McGhee said, "You're a professional, Brownie, your guitar goes in a case. And a necktie. You don't take your coat off on stage."[8]

On Friday, September 28, Lomax's son Johnny arrived from Birmingham with "a lady friend," and Ledbetter gave what Lomax described as a "concert." Lomax was critical, complaining that Ledbetter had "sung too much of late" – on his own at night – "and his voice is not up to standard." Regardless, Johnny returned the following day with colleagues from work, and Lomax and Ledbetter together performed for them at a hotel, "with Leadbelly singing and me interpolating." Lomax pronounced the event a "great success."[9] That he was already thinking of a future when he might go on stage and introduce Ledbetter in person, a big step up from his years lecturing and performing cowboy songs on his own, is further evidenced by a small but significant detail: Johnny and his friends had brought some additional clothing for Ledbetter,[10] but Lomax insisted that Ledbetter not dispose of the outfit he'd worn to Marshall, which Lomax called his "convict clothes." As he explained to Ruby, "[f]or exhibition purposes I had him put them away."[11]

Even as Ledbetter was getting a sense of how much Lomax valued his singing and the types of "performances" the two of them might do, he was also learning the scope of servitude expected of him, beyond driving and helping with the recordings – and certainly far different from anything Lomax had expected of his sons. "I found my first experience with a 'body servant' pleasant," Lomax wrote to Ruby. "Each morning he waked me and handed me a cup of hot coffee, made ready my bath, laid out my clothes, allowed no hotel porter to touch my shoes or valises, and, as we started our daily drive, opened for me the door of a freshly cleaned car."[12]

At the end of their first week on the road, the pair began seeking material at a relatively small prison farm at Pine Bluff, south of Little Rock. Not finding much there, they moved on to Tucker, which was about 4,500 acres (7 square miles). There, they made the first exciting discovery of the trip: a fast-paced song, new to Ledbetter, "Rock Island Line." Written and copyrighted in 1923 by Clarence Wilson, the song was originally titled "Buy Your Ticket over Rock Island Lines," according to folklorist Stephen Wade. It was created as part of a "booster movement" for "the Rock Island railroad's Arkansas–Louisiana division," Wade wrote, and meant to be performed by a quartet, as it was when Wilson sang it with three others in a group known as the "Rock Island Colored Booster Quartet." The singers were all employed by the railroad; they were not incarcerated.[13] The song had made its way into the penitentiaries because the rhythm lent itself to service as a work song, setting a pace for labor.

At the Cummins State Prison Farm, about seventy-seven miles southeast of Little Rock, they recorded "Rock Island Line" again. This version

3.1 Prisoners working with axes, Reed Camp, South Carolina, December 1934. Alan Lomax, photographer. Library of Congress, Prints & Photographs Division, Lomax Collection [number LC-DIG-ppmsc-00419].

was led by a smooth-voiced man named Kelly Pace, accompanied by seven others. "Their performance involved a closely-patterned call-and-response," wrote Wade, "their voices dispersed in three- and sometimes four-part harmony. Between the choruses one of them imitated a train whistle."[14]

> Pace: O the Rock Island Line
> Others: It's a mighty good road
>
> Pace: O the Rock Island Line
> Others: It's the road to ride.

Pace: O the Rock Island Line
Others: It's a mighty good road

Pace and others: If you wants to ride, you got to ride it like you find it
Get your ticket at the station on the Rock Island Line.[15]

Ledbetter soon added the song to his repertoire. In a preface to a 1937 recording at the Library of Congress, he described how the loggers he'd seen in Arkansas used the song to set a safe rhythm for a dozen or so men, standing on opposite sides of a log, to alternate chopping into the wood. "You can't cut your ax in there and leave it," he said. "You've got to pick it up in rhythm with the song. As I cut down, you bring it up."[16] Authors Charles Wolfe and Kip Lornell noted that over time, as he began performing in the folk music scene of New York in the late 1930s and early 1940s, Ledbetter "gradually dropped the work song references" in the story that preceded the song. Instead, he "replaced them with a narrative about an engineer who fools the 'depot man' about what kind of freight he is carrying."[17]

Already, and probably without Ledbetter's knowledge, John Lomax had begun to explore introducing Ledbetter's repertoire and talent to a wider audience. On Monday, October 1, 1934, just one week after leaving Marshall, he wrote to Oliver Strunk, a prominent young musicologist and head of the Library of Congress's Music Division. "Just now I am on the Arkansas river in the center of a Negro convict farm with 750 inmates," he said. "My driver and assistant (Alan is sick in Lubbock, Texas, having again fallen victim to the malaria of southern Louisiana) is a Negro ex-convict, Leadbelly by name, who two months ago sang a petition for pardon on a record, addressed to Governor O.K. Allen." As he would continue to do, Lomax implied credit for Ledbetter's release: "I carried the record back to Baton Rouge, a hundred miles away. The governor listened to it, and then pardoned Leadbelly." And once again, he feigned to have played no role in establishing this new partnership. "He came on to Texas and attached himself to me," he told Strunk. "He says that I will never again have to tie my shoes if I 'don't want to.' When I come to Washington in January I'll bring him along and give you and Mrs. Strunk a specimen of Negro music as interpreted by a real Negro."[18]

A day later, though, Lomax expressed doubts in a letter to his wife. The problem was not Ledbetter's driving, he wrote. "[H]e is very careful and

watchful. I am much safer with him at the wheel than I would be with Alan."
But he was worried, already, that he would "probably . . . not be able to keep
[him], partly because the praise of his music spoils him and partly because
of his Shreveport woman." These weren't Lomax's only issues. Having
expected from Ledbetter a role of almost pathetic subservience, he now
disparaged him. "If I better understood the nature of a Negro, I could
perhaps do something with him to the end that I could sell his product," he
told Ruby. "But he is too much of a child to wait." To Lomax, this was
particularly disappointing because he wanted Ledbetter to travel to Austin
to play for Ruby and for his thirteen-year-old daughter, Bess, who was living
with her. If this were to happen, Ruby could invite her women friends "to
hear a concert the like of which they have never before heard."[19]

If Lomax was having mixed feelings about the arrangement, so was
Ledbetter. Only two months had passed since he had walked out of the
18,500-acre Louisiana State Penitentiary at Angola, and there was little to
distinguish that from Cummins, where they now were: a vast, 16,600-acre
prison farm situated on former plantations, with armed trusties.[20] As
historian Robert Perkinson noted, southern states, including Texas and
Arkansas, had followed Louisiana's lead as they "similarly replaced [con-
vict] leasing with government plantations."[21] Cummins, operational in
1902, was the oldest prison farm in Arkansas. Like many others, it was
located miles from any substantial town and the possibility of finding
a hotel or guest cottage. Lomax was the guest of the head warden.
Ledbetter was bunking with trusties. The idea that returning to eat and
sleep in conditions that were deplorable, filthy, and at times dangerous
might have been traumatic for Ledbetter seems never to have occurred to
Lomax. To the contrary, after telling Ruby that Ledbetter would, on their
first night at Cummins, be performing at the women's camp "in order to
show them what kind of material I wish," he added, "Leadbelly I find plays
much better when in the environment of a penitentiary, perhaps his
native element, poor chap."[22]

Obviously, prison farms were not Huddie Ledbetter's "native element."
But it is not surprising that Ledbetter would pour his heart into performances for people trapped in a segregated and brutal system that he knew
all too well, or that, as a musician, he would be eager to learn new material
and compete with those who were the most talented, challenging them to
bring forth material to be recorded for the Library of Congress. This was

an audience that could understand and appreciate Ledbetter in ways that the Lomaxes never would. And yet it was the Lomaxes who were crafting his story, from the moment they met, and getting important details very, very wrong.

One of the most significant errors in the Lomaxes' narrative stems from their faulty chronology, which dated Ledbetter's birth to 1885 rather than 1889. This allowed them to pump up a racially stereotyped portrait of Ledbetter as a swaggering, violent, hypersexual teenager with no choice but to leave home at sixteen, which by their timeline was 1901.[23] In their book, they stated that in 1900, at fifteen, Ledbetter had fathered a child with his longtime friend Margaret Coleman. "The boys of his own age were jealous, the girls fearful and a little adoring, the old folks angry and resentful," the Lomaxes wrote. Ledbetter's parents would not let their son "be forced into an early marriage, but his school days were over," they said. "He went to work on his father's farm." When Coleman became pregnant again the following year, the Lomaxes claimed that Ledbetter denied responsibility, "but this time the community had turned against him. Soon he would have to leave Mooringsport."[24]

In the meantime, though, *Negro Folk Songs as Sung by Lead Belly* took a brief detour, describing a young Ledbetter acquiring his musical skills, and then, when he was around fifteen years old, playing "for parties and dances over the countryside" as his "fame . . . spread around."[25] Allegedly quoting Ledbetter, they wrote, "[M]y papa bought me a Puttection Special Colt [that] fit under my coat in a scabbid. He tol' me, says, 'Now son, don' you bodder nobody, don' make no trouble; but if somebody try to meddle wid you, I want you to puttect yo'se'f.'" According to the Lomaxes, Ledbetter said his father had also bought him a new horse and saddle. "I felt like a man, sho' 'nough."[26]

In the Lomax narrative, the two stories and the need to leave home merge after an incident, purportedly told by Ledbetter himself, about being at a "sukey-jump" (a house party or dance) and getting into a fight with another teen over a girl. Ledbetter pulled out his pistol and fired, but the gun jammed and no one was hurt. "[T]he sheriff knew my papa . . . and wouldn't do me nothing but fine me twenty-five dollahs fo' carrying concealed weapons," they claim Ledbetter told them. Suggesting that the fine was paid and the matter settled, the Lomaxes continued: "Now everything pointed to Fannin Street. His Protection Special Colt, his sexual precocity, his swaggering mannishness, even the songs he sang suggested Shreveport and the red-light district," they wrote, adding with a leer, "Something in his music, perhaps, had made him feel there were more exciting experiences in the way of womankind than Margaret and the other timid young girls of Mooringsport."[27]

These stories have played a big role in the Lead Belly mythology, and the Lomaxes' inaccurate summation of his character and experiences at sixteen (allegedly in 1901) would haunt him for the rest of his career. "Lead Belly, then, at sixteen had become the man he wanted to be and was to be," they wrote. "He was the best guitar-picker and songster in his part of the country. He was feared and respected by all the men who knew him, because he carried a pistol and was known to have an ugly temper. He was completely competent in a fight, with a terrible and calculating anger." They said that he "was thoroughly disliked by most of the men who knew him, because of his pride, his success, his conceit, and his way with women . . .. Any woman on Fannin Street would be proud to keep him in idleness because of his guitar, his voice and his charm."[28]

Primary source evidence and a corrected chronology paint a far different portrait. Born in 1889, Huddie Ledbetter did not turn sixteen in 1901, but in 1905. By then, he had already left school, most likely when he was about thirteen. This was not unusual – in fact, it was later than usual – for the children of farming families of any race, but especially Black share-cropping families. Those who knew Ledbetter agree that by the time he was sixteen, he was recognized as a talented and multifaceted singer, dancer, and musician, and as his teens stretched toward his twenties, his traveling range and the type of events at which he performed expanded. The allure of Shreveport, Louisiana, whose population rose from 16,000 in 1900 to 28,000 in 1910, was likely strong.[29] Ledbetter first visited the city as a child while on trips with his father, heading east from Leigh, Texas by horse-drawn wagon to sell cotton and other crops at local markets. His father would "lead me all around on Fannin Street and that's what I like," Ledbetter said, introducing the song "Fannin Street," "where the people dance and play and sing and pianos . . . and women dancing. . .. I wasn't much knee-high to a duck at that time, but I was watching. Shows you children don't forget nothing."[30] The official "red light" district, short-handed by Ledbetter and the Lomaxes as "Fannin Street," was not officially established until 1903, when Ledbetter was fourteen. It was created when city officials identified an area known as St. Paul's Bottoms, with its less desirable real estate, in which they would tolerate and thereby control illicit businesses including prostitution and gambling. "The low-lying 'bottoms' were far enough removed from the river to lack the benefit of breezes in the summer," wrote historian Cheryl H. White. The brothels "primarily attracted white clientele for white prostitutes," she noted, "although there were areas in the district that featured black or 'mulatto' girls."[31] Huddie Ledbetter, a maturing performer ready to seek larger audiences and the company of other musicians, composed a song about his eagerness to go, and his mother's fears that if he did, something bad might happen.

> My mamma told me, my sister, too,
> "Th' women in Shreveport, son,
> gonna be th' death o' you."

Speaking between stanzas, he said, "I looked at my mama and I couldn' stand to see my mama cryin' offa the words that I had spoke. I don' care how old you are – when you break your mother's heart it's gonna break your heart."

> I went to my mamma, fell down on my knees
> Cryin', "O' lordy Mamma,
> will you forgive me please?"[32]

As enticing as they may have seemed, "The Bottoms" presented challenges to a young performer, according to Monty and Marsha Brown. Some houses didn't hire musicians, but instead "had coin-operated player pianos which entertained clients waiting in the downstairs rooms." Huddie Ledbetter would have gotten "a taste of life in the Bottoms, but ... also found out that it was a tough place to make a living as a musician."[33] For a brief time, he returned home and seemed to settle down. On July 20, 1908, at the age of nineteen, he married Aletha "Lethe" Henderson, a seventeen-year-old from Kauffman County, east of Dallas.[34] The couple are documented in the 1910 census of Leigh village, enumerated in May, living next door to Wesley and Sallie Ledbetter and their now-married daughter, Australia Carr Davidson, who divorced soon after.[35] Also living nearby were Alonzo Batts and his family.[36]

It is true that Huddie Ledbetter fathered not one but two children during this period, and he did not deny his parentage of either of them. Both used Ledbetter as a last name throughout their lives, and he remained in touch with them and with their mother, Margaret Coleman. On January 28, 1909, about six months after his marriage to Aletha, twenty-year-old Huddie Ledbetter had a daughter, Arthur Mae, with Coleman. A year later, in January 1910, they had another daughter, Erma.[37] The Lomaxes' tale of a sixteen-year-old Huddie and his parents who "would not allow him to be forced into an early marriage"[38] is an invention.

Not long after the children were born, Margaret Coleman, her widowed mother,[39] and her children relocated to Dallas, where they can be found in the 1912 city directory and in census documents in the decades after.[40] The account of Ledbetter's two daughters with Margaret Coleman and their ongoing, if often distant, relationship with their father is supported by oral histories. Mary Patterson, for example, born around 1887, remembered that there were two children. Viola Batts Daniels and her sister Irene Batts Campbell remembered playing with Arthur Mae and her sister, suggesting that occasionally Margaret Coleman brought them from Dallas to visit family members who'd remained in Harrison County. Queenie Pugh Davidson, a cousin close in age to Huddie, said that Margaret's daughters stayed with Queenie's mother for a time. She remembered that Erma's nickname was "Plug." Sadly, Erma died on April 15, 1926, a little more than a year after Ledbetter's release from prison in Texas. She was sixteen years old and a student, and she died of septicemia, brought on by an abortion.[41] He attended her funeral, Davidson said; he "buried her."[42]

Sometime after the 1910 federal census, enumerated in their district in May (and not long after the birth of his second daughter), Huddie Ledbetter and his wife Aletha, like Coleman and her family, relocated to the Dallas–Fort Worth area. Rather than sharecrop, they worked as day laborers on the cotton farms of Rockwall County, a fertile agricultural area to the northeast of the city. Irene Batts Daniels, who'd picked cotton with her uncle at various times, admired his skills in the field. "He was a *professional* cotton picker," she said. Everyone they knew picked cotton, so they made as light work of it as they could. "Uncle Huddie had a game with it," she remembered. "He would have two rows. He had a long sack and had the strap so it would go over *both* shoulders, and he'd pick with both hands. He'd pick this row and he'd pick that row and he'd put it into his bag."[43] Ledbetter told the Lomaxes that he'd learned "Ain't Goin' Down to de Well No Mo'," a work holler, from a man named Will Darling "on a cotton pick" at Gus Edwards' farm in 1910. The "well," the Lomaxes explained, is prison. The song is "a field holler, typical of the loveliest of Negro folk songs – a pre-blues, pre-jazz, perhaps even a pre-spiritual type." A singer "can adapt the melody to anything he wants to say, or he can 'moan' his way through."

> Oh ain' goin' down, I ain't goin' down
> Oh, mama to de well no mo'.

Ledbetter told them that the song was a favorite of Aletha's. "We'd be down in de field' – she was a li'l', low woman, but, Godamighty, she could pick cotton!," the Lomaxes quoted him as saying. "An' she'd ask me to sing this song. I'd raise it up right sweet, an' we'd pick cotton till you couldn' hear nothing' but de bolls rattlin'."

> If I ever gets able, able,
> to pay dis debt I owe –
>
> I ain't goin' down, ain' goin' down
> to de well, no mo'.

As copyrighted, the song includes lyrics that reflect unjust incarceration.

> O somethin's funny, I can't understan', understan',
> Got me charged with murder,
> Oh Lawd, I ain' raised my han'.

And throughout, the refrain:

> I ain't goin' down, I ain't goin' down
> Oh, mama to the well no more.[44]

During the off-season, Huddie and Aletha Ledbetter spent time in Dallas, where Huddie worked to establish himself as a performer. There is a full-length portrait of him during this period, taken in a professional photographer's studio against a scenic theatrical backdrop. The image is undated, but it was likely taken between 1910 and 1915, when he was in his early to mid-twenties. His face, unmarked by scars and not yet rid of

3.2 Huddie Ledbetter, studio portrait, c. 1910–1915. Courtesy of the Lead Belly Estate, Murfreesboro, Tennessee.

its baby fat, is bright and open. He wears a bowler hat and formal suit, and he carries a cane, the kind used by vaudevillians. In later years, on his New York City stationery, he would use this portrait to advertise his "gun tap dancing."

It was a time of rapid growth in Dallas, as the city became "the first urban center of blues activity in the Southwest."[45] There is no available hard evidence (such as newspaper announcements, flyers, ticket stubs, and the like) to show exactly where around Dallas, and with whom, Ledbetter performed. "He said later that in Dallas he heard his first jazz band, and that may also be where he discovered the instrument that became his favorite: the twelve-string guitar, at that time associated mostly with Mexican musicians," wrote Alan Govenar and Jay Brakefield.[46] Many note-worthy Black performers in the South during this era drew crowds at open-air tent shows or vaudevilles, and they traveled by rail between cities. Ledbetter's contemporaries in the years between 1910 and 1915 would have included Gertrude "Ma" Rainey, born in Georgia around 1886, per-forming with her husband and various companies, including the "Rabbit Foot Minstrels." Certainly, he performed with Blind Lemon Jefferson, whom he met in the "Deep Ellum" area at least by 1912. "Deep Ellum" had a long history both as an African American neighborhood and as a site where industries established their centers, from a cotton gin built in 1888 by Robert S. Munger to a Ford automobile factory built in 1914.[47] When Ledbetter saw Deep Ellum "for the first time," wrote Kip Lornell, "he must have compared it to the more familiar Fannin Street and perhaps noted that it was not quite as unabashedly bawdy .... [It] was not an official red-light district, nor was it exclusively devoted to bars and bordellos." Blind Lemon Jefferson, born in Texas in September 1893, was then in his late teens, nearly five years younger than Ledbetter. As Kip Lornell noted, "his days with Jefferson ... [were] one of the few things about this era in his life that he would later discuss."[48] Ledbetter mentioned his partnership with Blind Lemon in songs such as "Silver City Bound":

> Silver City bound, I'm Silver City bound
> Well, tell my baby, I'm Silver City bound
> Me and Blind Lemon gonna ride on down.[49]

Later, in informal recording sessions at the New York apartment of Frederic Ramsey, Jr., Ledbetter said of Jefferson: "Him and I was buddies .... We used to play all up and around Dallas, Texas–Fort Worth. We'd just get on the train. In them times, we'd get on that Interurban line that runs from Waco to Dallas, Corsicana, Waxahachie, from Dallas. Then they had an interurban that runs from there to Fort Worth. I'd get Blind Lemon about on and we'd get our two guitars, ride anywhere and didn't have to pay no money in them times."[50] For "a year or eighteen months," Kip Lornell wrote, "the pair managed to make a decent living" performing in the area; "Sometimes their weekend take was as much as $150." Notably, "Jefferson attracted special attention by playing what was then called 'Hawaiian guitar,' a type of open guitar tuning with which he usually used a bottleneck, knife, or short metal cylinder to slide along the strings." With Jefferson, Lornell wrote, Ledbetter also "often played a mandolin or his 'windjammer' (accordion)."[51]

Ledbetter also said that he'd played with Bessie Smith, "Empress of the Blues," who was five years his junior. At a June 1949 concert at the University of Texas, he introduced his performance of Smith's 1927 hit "Backwater Blues" by saying it was a favorite of hers, and that they "used to go around in Mississippi."[52] Smith, born in Tennessee, was a street busker who joined Ma Rainey's retinue in 1912, and by 1913 was performing on her own. It was Ledbetter who introduced Smith to Esther Mae "Mother" Scott in 1914, according to Sean Killeen, in Scott's home state of Mississippi.[53] Scott's 1979 obituary noted, "In her youth, as she recalled in court proceedings two years ago, she often traveled to New Orleans, 'playing and having gigs and a good time with people like Bessie Smith, Lead-belly and Louis Armstrong.'"[54]

For Ledbetter, the years between 1910 and 1915 seem to have been busy, adventurous, and apparently happy. Working alongside Aletha in the fields during times of peak demand and pay, performing in Dallas when club dates and pick-up work could be arranged, and traveling throughout the region by train as he expanded his audience and repertoire, the couple was carving a future for themselves. They traveled back to Leigh, a distance of about 170 miles, to visit family and friends, and Ledbetter, whenever he was in town, was in demand to perform. The confident, talented young man in the full-length studio portrait would have had a hard time imagining that his world was on the verge of collapse.

After four long days at Cummins gathering songs during that first week in October 1934, "Lead Belly became restless and dissatisfied," John Lomax wrote, and wished they could go elsewhere.[55] He himself complained to Ruby that the days were long and hectic. "Up at 5! Coffee immediately, which makes that dismal hour cheerful," he wrote. He and Ledbetter often recorded well into the night, making the workday about sixteen hours long. On top of that, the recorder broke down repeatedly. As soon as he and Ledbetter "had one section repaired, down would go another. Four long trips to Pine Bluff and back finally brought relief." He was, he wrote, "dog-tired."[56] Both men needed a break, and so with Ledbetter at the wheel, they returned to Shreveport. They parted ways for a couple of days before heading, together, to Austin. On Friday, October 12, Ledbetter performed at a "party" in Austin that elicited "enthusiastic" reports, according to a letter that Ruby sent to her husband on Sunday, after he and Huddie headed out again that morning.[57] A day later, she mentioned a different event, reporting that a friend had said other women "of the Saturday evening audience, 'raved' to her about their impression of you, – how much they liked your personality and how interesting you are."[58] As another rehearsal for the future, with Lomax introducing Ledbetter and "interpolating" his music, Austin was a success.

Their return to the road got off to a tough start after Lomax decided to make a detour to spend Sunday, October 14, 1934, at the Imperial State Prison Farm, later known as the Central State Prison Farm, at Sugar Land, near Houston. Ledbetter knew the prison all too well, having been incarcerated there between 1920 and 1925. Monday, Lomax reported to Ruby, "was a most unpleasant day with Leadbelly."[59] But within a day, they resumed their old rhythms as they began their fourth week together, taking a winding route that skirted the Gulf of Mexico as they headed east and then north toward Montgomery, Alabama.

CHAPTER 4

1915: *The State of Texas v. Huddie Ledbetter*

In *Negro Folk Songs as Sung by Lead Belly,* John and Alan Lomax described three events that brought Huddie Ledbetter into conflict with law enforcement in Texas. The first was the fight at the sukey-jump, which they presented as happening when Ledbetter was about fifteen and which, allegedly in Ledbetter's words, led to "nothin' but" a twenty-five-dollar fine. The second is included in their brief summary of what they termed the "vague" years between 1901 and 1918: "And in Marshall somewhat later he attacked a woman who turned him down. He got a year on the Harrison County chain gang."[1] The third occurred in December 1917, when he was living under an alias. This chapter considers the first two events, which are connected. Clarifying what actually occurred, as opposed to what the Lomaxes described, is important because it offers a clearer understanding of this history and the context of what racial "justice" meant in the post-Reconstruction South.

As a young performer in Harrison County, Texas – before he and his wife, Aletha, moved to the Dallas–Fort Worth area in 1910 – Ledbetter often traveled alone through the countryside, with nothing but the night sky to light the way. He carried his six-string guitar and perhaps his windjammer. "I got fifty cents a night, and I played sukey-jumps when I was about fifteen years old because I had a horse and I could go out and ride," he said in the recorded introduction to "Corn Bread Rough," adding, "No white man in twenty miles."[2] As the Lomaxes reported, his father bought him a pistol, intended strictly to keep him safe. "[W]e didn't know the people, where he's going to play and have these suppers and things," his niece, Viola Batts Daniels, remembered. Her grandfather, Wesley (Ledbetter's father), used to lay into him about that, she said. "You don't carry that gun with you 'cause you're looking for trouble." Grandfather, she added, "was a lecturer."[3]

The Lomaxes offered a fairly detailed account about the event at the sukey-jump, allegedly resulting in a simple fine. The story is told as if in Ledbetter's words. He got into an argument with another teen who was trying to convince Ledbetter's date to leave the dance party with him. As they fought over her, Ledbetter pulled out his pistol. "I came down wid my pistol 'side his head, *Whop!* An' when he fell back I jump astraddle of him an' fire dat gun right in his face. But it didn' go off. Had hit a bad cateridge. He saw dat gun and was up an' gone," the Lomaxes – primarily Alan, who was responsible for this section – wrote. "I throw de pistol down on him an' give it to him twice, *Zow! Zow!* But he was already 'roun' de corner de house."

The story, with its italicized sound effects, makes little sense: The other boy saw the gun and was "up and gone" and yet Ledbetter was still hitting him, while at the same time the other boy was "around the corner of the house." Further straining credibility is "Ledbetter's" account that he went "right to" his father and told him what happened, and that his father went to the sheriff, only to discover that the other teen's parents had gotten there first.[4] In other words, John and Alan Lomax, both Texans, both white, expected readers to believe that two Black families, during one of the worst periods in Jim Crow America and in Harrison County, known for its racial violence,[5] went miles out of their way to meet with a white sheriff expecting a resolution. The Lomaxes' portrayal of a neutral and even benevolent system of justice is underscored by the statement, attributed to Ledbetter, that the sheriff "knew my papa anyhow," and as a result he was merely fined for carrying "concealed weapons."[6] In the Lomaxes' telling, it has become a story of rowdy teenagers, an understanding sheriff, and a slap on the wrist. It is as if neither John nor Alan Lomax comprehended the ways in which, beyond geography, the Texas they knew bore little resemblance to the Texas inhabited by Huddie Ledbetter and his family.

The other event, presented by the Lomaxes as occurring sometime between 1910 and 1918, was prefaced with yet another impeachment of Ledbetter's character. He had bought himself a twelve-string guitar, they wrote. "Then ... he became the king sure enough. He had more whisky than he could drink, more money than he could put into his pockets, and more women than he could possibly ever make love to," they wrote. "Lead Belly's attitude toward women had become completely arrogant and domineering. He kept one at home to clean his house and give him comfort when the world turned sour on him, and he believed that all other women belonged to him by rights. The truculent Dallas prostitutes had nearly chopped his head off because of his swaggering 'I wouldn't give two bits for you,' but he had learned little from this experience. And in Marshall somewhat later he attacked a woman who turned him down. He got a year on the Harrison County chain gang."[7]

In fact, both the weapons conviction and the sentence to serve on a chain gang happened in 1915, when Huddie Ledbetter was not a teenager but a twenty-six-year-old man. That year, he faced charges in two separate Harrison County courts: *The State of Texas v. Huddie Ledbetter*, case number 14185, in district court; and *The State of Texas v. Huddie Ledbetter*, case number 8455, in county court. In both, the circumstances are far different from those presented in the Lomax book.

In June 1915, Huddie and Aletha Ledbetter were home from Dallas, visiting in Leigh and likely staying with Wesley and Sallie Ledbetter. They may have come to help with the farm, but it was also a special occasion: family and friends would be gathering to celebrate the fiftieth anniversary of Juneteenth – June 19, 1865 – the day enslaved people in Texas finally learned that they were free. Even more than usual, news that Ledbetter and his wife were back in town would have spread quickly, with many requests for Ledbetter's time and talent. On Saturday, a week before the holiday, *The Marshall Messenger* was advertising peaches at 50 cents a bushel, the Hawley Motor Co. was selling a "Seven-Passenger Chandler Touring Car or Roadster" for $1,295, a short "Chas. Chaplin" reel was playing at the Grand, and both Harvey's and The Russell-Graham Company were promoting sales to Saturday night shoppers. Ice, ice cream, garden hoses, and sprinklers were suggested as ways to combat weather described as "awful hot and dry." With one exception, temperatures had been in the nineties in Marshall (the seat of Harrison County) every day since June 3. The high on June 12 was 95 degrees, and it wouldn't get below 74 degrees that night. Other than a half-inch of rain on June 8, it hadn't rained in nearly three weeks. That night, Ledbetter was attending or, more likely, performing at a party just north of his parents' farm, in an area between Leigh and Karnack.

Sometime between Saturday night and Sunday morning, according to a report published in *The Marshall Messenger*, there was a "shooting at Leigh."

> News was given out at the sheriff's office Tuesday [June 15] to the effect that a shooting scrape occurred Saturday night near Leigh between two negroes, one of whom was badly wounded. The name of the injured man is unknown here. Huddie Ledbetter was arrested by Deputy Hope, charged with having done the shooting. Deputy John Scott has gone to Karnack after the prisoner and lodged him in the county jail. It is reported officially that Ledbetter admits having done the shooting. The injured negro hails from Louisiana and was a stranger at Leigh.[8]

Two days later, *The Shreveport Times* reported that "a negro named Huddy Ledbetter, who is charged with shooting another negro near the Louisiana state line Sunday" had been arrested in Karnack on Wednesday night, June 16, and was now in jail.[9] The victim's name was Jim Coleman, but he does not seem to have been related to Margaret Coleman. If the newspaper was accurate in stating that Ledbetter admitted to the shooting, perhaps it was because he felt it was justified, to protect either his own life or someone else's. It's also possible that Ledbetter never made this admission, and that Robert Hope, a stout, twenty-eight-year-old farmer[10] who had been appointed "riding bailiff" for Karnack in January 1915,[11] merely claimed that Ledbetter confessed, or had even coerced a confession.

This shooting was the event that became case number 14185, in the district court. On Thursday morning, June 17, 1915, the all-white, all-male grand jury, appointed to a two-month term beginning in May, convened to consider three cases: "Junius Furrh who is charged with having killed Charles Hendrix at Elysian Fields two weeks ago, a negro shooting scrape at Karnack [this is the Ledbetter case] and the Pete and Ed Moore shooting."[12] The grand jury adjourned Friday afternoon, June 18, and was in recess until Tuesday morning, June 22, *The Marshall Messenger* reported, "on account of it being so difficult to get negro witnesses while the carnival spirit of Emancipation Day prevailed."[13]

In the meantime, on Monday, June 21 – before Ledbetter's indictment was made public, and possibly before he had even *been* indicted – Wesley and Sallie Ledbetter hired two white attorneys, Walter Clough Lane and his son William Henderson Lane, of the law firm Lane & Lane, to defend their son. Walter C. Lane, the senior partner, was not only an attorney, but had also been appointed by the governor, sometime between 1907 and 1911, to serve as a "special judge" in the Harrison County court. The Lanes were a large and prominent family in the region, and they appeared frequently in the society pages. In exchange "for legal services rendered and to be rendered in the future," the Ledbetters conveyed to the Lanes the deed to 30 acres of their hard-won 68.5-acre farm.[14] Wesley Ledbetter signed the document; Sallie signed with "her mark," an X. In what seems like an extraordinary conflict of interest, R.L. Sypert, that term's grand jury foreman and a prominent landowner from Hallsville,[15] witnessed Wesley's signature. Sallie's signature was witnessed by E.L. Vance, an attorney who had just moved to the area.[16]

By Wednesday, June 23, the grand jury had completed its work for the May term, and its report to Judge Henry Thomas Lyttleton, submitted by Sypert, stated that "bills of indictment have been brought in where we thought proper and right."[17] Three days later, *The Marshall Messenger* listed the indictments on its front page, including "Huddie Ledbetter, assault to murder, out on bond" and "Junius Furrh, murder, out on bond."[18] The Furrh case, involving two white men, was the attention grabber: Twenty-five-year-old Junius Furrh was accused of fatally shooting twenty-eight-year-old Charles Hendrix "three times with a 32-caliber automatic pistol . . . [at] about 7:30 o'clock in front of Furrh's store in Elysian Fields" on June 4. According to *The Houston Post*, Furrh pleaded self-defense in the incident, which was "a dispute over management of a baseball team of which Furrh was owner and on which Hendrix had formerly been a catcher."[19] The "tragedy caused a profound sensation as both the parties are of the oldest and most prominent families in Harrison county," reported the *Fort Worth Record-Telegram*. "Junius Furrh is the son of J.M. Furrh, a merchant at Elysian Fields, and a brother of Representative Furrh of Harrison County," while Hendrix was "married and leaves a widow and two children."[20] Furrh was released on a $10,000 bond and continued to appear regularly in the Harrison County society pages while out on bail. In December 1915, Judge Lyttleton continued his case to the next term of court, and in April 1916 it was reported that Furrh was acquitted.[21] He left for officer training camp in the middle of

May 1917, a month after the United States declared war on Germany, thus entering World War I.

Huddie Ledbetter's "shooting scrape" was handled very differently. The state's case envelope is marked, "In District Court, Harrison County. No. 14185, *The State of Texas v. Huddie Ledbetter.*" The memorandum of papers filed lists: (1) Indictment, (2) Capias (a bench warrant), and (3) Bond. Unfortunately, as of 2019, the bond information was no longer included among the records. In the indictment, a true bill signed by grand jury foreman R.L. Sypert, the jurors presented that Huddie Ledbetter, on or about the "13th day of June" 1915, "did then and there unlawfully and with malice aforethought make an assault in and upon the person of Jim Coleman with the intent then and there on the part of him the said Huddie Ledbetter to kill and murder him the said Jim Coleman." The witnesses identified were Jim Coleman, John Lee, T.J. Miles, Charles Jones, Celeste Lee, and Tobe Jerry.[22] Jim Coleman's presence before the grand jury, just days after the shooting, suggests that his injuries were minor. Some of those who testified can be found in the 1910 census for Leigh. Others may be misidentified. "John" Lee is perhaps George, Celeste Lee's husband; Celeste is forty-two, a farm laborer. "T.J. Miles" might be Tommy Meyers, twenty-two. There doesn't seem to be a Tobe Jerry, but there is a Jerry Meyers, thirty, next door to Celeste.[23] All of them lived in the proximity of the Ledbetters' farm, and all were Black. None are present in the 1920 census for the same area.

The second document, the capias, also dated June 23, 1915, is the arrest warrant for Ledbetter. On the reverse side, Sheriff John C. Sanders and Deputy Sheriff J.B. Henderson signed that they had executed the capias by arresting Ledbetter on June 25 in Harrison County. It listed six dollars in costs, including one dollar as a "fee for arrest" and five dollars for "mileage by private conveyance." As noted in the newspaper, Ledbetter was released on bond, although the amount of money and its source are unknown. He was to appear in Judge Lyttleton's court on July 5, 1915, to be tried on the charge of assault to murder.

Curiously, the July 5 trial did not take place. Twelve weeks later, on September 28, 1915, Clerk William Rudd, on behalf of the district court, issued another subpoena. It charged Sheriff Sanders and Deputy Sheriff John Scott to again summon the six witnesses identified in the grand jury

records. All of the individuals were apparently found, as there are penciled checkmarks and the date "10/5" next to each of their names, and all
were "at Leigh." They were to appear in court on October 11. For carrying
out this summons, the sheriffs charged another six dollars: a three-dollar
fee, plus three dollars for mileage: sixty miles at five cents per mile. Once
again, though, the trial did not take place. On December 10, according to
The Marshall Messenger,[24] the district court of Judge Lyttleton, concerning
the case of *The State v. Huddie Ledbetter*, issued an alias capias – the warrant
issued when a subject fails to appear in court. The court issued yet another
subpoena for the same six witnesses, who were to appear in court on
February 11, 1916. From there, the case disappears and was apparently
dropped. In 1930, when the state of Louisiana checked in with the state of
Texas, they were told that Texas had no outstanding charges against
Huddie Ledbetter.

But Huddie Ledbetter's trouble with Harrison County law enforcement had not ended. On July 26, 1915, three weeks after the first district
court trial was supposed to take place, he was charged with "carrying
a pistol," case number 8455, *The State of Texas v. Huddie Ledbetter*. For this
offense, he would face not Judge Lyttleton, whose *district* court generally
handled criminal cases and felonies, but Judge George L. Huffman,[25]
Lyttleton's successor in the *county* court, which handled misdemeanors
and lesser crimes. Lyttleton's court required a twelve-person jury, while
Huffman's required only six.

Texas had long had laws regulating the carrying of weapons, including
not only pistols but also daggers, brass knuckles, and bowie knives, which
in 1911 was punishable by a "fine of not less than one hundred dollars . . .
or by confinement in the county jail not less than thirty days . . . or by
both."[26] But enforcement was highly selective.[27] As a matter of routine,
for example, John Lomax packed a pistol to bring with him for his first
semester at the University of Texas at Austin in 1906.[28] Notably, Junius
Furrh, who shot Hendrix "three times with a 32-caliber automatic
pistol,"[29] was not charged with carrying a weapon. It is also not clear
from the records whether or not the weapons charge levied against
Huddie Ledbetter was separate from or connected to the "shooting
scrape" at Karnack. What is clear is that Harrison County officials seemed
determined to convict him for *something*, because, on September 2, 1915,
Ledbetter was arrested again, on a new charge of carrying a pistol. "Pistol

Toting Arrest," read the headline in the September 3 issue of *The Marshall Messenger*. "Haddie [*sic*] Ledbetter has been arrested by the sheriff's force on a charge preferred in the County Court in which he is alleged to have carried a pistol. He was released on $250 bond."[30] Six days later, the official records for county court judge George L. Huffman, *State v. Haddie Ledbetter*, carrying a pistol, noted that "the defendant's motion for continuance was overruled."[31] That there really were two cases against Ledbetter for carrying a pistol, and not just one, is confirmed by a story that ran in *The Shreveport Times* on Friday, September 10: "Huddy Ledbetter, a negro from the east end of the county near Leigh, was tried in the county court yesterday for carrying a pistol and was convicted and given 30 days in jail and costs," the story read. "A second case against Ledbetter for carrying a pistol is on trial again today in county court."[32] With respect to the second case, *The Marshall Messenger* on September 10 reported the official ruling of the County Court, G.L. Huffman, Judge: "State vs. Haddie Ledbetter, carrying a pistol, jury verdict of not guilty."[33]

In other words, despite Wesley and Sallie Ledbetter's payment of thirty acres of farmland to the law firm of Lane & Lane, their son continued to face the charge of attempted murder in district court, which could send him to state prison, even as the county court judge sentenced him on the weapons charge. For carrying a pistol, Ledbetter was given thirty days of "jail" time, to be served in chains on a county road crew – in other words, on a chain gang – and he had to reimburse the county for fees totaling $73.50: trial fee ($5.00), jury fee ($3.00), county clerk's fee ($6.50), sheriff's fee ($15.00), county attorney's fee ($10.00), and witness fee ($34.00).[34] It's possible, even likely, that Ledbetter himself had sought to minimize what occurred by suggesting to the Lomaxes that a twenty-five-dollar fine was "nothing," but even that amount would have been worked off in hard labor. In nearby Camp County, Texas, imprisoned roadworkers were credited fifty cents per day.[35] If this was also true in Harrison County, Ledbetter's thirty days on the chain gang would be extended by at least five months, from the end of September to the end of March, to pay off the debt. Any additional costs he incurred, such as medical expenses, would add to the sentence. On Monday, September 27, 1915, *The*

Shreveport Times reported that Deputy Sheriff John Scott "left for Longview with two negro prisoners, Huddie Ledbetter and Odell Maneyfield, who he will turn over to the road gang foreman at Longview to work on the Harrison county roads in the west end of the county."[36]

There is a suggestion in some "Lead Belly" biographies that perhaps the law firm of Lane & Lane had secured the weapons charge(s) as an alternative to the more serious charge of attempted murder, but that is contradicted by the fact that the original charge was not dropped. A question that has not been asked is whether or not the Ledbetters – the outspoken and self-confident Huddie Ledbetter, in his mid-twenties, and his parents, independent landowners in their fifties – were instead the victims of white corruption. "In a country of share-croppers and large plantations, like the Red River bottom country, old man Wess Ledbetter was conspicuous for his independence and success," the Lomaxes wrote in *Negro Folk Songs as Sung by Lead Belly*. "He had risen from the position of a renter to that of a small landowner. He voted at every election – always the Republican ticket. The whites of the community respected him, and the sheriff was always easy on his son."[37] Historically, there is little to support this portrait of easygoing race relations during this era. In 1900, four years before the Ledbetters finally owned their land outright in Harrison County, roughly 90 percent of the nation's African American population, about 8.26 million people, still lived in the South.[38] The political gains of Reconstruction had been steadily dismantled in an effort to restore white supremacy, and Black men (and, as of 1920, Black women) were effectively barred from voting, serving on juries, or running for political office. "It would be sixty-five years," with passage of the Voting Rights Act of 1965, "before African Americans could vote freely throughout the country, seventy-two before a southern state would elect another black member of Congress," wrote historian Morgan Kousser.[39]

Notably, this retrenchment included both Harrison County, Texas and nearby Caddo Parish, Louisiana. Caddo Parish imposed rigid property and literacy requirements on voters in general, while carving out exceptions for whites who didn't meet the requirements. They also placed polling locations far from Black communities, and potential Black voters often faced intimidation and violence. In 1898, the state adopted a new constitution which directly limited Black voting. "As a result, in a state with 650,804 Black residents, the number of Black registered voters dropped from 130,000 before the new constitution to just 5,000 by 1900," noted the Equal Justice Initiative. "By 1904, the number dropped to just 1,000."[40] The Ledbetters' 1894 move to nearby Harrison County, Texas, another stronghold of white power, would not have positioned Wesley Ledbetter in a better or safer position to vote, even after he owned property. By 1878, Harrison County whites had succeeded in "redeeming" their political and economic power.[41] It's possible that Wesley Ledbetter voted Republican in 1900,[42] but in 1902, the Texas state legislature created more hurdles for Black voters by adding a yearly poll tax of between $1.50 and $1.75, which had to be paid in advance. From that point on, despite a continuing Black majority, "the county voted solidly Democratic in all elections until 1948."[43] If Wesley Ledbetter continued to vote Republican, it was at considerable inconvenience, expense, and risk.

Along the same lines, it seems impossible that the Lomaxes were unaware that for a Black man like Wesley Ledbetter to be "conspicuous for his independence and success" might be problematic for whites. There might be co-existence, and even friendship, but the significant power imbalance was always present. "In rural areas, blacks and whites necessarily worked side by side, and despite white supremacy, friendly relationships developed across the color line," wrote historian Pete Daniel. "Industrious African American farmers deferred when necessary and earned the respect of their white neighbors," he noted. "A combination of husbandry, diplomacy, and ambition allowed black farmers to secure land, and the fact that so many succeeded during some of the darkest years of racist violence testifies to their character and determination."[44]

There is an additional complication that the Lomaxes neglected to mention. In the early 1900s, oil was discovered beneath Caddo Lake, and explosive economic growth permanently changed the region. By 1910, "[a]ll the land along the lake, on both north and south shores, had been leased, every foot of it."[45] With their own stake just a mile south of the lake in Texas, the Ledbetters were among those approached by speculators. Sallie and Wesley – her with a mark, him with a signature – executed a handful of oil, gas, and mineral leases, most of which offered nominal payment in exchange for some part of what, if anything, was discovered below their land. Any hook ups to take advantage of the findings were the Ledbetters' responsibility. They entered into an "Oil, Gas and Mineral Lease" to R.D. Elmore and J.L. Breathwit (February 5, 1906);[46] to Phil Draiss (May 25, 1908);[47] to Henry Coyle (December 9, 1908);[48] and to J. M. Guffey Petroleum Corporation (April 11, 1910).[49] In 1911, the Gulf Refining Company constructed the nation's first over-water drilling platforms, which soon dotted Caddo Lake.[50] Gulf also erected a dam near Mooringsport, "in order to raise the water level to accommodate drilling equipment when oil was found under water," according to the Texas Water Development Board.[51] A drawbridge was installed at Mooringsport, replacing the ferry and allowing vehicular traffic to cross the lake. Built into the bridge was a "Vertical-Lift" that allowed waterborne vessels through, especially "tall oil equipment" such as "Gulf Oil Company's pile driver."[52] Oil City, opposite the lake, was soon a tough, frontier-style town, a haven for men who flocked to the area in search of work.[53]

With an influx of people and heavy-duty equipment, the push for more and better roads throughout the region, including Harrison County, Texas, intensified. District Court Judge Henry T. Lyttleton was a leader in these efforts. Born in Kentucky in 1852, he had served as a "a surveyor and civil engineer" whose "skill along these lines enabled him to set up the present system of good lateral roads in Harrison county," reported *The Marshall News Messenger*.[54] From 1898 to 1911, he served as county judge, during which time "he began his roads program that is still benefitting the county today," earning him a reputation as the "good roads judge."[55] He was even given a twenty-horse-power Maxwell automobile by "the good roads advocates of Marshall."[56] In 1911, four years before Huddie Ledbetter's arrest, Lyttleton became the first judge of the "newly-created" 71st Judicial District court,[57] a position he held until December 1916. He was also president of the Caddo–Clinton Oil & Gas Company, which began "active drilling" in October 1915,[58] and a prominent landowner, whose holdings, since the end of 1913, included the development of an exclusive, lakefront private club, "the Port Caddo Club." Elected officers included "H.T. Lyttleton, president; E.B. Wilson, vice president; W.H. Lane, Jr., secretary,[59] and G.M. McDaniel, treasurer." The group regularly advertised shares in the club, which owned a seven-room club house and twenty-five acres of land.[60]

In Texas overall in 1914, there were about "40,000 motor vehicles"[61] and "a total of 10,527 miles of roads" – but, of these, only 703 miles were of medium or high quality as measured by the US Geological Survey. The rest of the roadways were either just compacted dirt or a layer of crushed stones. They were often in disrepair and at times unnavigable due to damage caused by wear and tear and by inclement weather, especially rain. At the county level, elected officials, businesspeople, and voters haggled over where to prioritize roadbuilding, how to pay for it, and how quickly it could be done. Early in 1915, Texas amended its 1905 "Act creating a special road system for Harrison county," in order to give county commissioners "full power and authority" over road work. The day

4.1 Prisoners breaking up rocks at a prison camp or road construction site, c. 1934–1950. Library of Congress, Prints & Photographs Division, Lomax Collection [LC-DIG-ppmsc-00662].

rate for "any hands or teams to work on the road" was not to exceed "three dollars per day, or nine hours per day, for a team and driver, and not to exceed one dollar and a half per day for day hands." The road commissioners would make four dollars per day, or a maximum of forty dollars per month. The ruling, which passed the Texas house and senate unanimously, was enacted on February 16, 1915.[62] Also on February 16, 1915, *The Marshall Messenger* noted the ongoing interest among white men to secure employment as "overseers" of road crews, which "all goes to show an interest in good roads." The list of overseers appointed "just this week" – in the middle of February 1915 – included twenty-nine-year-old Robert Hope, "a member of the Karnack Baptist Church" and the "son of ... pioneer settlers of Karnack."[63] Hope was the deputy sheriff who would arrest Huddie Ledbetter just three months later.

The state began releasing funds for road work. In early March, for example, it was reported that "County Judge George L. Huffman wired from Austin Saturday morning that the $300,000 bonds of road district No. 1, Harrison county, had been approved by the attorney general and registered by the comptroller."[64] On March 4, the largest headline on the front page of *The Marshall Messenger* read, "Good Roads Money Is Now in Marshall Banks." By May 13, the county was seeking "sealed bids for the construction of approximately twenty-five miles of graveled and macadam highway in Road District No. 1 of Harrison county."[65] The remaining issue for Harrison and other counties in Texas, as it was for counties throughout the South, was finding laborers to do the dangerous, back-breaking work of actually clearing dense forests, digging and grading hard earth, crushing rocks into ever smaller pieces, and laying and pounding rock and asphalt. This work fell to "convicted" Black laborers, women as well as men.[66]

No longer able to lease convicted prisoners to private industry, states and counties were legally able to use them, at minimal cost, for public projects, including the construction of municipal buildings, bridges, and, most ubiquitously, roads. Writing in 1924, prison reformer Frank Tannenbaum reported that there were "two types" of such road crews: one, where the prisoners "live in cages set on wheels," and the other, "where they live in tents set on the ground." The prisoners – mostly but not always male – were shackled in chains twelve to twenty-four inches long, he wrote. One chain was riveted to both

4.2 Chain gang of convicts engaged in road work, Pitt County, North Carolina, 1910. Wagons were equipped with bunks and moved from place to place as labor was utilized. Library of Congress, Prints & Photographs Division, FSA/OWI Collection [LC-USF344-007541-ZB].

ankles, and another was used to lift this chain off the ground when the crew was working; at night, it was used to "to chain the men together" in groups of a "dozen men and more." In 1933, the steel-cage wagons were described in a *Harper's* exposé by journalist Walter Wilson.[67] "This wagon is ordinarily about 18 feet long, 8 feet high, and 8 feet wide with two or three tiers of bunks in each cage," he wrote. "This is the sleeping and living room for about twenty men" and, because it is movable, it "is especially suited for road work." Only a tarp kept out rain; "it also shuts off ventilation and light." A hole in the floor, leading to a tub, was the only toilet. Days "off" did not mean freedom. "On Sundays, nights, and holidays the men are locked in the cages. A long chain passed through the leg chains of each prisoner – these latter are permanently riveted on by a blacksmith."

Business leaders and wealthy landowners benefited from the relatively low cost of roads that helped them to maximize profits and growth. So, too, did the sheriffs, judges, and clerks, Wilson wrote. "Under the notorious fee system [of] law-and-order enforcement, officials are paid a commission on the basis of the number of arrests and convictions they secure. The prisoner is made to pay these fees or 'court costs' in addition to fines and jail sentences." For men like Robert Hope, recently deputized and also employed as a road overseer, there was a clear incentive to arrest young, healthy Black people, even on flimsy charges, because, as prisoners, they could be forced to work in almost unbearable conditions. Without political or legal power, how could those arrested defend themselves? Hopping trains, being insolent, carrying a weapon, drunkenness, vagrancy, and gambling could all land someone on a road crew. "The mill of criminal justice grinds most industriously when men are needed for a big road-making job," Wilson noted. Story after story in *The Marshall Messenger*, in the months surrounding Huddie Ledbetter's arrest, supports this. In some, the individuals and purported offenses aren't even named:

- August 19, 1914: Wednesday afternoon Sheriff J.C. Sanders and Deputy Sheriff John Scott carried four negroes to Jonesville where they were turned over to Sam Long, overseer of the county road gang. They were convicted in the courts here on the following charges: Emma Price, vagrancy; Sylvestus Rhodes, theft; Mozella Turner, vagrancy; Roy Thompson, train riding.
- October 28, 1914: Several negroes were sent to the county road gang Wednesday afternoon on train No. 58, by Sheriff John C. Sanders.
- November 4, 1914: Sheriff John C. Sanders left Wednesday afternoon for Waskom with three negro prisoners in custody, which he will deliver to the county road gang. Tuesday the sheriff delivered three negroes to Road Overseer Sam Long, and Thursday he will deliver three more. Last week there were about seven or eight sent to the gang, making in all a total of about seventeen negroes to be placed on the road within one week.
- November 24, 1914: County officials are contemplating transferring the county road gang from their present location on the Shreveport road near Jonesville to the west end of the county, near Hallsville. The road gang has been stationed on the Shreveport road during the past year and has built several miles of fine road.
- February 12, 1915: Negroes convicted of different misdemeanors and sentenced by the county and justice courts have been sent to the road gang ...

Jailer Cain took them to Hallsville where they were sent to the gang north of that town.

- June 9, 1915: Fred Johnson, colored, convicted Wednesday in Judge G.L. Huffman's court on a charge of theft of a watch was given a fine of $25 and costs and 30 days in jail. The defendant was unable to pay the fine and was sent to the road gang.
- June 29, 1915: Deputy Sheriff John Scott carried two negroes to Hallsville Monday afternoon, where he delivered them to Beecher Newman, foreman of the county road gang. The names of the prisoners are Mary Belle Summerland and Tim Wood. At present the road gang is working on the Longview road near the county line.
- July 27, 1915: Roy Williams, convicted in the County Court, and sentenced to eight months, Roxia Crow and Dora Crockett, convicted in the court of Justice Steelman and fined $50 and $10 respectively and costs, were delivered to the road gang Saturday.
- August 3, 1915: Because he became intoxicated, possibly on bootleg liquor, Dillard Donoho was arrested Sunday and brought to Marshall to answer charges of assault, disturbing the peace and intoxication. The assault charge was dismissed, but [the fine and costs] totaled $24.55. Donoho will hold a steady job with the road gang for a long time just because of a few drin[k]s. He is a negro.
- September 3, 1915: Three more Negro train riders have been hauled up before Justice Pace and each fined $5 and costs, failure to pay which assures labor for the improvement of the roads.

All these years later, it is impossible to prove that a dual goal was achieved through the arrest of Huddie Ledbetter: putting the brash young performer in his place, and acquiring, through deception, thirty acres of his parents' potentially lucrative land. Other Black landowners in the area successfully held onto their land, including Queenie Davidson (Sally's niece) and her husband Early. But many, many Black landowners throughout the South did not. According to Pete Daniel, "African Americans held title to some 16 million acres of farmland" in 1910 (nearly all of it in the South), and, "by 1920, there were 925,000 black farms in the country." From there, though, "the trajectory of black farmers plunged downward."[68] In part, the trend reflected a general urban-to-rural movement; it also reflects the Great Migration of Black families, in part in response to "the restriction of foreign immigration; to the call of industry for additional labor during the period the [first] World War and since; [and] to the widespread ravages of the boll weevil," wrote Charles E. Hall, analyzing the 1930 federal census in comparison with earlier ones, notably that of 1920.[69] But he found it "quite significant" that while the farming population decreased overall, "the land operated by Negroes decreased by 3,835,050 acres ... as compared with a very substantial increase of 34,743,840 acres ... for the white farm operators."[70]

This decline in Black land ownership continued throughout the twentieth century, as reported in an eighteen-month study conducted by the Associated Press. It "documented a pattern in which black Americans were cheated out of their land or driven from it through intimidation, violence and even murder." By the time the three-part investigative series was written, Black people owned "only 1.1 million acres of farmland" in the United States, and they were "part owners of another 1.07 million acres." While the "number of white farmers" had also declined, "as economic trends" concentrated land ownership over-all, the series cited the 1982 Census of Agriculture to note that Black ownership declined at a rate more than double that of white ownership.[71] More than half of the instances of land-taking docu-mented by the Associated Press report, 57 out of 107, involved violence, including "lynchings and white mob attacks." The others involved "trickery and legal manipulations."[72]

In 2023, the American Bar Association reported that, in addition to "theft by state-sanctioned violence, intimidation, and lynching, Black farmers also lost land due to discrimination by banks and financial institutions."[73] This included "the denial of access to federal farm benefits by local administrators who funneled those benefits to white farm owners; through forced partition sales brought about by predatory third parties; through government misuse of eminent domain, including many cases in which Black landowners were compensated well below market value; through discriminatory tax assessments and non-competitive tax sales; and through longstanding, coordinated discrimination by U.S. Department of Agriculture agents who wield power and control over access to credit and essential resources." In this way, the authors clarified, "many Black landowners lost a valuable tool for wealth creation" for succeeding generations.

Wesley and Sallie Ledbetter were among those to lose their land, and their risky efforts to fight back suggest that they felt they had been cheated. In September 1916, nearly a year after their son was taken away in chains to serve on the Harrison County road crew, they tried to recover their thirty acres. Reviewing the documents in Marshall, Texas, attorney Michael Warwick thought that perhaps the Ledbetters had been led to believe that they were simply posting their land as a "security interest (mortgage) to secure payment of lawyer's fees." That would mean that if they paid their fees, "the lawyers would then re-convey title." But "that's not how the instrument reads," he said.[74] Instead, the Ledbetters had conveyed the full fee title, all thirty acres. Now, the Lanes said that if they wanted it back, they would have to buy it. And so, on September 13, 1916, the Ledbetters entered into an agree-ment to buy their land back for $200, or about $6.67 an acre. (This was nearly double the price they had paid the Waskoms: $240 for the entire 68.5-acre property, or about $3.50 an acre.) The Ledbetters didn't have $200 in cash, and so they entered into an agreement through which the Lanes loaned them the $200, with a promissory note that the Ledbetters would repay that amount plus interest.[75] Around the same time, they seem to have left Harrison County, relocating back to Caddo Parish in Louisiana. It seems that Sallie Ledbetter and her grandchildren stayed for a time with relatives of Sallie's mother in the Mooringsport area, while Wesley worked to earn money driving a grocery wagon in Shreveport.[76] By 1919, the Ledbetters had been able to pay only about $41.50, roughly a fifth of the $200 owed (not including interest), when they were served notice that they were being sued. Walter Lane had died the previous fall, and his widow, Nannie, and son, William, sought to collect the balance due and, at the same time, to foreclose the vendor's lien on the thirty acres – in other words, to return the property to the Lanes.[77] It was another terrible blow. When Wesley Ledbetter did not appear or answer the suit, the court entered a default judgment in favor of the Lanes for $158.51 (the balance due), plus interest, plus the costs of the lawsuit, including clerk's fees ($7.55) and the sheriff's fee ($3.00).[78]

A month later, in March 1920, by virtue of an order of the court, Harrison County Sheriff John C. Sanders and Deputy Sheriff R.K. Turner began publicizing an upcoming auction to settle the suit filed by the Lanes. For sale were the Ledbetters' thirty acres of land, "situated in the county of Harrison and state of Texas, about one mile south of Caddo Lake and about nineteen miles north of east from the City of Marshall, Texas."[79] On May 6, the property sold for $225 in cash to the highest bidders,[80] Robert Hope and Charles Carney. Hope, in his capacity as "riding bailiff," was one of the men who arrested Ledbetter in Karnack in June 1915. In 1919, he married Christine Carney, daughter of Charles Carney, "one of the best known railroad men in the state."[81] The groom "is a splendid and enterprising young businessman," the local paper announced. "He is manager of the Puro Oil company, a Marshall concern recently organized for the sale of petroleum and its products."[82]

Wesley and Sallie Ledbetter had lost this battle, and they had lost their son. In the midst of their efforts to reclaim their thirty acres, he was arrested again, while living in northeast Texas under an alias. From February 1918 to early 1920, he was incarcerated near DeKalb, Texas. That May, as his parents' land was sold to the highest bidder in Marshall, he was transferred to a vast prison farm in Sugar Land, about twenty-five miles southwest of Houston.

CHAPTER 5

Frayed Nerves

The relationship between John Lomax and Huddie Ledbetter, built less on honesty and more on two people trying to get the most they could out of each other, was already fraying as they reached Alabama, the second of four states in which they planned to record in the fall of 1934. On Friday, October 19, they arrived in Montgomery, where Lomax met with the governor and prison authorities. They then headed ninety miles north toward Birmingham, which was "football wild," Lomax complained to Ruby. On Saturday, they would meet up with Johnny, still employed in Birmingham. Except for the brief break from each other earlier in the month, they had been traveling together for nearly a month. Perhaps to ease the mood, Ledbetter played to Lomax's vanity as they anticipated Johnny's arrival. He woke Lomax up early, "saying, 'I come early to fix you up pretty for Mr. Johnny,'" Lomax reported to his wife. Ledbetter brushed Lomax's clothes and polished his shoes, apparently telling Lomax that he "looked well" and that the previous night he had "seemed tired."[1] Somehow, this wasn't enough; Lomax wanted Ruby to enclose in a future letter "a sealed note to him telling just what he is to do for me," Lomax wrote, although he added, "I have managed him happily for the last few days." Lomax and Johnny attended a game between the University of Alabama's Crimson Tide and the University of Tennessee's Volunteers, which Alabama won. (Both universities were segregated: Alabama didn't enroll Black students until 1963 and didn't have Black players on the team until 1971. Tennessee admitted its first Black undergraduates in 1961, and its first Black player joined the team in 1968.) The following day, the three of them went "ballad hunting in the convict camps around Birmingham," where Lomax and Ledbetter did some recording.[2]

5.1 Recording equipment in the back of John Lomax's car, 1930s. Library of Congress, Prints & Photographs Division, Lomax Collection.

On Tuesday, they left Johnny behind as they headed south to Tuscaloosa. As they woke, the weather was chilly, with "a heavy dew," Lomax said. He had stayed in a tourist cabin outside the city; Ledbetter was somewhere nearby. They had breakfast together before heading to the post office, where Lomax posted a note to Oliver Strunk at the Library of Congress. He included positive news – "I'm in the midst of . . . getting some of [the] best of the Alabama folk songs" – and negative: "My convict 'n[–]' (so he calls himself) is yet with me though I find him hard to handle. His freedom and apparent prosperity came too suddenly for him and he's misinterpreted kindness and consideration."[3] Lomax's constant evaluation of Ledbetter's temperament, which was clearly grating to Ledbetter, was likely motivated in part by his determination to present Ledbetter at that year's gathering of the Modern Language Association (MLA), to be held in Philadelphia in late December. The group, founded in 1883 and still in operation, "provides opportunities for its members to share their scholarly findings and teaching experiences with colleagues and to discuss trends in the academy."[4] Lomax first presented at the MLA gathering in 1909, as a forty-two-year-old academic newcomer discussing "Cowboy Songs of the Mexican Border" – a preview of his 1910 book – and leading attendees in singing "Git Along Little

Dogies."[5] The previous December, 1933, he had again given a presentation at the annual meeting, titled "Songs from Negro Convict Camps," which helped to advertise the forthcoming publication of his and Alan's *American Ballads and Folk Songs*. Biographers have noted that Lomax was a compelling speaker, "what with that resonant voice, the measured phrases, his imposing Texas girth and swagger, the Stetson that he never removed from his head (except when he swept it off in the presence of a lady), his cheap cigars, and his I-alone-have-returned-to-tell-the-tale narrative."[6] But his solo presentations could not compare, in terms of impact, to a performance by "Lead Belly," an actual former convict from the South.

In Tuscaloosa, Lomax was scheduled to give two lectures at the University of Alabama, October 24 and 25, and in a sort of audition, he included Ledbetter in the presentations. "Lecturer Seeks Old Folk-Songs: Library of Congress Representative Speaks Here," reported *The Crimson-White*, the weekly student newspaper. The first sentence: "Accompanied by Ledbetter, negro musician rescued from a Louisiana State chain-gang, John A. Lomax, representing the Library of Congress, Washington, D.C., in a quest for old negro folk-songs and ballads, lectured at the University of Alabama Wednesday and Thursday." This was the only reference to Ledbetter in the piece, which discussed Lomax being "a graduate of Harvard University" and for "a number of years [serving as] alumni-secretary of the University of Texas."[7] With Lomax's encouragement, Ledbetter passed a hat at the end of the performances, gathering tips. Lomax determined that Ledbetter had "seemed to please his white hearers."[8] Emboldened, on October 25 he sent a letter to President Frank Aydelotte of Swarthmore College, which was hosting that year's MLA meeting, and proposed that Ledbetter perform there.

While Lomax was pleased by the Tuscaloosa presentations, something about them troubled Ledbetter. Given the ways in which he was later introduced to audiences, it's likely that Ledbetter had his first real sense of the limited and racist ways in which Lomax would publicly present him, as he sat in silence, waiting to perform. Lomax noticed the tension enough to mention it to Ruby,[9] but thought it was because he had offended Ledbetter by offering to drive the 150 miles back to Montgomery. He said that Ledbetter kept saying that he wanted to "go home to Martha." The moment passed, but to Lomax, the key takeaway, noted in *Negro Folk Songs as Sung by Lead Belly*, was that "this was his first voiced complaint against me."[10]

After their return to Montgomery, the two nearly parted ways for good. Lomax had settled at the Roosevelt Hotel in Court Square, formerly the Conyers Hotel.[11] Ledbetter stayed at a rooming house at 14 South Decatur Street, about a half-mile away. To get there, he would have walked across the square and then five blocks along Dexter Avenue, turning right just after the Dexter Avenue Baptist Church. Founded in 1877 as the "Second Colored Baptist Church" and renamed soon after,[12] the church was the site of the Rev. Dr. Martin Luther King, Jr.'s "first full-time pastorship."[13] King remained there from 1954 to 1959, and the church served as the hub for the 1956 Montgomery Bus Boycott. All of this, of course, was two decades in the future. As Huddie Ledbetter walked between his accommodations and Lomax's hotel in October 1934, Dr. King was just five years old, living in Atlanta, Georgia.

Ledbetter and Lomax scouted and recorded at multiple prison facilities in the Montgomery area, including Speigner. From there, they planned to spend Saturday and Sunday, October 27–28, recording at the Kilby Prison, an imposing facility spread out over 2,550 acres of farmland, located about four miles from Montgomery's downtown area. It is not mentioned by Lomax, but among those held at Kilby in the fall of 1934 were the nine so-called "Scottsboro Boys": Olen Montgomery, Clarence Norris, Haywood Patterson, Ozie Powell, Willie Roberson, Charlie Weems, Eugene Williams, and brothers Andrew and Leroy Wright. Ranging in age from thirteen to nineteen, they had been arrested three years earlier, in March 1931, after being falsely accused of rape by two young white women in Scottsboro, Alabama. Within a month, all but the youngest were found guilty by all-white, all-male juries and sentenced to death. The group arrived at Kilby on April 27, 1931, and they remained there as their cases wound through the judicial system, including the Alabama and US Supreme Courts. In 1937, after he and Martha were settled in New York City, Ledbetter called attention to the injustice of their treatment with a song he wrote, "Scottsboro Boys."[14] He prefaced a recording of the song by stating, "That Alabama is a hard world down there." At the end of the song, speaking to Alan Lomax, he added, "I'd advise everybody to be a little careful when they go down through there. Best stay woke, keep their eyes open."[15]

On Saturday, probably during a break from their first day of recording at Kilby, Lomax wrote to Ruby, telling her that he was upset not to have heard from Alan, whom he hoped would be well enough to join them soon. He saw "ten days of work already ahead in Alabama" and grumbled that he was "much disappointed in the amount and quality of the material current in this state."[16] He returned to the prison, where he and Ledbetter worked until late. Ledbetter drove Lomax back to his hotel on Saturday night, parked the car, and handed Lomax the keys. The next morning, according to Lomax, Ledbetter didn't show up at 7:00 as they had agreed. He waited until nine and then drove to Ledbetter's "boarding house" where "[t]he Negro proprietress told me that my man had spent the night there, [and] that at that moment he had gone 'somewhere' to get a shave." Lomax drove to the prison alone and worked until night time, after which he wrote again to Ruby, stating that the day had been "the busiest and best" since he'd left home.[17] In *Negro Folk Songs as Sung by Lead Belly*, however, he reported that he had returned to the hotel "tired, worn, and disturbed, too, at the conduct of Lead Belly,"[18] and found a penciled note waiting for him. The note is in the Lomax files at the University of Texas. It reads (in full):

> Boss i haven had anything to eat to Day you left me i was here in plenty time but you left me and got your suit case That is all right Pleas give me money to go home an[d] so i think you for what I had did for you.
>
> Huddie Ledbetter
>
> *[reverse side]*
>
> i have all ready Telegram Martha i am ready to go Please if you dont give me my fair [fare] take me home Pleas[19]

Ledbetter was clearly asking Lomax to give him enough money to get back to Shreveport on his own or to drive him there. As included in the Lomaxes' book, however, the note has been changed, with Ledbetter asking *Martha* to send money for his return.

> Boss, I come here this morning in plenty time. You was done gone and left me. That is all right. I telegram to Martha for money to come home. I aint got no money. I am hungry.
>
> Your servan, HUDDIE LEDBETTER[20]

According to Lomax, an hour after finding the note, he was notified by the hotel that "my boy" was at the desk, waiting for him. Told that

Ledbetter needed money to buy a meal, Lomax responded as if to a child: "Don't I give you a dollar the first thing every morning?" Whether the conversation exactly reflects what occurred, it is telling that Lomax thought he was portraying himself in an accurate and reasonable light. He described lecturing Ledbetter about "how no business could be carried on anywhere unless men could trust each other." He wrote that he "silenced" Ledbetter's "frequent attempts to interrupt" him, and then says he finally stopped yelling at him "partly through weariness, partly through pity." According to Lomax, Ledbetter chose to grovel rather than fight, and the strategy worked. "He got his money," Lomax wrote, adding, "This was the first, in fact the only time, in all my experience with him that he voluntarily confessed to a fault." There was no consideration of Ledbetter's position, or the fact that he had been working without pay for five weeks. Instead, according to Lomax, he tightened his control even more. "As a punishment and because he often spent his allowance for drink, the next day I only gave him money before each meal. I paid his lodging in advance, but held him to a fixed amount, one meal at a time."[21]

Not surprisingly, Ledbetter "chafed under these restrictions and grew morose and nearly sullen on our next two or three trips," Lomax reported. Finally, his last nerve shot, Ledbetter decided to precisely follow the driving instructions Lomax gave him, and as a result drove through a red light, nearly causing an accident. When Lomax yelled, Ledbetter calmly said he'd been following orders. As the fight escalated, Ledbetter left Lomax in the car and "disappeared in the traffic." When Lomax checked, he had also moved out of his rooming house.[22]

Two days later, Lomax stopped at the post office in the midst of a downpour,[23] and Ledbetter appeared. This time, Lomax repented. "It may be that you misunderstood me," he said. "If that be true, I owe you an apology which I now make …. Do you want to drive for me again?"[24] Ledbetter considered. Marshall, Texas was 500 miles behind him; New York, New York was 1,000 miles ahead. He had faced far worse than the indignities of working for John Lomax. He got back into the driver's seat.

CHAPTER 6

1918: *The State of Texas v. Walter Boyd*

It is part of the Lead Belly lore – and also true – that Huddie Ledbetter managed to escape from the Harrison County chain gang to which he'd been sent in September 1915. The Lomaxes (and quite possibly Ledbetter himself) claimed that he broke free just three days into his sentence. In *Negro Folk Songs as Sung by Lead Belly*, the Lomaxes spent four breathless paragraphs describing Ledbetter, his legs chained together, evading guards, horses, bullets, and dogs, and then hiding in a cane patch on his father's farm before deciding that it was safe to move on. Yet, looking at the payment records related to the $73.50 in court fees that Ledbetter owed to the county court in Marshall, Texas, it seems likely that he spent far more than three days under the terrible conditions of the Harrison County road crew. He, or someone on his behalf, paid "cash to officers" against this debt on November 1, 1915; January 6, 1916; and January 26, 1916, for an amount totaling $16.25.[1] These dates suggest that Ledbetter may have been on the road crew for up to four months before he managed to run. How he ran is not clear, but the description in *Negro Folk Songs as Sung by Lead Belly* seems unlikely. An article from *The Marshall Messenger* reported one escape by prisoners using what the newspaper called an "old-time practice." "The eight negroes in the jail wagon, who were all locked to the bull chain, were located just in the rear of the dining tent." While the guards were eating, the men in the wagon asked for water, and a trusty brought them water and pine sticks before returning the keys to where they were kept. "During the night, the negroes started a fire on the floor of the jail wagon and got away through the hole they burned."[2]

Ledbetter and his wife Aletha then fled to Bowie County, on the northeast border of Texas, flanked by Arkansas and Oklahoma, with the boundary marked by the meandering Red River. Just two counties, Marion and Cass, separate Bowie County from Harrison County, but it must have seemed far enough. They settled into a large Black community known as Beaver Dam, about five miles outside DeKalb, and began again as Mr. and Mrs. Walter Boyd.[3] And then, on December 18, 1917, Huddie Ledbetter's luck again ran out: He was arrested and charged with the murder of thirty-five-year-old Will Stafford and remanded to the Bowie County jail.

It's not known exactly when, in 1916, Huddie and Aletha Ledbetter, as Walter and Aletha Boyd, arrived in Bowie County. In addition to finding day work in the fields when extra hands were needed, and, in Ledbetter's case, helping to break in wild horses, they sharecropped on a 391-acre farm owned by John Cowan, a white man who turned seventy in July 1917. Widowed twice, he lived with his wife Cora, about twenty years younger, and their children.[4] One of Cowan's farm ledgers was discovered at a yard sale a few years ago.[5] It's about fourteen inches tall and nine inches wide with a worn, black cover and blood-red binding, and its pages are yellowed with age and dirt. On lined pages, there are penciled calculations, with an occasional child's doodle in the margins. The entry on the first page of the book (a carryover from "old book page 312," as noted in the upper right), is dated "2/9/1916" and documents dealings with "Stafford, Dick" (Richard), the younger brother of Will Stafford. The book continues to page 138, although other pages may have been torn out. Individuals have their own pages, so the dating is by individual rather than by page. The date on the final page, for example, is "1920/10/6" (the name of that account is difficult to read), while the oldest *entry* in the book is "2/1/1921." By that point, the handwriting had noticeably declined; Cowan died on January 30, 1923, at the age of seventy-five.

The ledger book displays a series of interactions between Cowan and Will Stafford, Nick Boyd, Alex Griffin, and "Walter Boyd," whose lives intersected on the night Stafford was killed. Will Stafford's first entry in the ledger is dated February 9, 1916; the last is September 19, 1917, about three months before his death. Walter Boyd, who lived about a quarter-mile from Will Stafford, first appears in this book in an entry dated January 26, 1917, and last appears on September 28, 1917. Nick Boyd, in his mid-forties,[6] did some business with Cowan while primarily living and working on a sixty-four-acre farm owned by Jim Jones, a Black farmer who had close dealings with local white business owners, possibly including gambling.[7] "Alex" (sometimes spelled Ellic and Alec) Griffin, in his late forties,[8] also appears; his family lived and worked on a 140-acre property owned by John Wright, another white farmer. At times, Cowan seems to have served as a sort of banker between the men as they borrowed cash to pay each other as well as Cowan.

Ledbetter's brother's children, Viola and Irene, by now in their early teens, and Alonzo, about eight, lived with him and Aletha in Beaver Dam for several months between 1916 and 1917. Their lives on the Leigh, Texas farm of their grandparents, Wesley and Sallie Ledbetter, had been upended after their uncle's 1915 arrest and the conveyance of nearly half the Ledbetter farm to the law firm of Lane & Lane. The girls remembered traveling with Sallie Ledbetter to the Shreveport area, where they stayed with her relatives.[9] Their aunt Aletha, whom they adored, visited and brought the three of them back with her and their uncle Huddie in Beaver Dam. In addition to working in the fields, they were there long enough to attend school. Margaret Cornelious, born in 1903 (within a year of both girls), remembered attending school with them, and also remembered being with them and "Walter and Aletha" as they picked cotton for Jim Jones.[10]

As in Harrison County, the experiences of white Texans in Bowie County differed significantly from those of Black Texans. White children in DeKalb went to a well-built brick school, joined the Girl Scouts and Boy Scouts, and played on athletic teams sponsored by local businesses. There were some Black-owned businesses in DeKalb, including a hotel and barbershop, but for the most part Black residents lived in sharecropping and tenant farming communities outside of town. Their homes were heated with wood, and lamps were lit by coal oil. Meals were cooked over open fires. Working and living conditions were subject to extremes of weather, from droughts to tornadoes. The cycle of agriculture was relentless and unending: cotton and corn, corn and cotton, marked by the near impossibility of getting ahead. In the meantime, in Texas and throughout the South, generations of white southerners, including those not born into wealthy landowning families, were gradually moving into the relative prosperity of a growing middle class.

There were also, of course, the rhythms of life with its attendant loves and laughs, joys and triumphs. Black children of all grades attended the same one-room schoolhouse, and years later still spoke with admiration and gratitude for the teachers they remembered. People worked together ("sun to past sun"), looked out for each other, and celebrated together, whether it was the end of another long week in the fields or the annual multi-day celebration of Juneteenth, when Jim Jones' farm was the place to be. His daughter, Zeola Jones Vaughn, said that her father "would give maybe a two- or three-day picnic" at a space known as Ellum Park, at the foot of "Jim Jones Hill." Born in 1912, Vaughn was a small child when "Walter Boyd" lived in the area, but she heard stories about the man who played an unusual, twelve-string guitar from her oldest brother, Zollie Jones,[11] who was just five years younger than Ledbetter. "Everywhere he went, he carried this guitar," Vaughn said. "If he went to the field, he had it, that was his life." Walter Boyd was a popular entertainer: "If he was going to be there, everybody knew he could pick and sing and they were anxious to get there." Among the places he played was "Ellum Park," she said, and there are stories that he was joined there at least once by Blind Lemon Jefferson.[12]

It was children, making their way to the schoolhouse in Beaver Dam, who discovered the lifeless body of Will Stafford on Friday morning, December 14, 1917. Within a week, "Walter Boyd," a month shy of his twenty-ninth birthday, was arrested and charged with his murder. The Lomaxes' version of events was that Ledbetter, Alex Griffin, and Will Stafford "started out through the river bottom one evening late to a dance." They said that "Alex Griffin began to 'jive' Will Stafford about the way his girl had been playing around with other men. Walter Boyd's name was drawn into the talk and Stafford drew a pistol. Walter Boyd shot Stafford through the middle of his forehead, and Alex Griffin ran off into the woods believing that Walter had tried to kill him, too."[13] It is not clear where or from whom the Lomaxes got these details, and the lack of clarity in their description is mirrored in documents from the period. Were the Lomaxes suggesting that Boyd – Huddie Ledbetter – had shot Stafford in self-defense? That he had used Stafford's gun against Stafford, or that both men were armed? No death certificate has been found, nor is there any report of the death in the usual county or state documents, and there is no mention of the shooting or Stafford's death in the area's main newspapers. No arrest warrants for Walter Boyd have been found, or subpoenas for witnesses. There is no tombstone for Stafford in the Beaver Dam cemetery, although that's not unusual. But surviving documents strongly suggest that in an impartial system of justice, Huddie Ledbetter might not have been convicted.

Huddie Ledbetter and Will Stafford were distant cousins, and they were also related by marriage. Stafford's wife, Mary "Pig" Walker, was Ledbetter's cousin, the daughter of Wesley Ledbetter's sister Delia and her husband, Wright Fisher.[14] The Staffords were married in October 1903, when Will was twenty-four years old. Pig was twenty-three, a widow with a three-year-old daughter, Willie Kate. Ledbetter's niece, Viola, remembered Stafford as being tall, about six-foot-three. "Wore a big western hat," she said. He and his brothers were very light-skinned, and are listed in census records as "mulatto," or mixed-race. He was "tough," Viola added, "like a western guy. Rode a good horse. He was also a farmer, and a good one."[15]

When they were first married, the Staffords lived near the Louisiana side of Caddo Lake.[16] Sometime by early 1913, they moved to Beaver Dam, and shortly afterward, Will, then thirty-five, fathered two children outside of his marriage. On January 28, 1914, thirteen-year-old Clara Boyd (daughter of Stafford's friend, Nick Boyd),[17] gave birth to Stafford's son, Presley.[18] On June 2, 1914, fourteen-year-old Willie Kate, Will Stafford's own stepdaughter (Pig's daughter), gave birth to his daughter, Acie. At some point, Stafford also became involved with Chammie Jones,[19] four years younger than him, and moved her into the house he shared with his wife. (Willie Kate and her infant daughter may have moved out by then. In November 1916, she married Stafford's younger brother, Dick.) Chammie Jones was still part of the Stafford household when Will was killed in December 1917. Margaret Cornelious, who lived with her mother at the home of her uncle, Alex Griffin, remembered the odd procession as a wagon carried Stafford's body to the Beaver Dam cemetery. "It was a team and a wagon; that's the way they carried the corpse to the cemetery," she said. "Miss Chammie was sitting on the false box, on the coffin in the wagon." Stafford's widow rode up front with the driver, on the spring seat.[20]

An often-reported story, based on the Lomaxes' book, is that when Ledbetter was arrested in December 1917, "Old Man Wess Ledbetter turned up right away with his pocket full of the money he had got by selling some of his hard-earned sixty-eight acres. Mahaffey and Keeney, criminal lawyers, were retained."[21] The first part is not accurate; the only land transaction of that nature occurred in 1915, between the Ledbetters and the firm of Lane & Lane. In 1917–1918, Ledbetter *was* represented by the law firm of Mahaffey, Keeney, & Dalby, almost certainly pro bono.

What happened on the night of the murder remains unclear. The Batts children had already returned to live with their grandparents, Wesley and Sallie Ledbetter, now in Mooringsport. Later, the nieces remembered, Wesley Ledbetter traveled alone to Beaver Dam to gather up their belongings.[22] Margaret Cornelious, interviewed in 1991,[23] thought that after the shooting, Nick Boyd, Walter Boyd, her uncle Alex Griffin, and a man named Lee Brown (who, like Griffin, lived on the Wright place), remained together, walking a relatively short distance north from where Stafford's body was found to an area along the Red River known as the Pat Gibbons Bottoms. This was the site of a 457-acre farm owned by a white farmer, Pat Gibbons. Several small houses stood on the land, including the one where Nick Boyd lived with his family. There were a number of trails leading from the bottoms to the Red River, which authors Kip Lornell and Charles Wolfe reported was "often little more than a trickle" at that time of year: In December a man can literally walk the forty yards across to Oklahoma," they wrote.[24] In fact, Texas was experiencing a drought that December. "A thin sheet of ice is said to have formed clear across Red River once or twice during the past week, on account of the water being shallow and narrow," reported *The Paris Morning News*.[25] None of the men crossed, however.

Margaret Cornelious believed that Walter Boyd had forced the men to stay together in the bottoms for a time, but it's not clear what would be gained by this. In any event, at some point, the men set out for home, although it's also possible that, as was the custom, white farmers held one or more of them in make-shift jails, such as a feed crib. On Tuesday, December 18, 1917, Bowie County Sheriff Jim "J.D." Baker, a white man in his early forties, arrived from Texarkana, Texas, a distance of about fifty miles, and arrested "Walter Boyd." They also went to the home of Alex

Griffin, about three miles farther. His niece remembered being at home on a winter night and studying by the light of a coal-oil lamp when "the laws" came and "picked him up." Cornelious said that her uncle was away overnight but returned the following day.

Huddie Ledbetter was transferred to the Bowie County jail in Boston, Texas. Today the jail is a grim, crumbling brick structure, perched at the edge of a large, grassy square where the county courthouse, now located in New Boston, once stood. Ledbetter was held for six long weeks, through Christmas and New Year's Day, before facing a grand jury on Tuesday, January 29, 1918. He was indicted: The jury found that Walter Boyd, on or about December 13, 1917, "did then and there unlawfully, with his malice aforethought, kill Will Stafford, by then and there shooting the said Will Stafford with a gun, against the peace and dignity of the State."[26] Three weeks later, on Wednesday, February 20, 1918, the trial – The State of Texas v. Walter Boyd, docket number 4890, Fifth Judicial Court – got under way.[27]

> When a man git in trouble,
> Ev'rybody turns him down.
> When a man git in trouble,
> Ev'rybody turns him down.
>
> Now I b'lieve to my soul
> that I'm prison bound.[28]

Walter Boyd's was the first of nine capital cases to be considered at the "present session" of the Bowie County district court.[29] "To the charge of murder," records note, "the defendant, Walter Boyd, pleaded not guilty." Presiding over the case was Judge Howard Franklin O'Neal. One of the organizers of the Atlanta National Bank in Atlanta, Texas, O'Neal was born in Harrison County in 1853 but grew up in Cass County, where he practiced law throughout his life, including eight years as a judge and eight as a district attorney.[30] Representing the state was District Attorney Hugh Carney, who was also from Atlanta, Texas and was a nephew of Charles Carney,[31] who – two years later – would partner with Robert Hope to buy the Ledbetters' thirty acres at auction. Representing Walter Boyd, as noted, were lawyers from Mahaffey, Keeney, & Dalby, a general practice

firm based in Texarkana, Texas. White lawyers John Q. Mahaffey, Luther
E. Keeney, and Norman L. Dalby also brought on another attorney,
a "Mr. Thomas."

Records of the trial itself begin with a document of the "court's charge"
(the judge's instructions to the jury before their deliberation), followed
by a series of documents recording the "defendant's exceptions to court's
charge" (Ledbetter's lawyers' objection to the court's charge), along with
efforts to secure a new trial based on the judge's overruling of objections
they had made throughout the one-day trial.[32] The prosecution,
Ledbetter's attorneys argued, had not "clearly, affirmatively and with
sufficient fullness" presented to the jury the defendant's theory of the
killing as testified to by him. Further, the defense had been overruled
when they objected to District Attorney Carney asking "Peggy" (Pig)
Stafford if the defendant (Boyd) "did not tell her a short time before
the alleged commission of the offense in this case that he had been
convicted for shooting a man in Louisiana, that he had made his escape
from the road gang, raped a woman, and had come to Texas and had
changed his name from Huley [sic] Ledbetter to Walter Boyd." Then, still
over the defense's objections, the judge allowed the District Attorney to
ask white landowner John Cowan the same question. Not only was the
court assuming "as true" these testimonies, Ledbetter's attorneys argued,
but it would also be in error if the judge told the jury "that such testimony
may be considered by them in so far as it may or may not affect the
credibility of the defendant as a witness."

Additionally, the lawyers argued, the court had erred by not telling the
jury that Alex Griffin and Nick Boyd were accomplice witnesses and had
not charged the jury as to the "rule of law applicable to the testimony of
accomplice witnesses."[33] (Lee Brown's name does not show up in the
surviving court documents.)

Lastly, Ledbetter's attorneys wanted the judge to instruct the jury that
they were to "disregard the remarks of the District Attorney to the effect
that defendant had a right to bring his neighbors here and prove his
character as a law abiding citizen and that he has failed to do so." The
"State could not show it," the attorneys argued, because their client "had
not put his character in issue." Judge O'Neal overruled all of the defense's
objections, and the jury soon returned with a verdict, announced by
foreman P. Cookman: "We, the Jury, find the Defendant, Walter Boyd,

guilty of murder, and assess his punishment at twenty (20) years confineme[n]t in the State Penitentiary." In addition, the state of Texas would recover from "Walter Boyd" all of the costs spent to prosecute him. Ledbetter was remanded to the Boston jail "to await the further order of the Court."

In its reporting, *The Daily Texarkanian* seemed to be sharing a summary from prosecutors, rather than direct observation of testimony. "Boyd put up a rather novel defense, attorneys state, wherein he tried to fix the responsibility on two other negroes for the killing," the paper reported. "The claim was made that Boyd and three other negroes were out at night on the date of the killing, when they had some words with Stafford." Prosecutors apparently told the press that "[Walter] Boyd was walking ahead of Stafford, and the evidence showed that he turned and shot Stafford." As evidence of Boyd's guilt, the lawyers claimed it was "proven" that neither Nick Boyd nor Alex Griffin was carrying a weapon. Yet the paper also noted that Ledbetter "is said to have asserted that the one who really killed Stafford overpowered and disarmed him and shot him with his own gun."[34] Forensic technology was not advanced enough in 1918 to identify bullet types,[35] and the records don't indicate whether or not the defense tried to prove that Will Stafford carried a gun, although oral histories state that he did. His son Presley inherited the pistol, according to Presley's cousin, Willie Richard.[36]

Margaret Cornelious said that her uncle Alex never discussed the shooting, although she had some idea that the men had been gambling and arguing about money. Queenie Davidson, the cousin who grew up in Texas near to Huddie, said that she knew Will and Pig Stafford before they moved to DeKalb. She learned that Stafford had been shot from Alan Fisher, Pig's brother-in-law, who was visiting DeKalb when it happened. Davidson said that Fisher told her "Huddie didn't kill Will – some other men did."[37] The lawyers at Mahaffey, Keeney, & Dalby were very dissatisfied, and on February 23, 1918, they returned to the District Court of Bowie County to file a motion for a new trial. On March 13, their motion was denied, but it was "further ordered, adjudged and decreed by the Court that the defendant be allowed 90 days from this date in which to prepare and file in this cause a statement of facts and bills of exceptions, which order is here entered upon the docket of said Court, and upon the

Minutes of said Court, and Defendant's bond on appeal is fixed by the Court at the sum of $5000.00."

As his lawyers worked to prepare their case, Huddie Ledbetter, still being held in the Boston jail, made an understandable but fateful choice. On the morning of Monday, April 1, about five weeks after the trial, he and seven other Black men were transferred to a "safety cell" to await their breakfast. When the jailor, Henry Brooks, arrived with a tray, James Mosley and another man, "who had hidden under a pile of blankets in the corner of the cell, jumped upon him, knocked him down, and took his revolver." Hearing her husband's yells, Brooks' wife unlocked the jail's exterior door "and screamed for assistance" before being locked into a room with her husband. At that point, four of the men – Mosley, Walter Boyd, Elbert Jones, and Dave Williams – ran. (It is not stated which man was under the blanket with Mosley, and Ledbetter was never named as such.) The escape was quickly quelled. Mosley was shot and killed by a deputy sheriff. Ledbetter was chased and captured by "a rural mail carrier." He was only "about a mile away," unarmed, and had been at large for just three or four hours. Elbert Jones was also captured, and the fourth man was still missing as of the news report.[38]

Those brief hours of freedom would prove enormously costly. On April 22, "Walter Boyd" was in court again, charged with attempted murder for the attack on the jailor. The trial, *The State of Texas v. Walter Boyd*, number 4945, lasted less than a day. He was convicted, with the jury recommending "not less than two, nor more than ten" years' confinement.[39] Ledbetter's attorneys from Mahaffey, Keeney, & Dalby continued to appeal the first conviction, arguing that the escape attempt should not count against Walter Boyd with respect to the Stafford murder trial because, given how flawed the conviction was, he shouldn't have been in the Boston jail to begin with. But their efforts were doomed. In the case of *Boyd v. State*, number 5040, the Court of Criminal Appeals, Texas ruled on May 22, 1918, that: "Where appellant from conviction of murder, as appears by the affidavit of the deputy sheriff and jailer, made his escape from jail by overpowering the jailer, and was later arrested and returned to custody, motion to dismiss the appeal will be sustained."[40] Despite the six-month legal battle waged on his behalf by a prestigious white law firm,[41] Walter Boyd would serve two sentences: docket 4890, murder, "not less than five, nor more than 20 years"; and docket 4945, assault to murder, "not less than two, nor more than ten" years. The second sentence would begin when the first had expired, meaning that he was facing a total of seven to thirty years in prison.

On June 7, 1918, Walter Boyd, prisoner number 42738, arrived at Shaw State Prison Farm, about ten miles north of DeKalb, at the north end of Farm Road 992. His sentence would not expire until May 24, 1948, when he would be nearly sixty. In the meantime, life in Beaver Dam went on. On August 7, 1918, two months after Ledbetter arrived at Shaw and eight months after Will Stafford's murder, Iola Boyd (Nick Boyd's daughter, and the sister of Clara) gave birth to a daughter, Taleta "Panthy" Boyd. Among locals, she was rumored to be the child of "Walter Boyd." Counting backward, it seems possible that Iola didn't know at the time of the murder that she was pregnant. The following year, she married twenty-year-old Haywood Johnson, and in the 1920 census Taleta is listed with Johnson's last name.[42] In June 1991, about six months before she died, Taleta Boyd King was interviewed.[43] Then seventy-three years old, she said that her mother had told her that Haywood Johnson was her stepfather. "She told me, 'Now your real Daddy, he's in the pen and he plays a twelve-string guitar.'" King said that her mother, who died in 1972, called him Walter Boyd, and that she herself didn't connect her father with "Huddie Ledbetter" until perhaps the 1960s, at least a decade after Ledbetter's death. It seems possible that Ledbetter never knew about her.[44]

Aletha Henderson Ledbetter left Bowie County after her husband was sent to Shaw. Queenie Davidson, who years earlier had turned down a marriage proposal from Aletha's brother Gritt Henderson, said that Aletha became a preacher, starting out around Terrell, Texas. Irene Batts Campbell said that her uncle Huddie told her much later, possibly after he'd moved to New York City, that Aletha moved on to Kansas City. "And he went through there and saw her," Campbell said, likely referring to a visit Ledbetter made to Kansas City in 1926, "and that's the last I ever heard of her."[45]

Nick Boyd, the father of Iola and Clara, experienced a mental health crisis within a few years of the shooting, according to Zeola Vaughn, and was said to have drowned in Mill Creek. His widow remarried in 1922.[46] Alex Griffin died in 1939, at the age of sixty-nine.

The Huntsville, Texas intake records for June 7, 1918, described "Walter Boyd" as being thirty-one years old; he was actually twenty-nine. He was 5′ 7″, 164 pounds, with black hair and dark brown eyes. He was listed as Baptist, a non-smoker, with a scar on top of his left shoulder and a size 7 shoe.[47] A second form, "Texas State Penitentiaries, Description of Convict When Received," also dated June 7, 1918, noted "Heavy scar on left cheek. Scar on left arm near elbow."[48] Shaw, the prison farm to which he was sent, spanned 4,688 acres – more than 7 square miles – along the Red River in Bowie County, not far from DeKalb.[49] At its core was a 2,715-acre plantation sold to the state in 1915 by the Honorable N.A. "Gus" Shaw, a planter and lawyer who served in the twenty-second Texas legislature.[50] Ledbetter was one of 160 prisoners at Shaw in 1918.[51] Given the wartime conditions – the United States had entered World War I in April 1917, and the Armistice was not declared until November 1918 – the state faced pressure to maximize the output of those incarcerated on prison farms, "to produce sustenance for ourselves and our allies."[52] By August 1919, Ledbetter had seen enough suffering and death for a lifetime. According to the Lomaxes, he had seen other prisoners being whipped, but they hadn't hit him "'cause I was a good worker – but I didn' want to 'low 'em no chance at me."[53] Still, faced with three decades of incarceration, he decided to risk an escape or die trying. It was a desperate decision; if the guards didn't shoot and kill him, their punishment upon his recapture would be brutal. In the meantime, they would unleash trained dogs to find and attack him.[54]

> Sometimes, I live in the country,
> Sometimes, I live in the town.
> Sometimes I get a great notion,
> To jump in the river and drown.[55]

According to the story he allegedly told the Lomaxes, Ledbetter had reached a body of water when the authorities and vicious prison dogs caught up with him. He plunged into the water and nearly drowned before he was rescued and resuscitated. He was then taken back to Shaw and confronted by John C. Francis, a white guard in his late forties.[56] According to *Negro Folk Songs as Sung by Lead Belly*, Ledbetter told the

Lomaxes that Captain Francis was "a good cap'n" who kept him out of the field for a week, after which he gave him a pep talk. He told him to stop thinking about running, and that someday he could be "one of the best workers in de penitenshuh." From then on, the Lomaxes quoted him saying, "I was a rollin' sonafabitch. Dat's where I learned to work – down on de Shaw farm."[57] In fact, records show that after he was resuscitated, Ledbetter was whipped, possibly so badly that he *couldn't* work for a week. The "Conduct Register," page 536, under "Punishments," reads: "Escaped and recaptured at Shaw Farm, August 15, 1919. Lash 12 [*or possibly 14, it's difficult to read*]. Punishment set aside and lost time restored by order B. of P. C. 8–25–1924."[58]

The laudatory portrayal of Ledbetter as a hard worker and "number one roller" permeates the Lomaxes' narrative. The notion aligns with John Lomax's views about the transformative power of hard work in fresh, outdoor air, a sentiment echoed throughout the South by white politicians justifying the prison farms. To Lomax, the outdoor labor of prisoners was comparable to his decision to send ten-year-old Alan, frail even as a young boy, to spend a summer living and working with family friends on a sprawling ranch outside Fort Worth. "Lomax, imbued with the legend of his hero Theodore Roosevelt [who wrote the introduction to Lomax's 1910 book, *Cowboy Songs*], placed great stock in the restorative powers of the great outdoors as a cure for sickly boys," wrote biographer Nolan Porterfield.[59] The Lomaxes were boasting when they said that Ledbetter "became the best worker on the farm," adding: "His cunning, his body, his strength, his will, fitted him well to survive; and, under the hot sun, through the long driving days, in the course routine of the prison system, Lead Belly flourished."[60] The notion is deeply offensive, completely erasing a history in which failure to work at a set pace, no matter how unreasonable, could result in punishment or death; striving to meet that pace could also prove fatal. Through "most of the 1910s and 1920s," wrote historian Robert Perkinson of the Texas prison system, administrators "aimed for retribution, deterrence, and most of all production. They conceived of prison properties as for-profit state enterprises, and, as had lessees, they sought to wrest maximum exertion from convicts."[61] Death was a constant presence in prison songs from this era, in lyrics such as *Ought to come on the river in 1904 / you could find a dead man on every turn row* ("Ain't No More Cane on the Brazos") and *I told the captain / That old Ben was dead / And the captain didn't do nothing / But nod his head* ("Go Down, Ol' Hannah"). The song "Billy in De Lowlands," which the Lomaxes said was Ledbetter's second-favorite work song, after "Julie Ann Johnson," describes a man – "a sundown man . . . a number one man" – dying in the field.

In May 1920, Ledbetter and all of Shaw's other Black prisoners were moved to the Imperial State Farm at Sugar Land, renamed "Central State" a decade later. It was a journey of about 300 miles, and he was likely brought there, chained to other men around the neck or legs, by Bud "Uncle Bud" Russell, the chief transfer agent for the Texas prison system from 1905 to 1944. Over the course of his career, Russell transported "more than 115,000 persons to the penitentiary," generally "from 26 to 28 prisoners at a time." He was also "a crack marksman."[62] Russell is featured in some versions of the song "Midnight Special":

"Yonder come Bud Russell."
"How in de worl' do you know?"
"Tell him by his big hat
An' his 44.

He walked into de jail-house
Wid a gang o' chains in his han's;
I heard him tell de captain,
"I'm de transfer man." [63]

Even Shaw State could not have prepared Huddie Ledbetter for incarceration at the Imperial State Prison Farm, which stretched along 5,235 acres in Fort Bend County, Texas, near the Brazos River and Oyster Creek. The region had a long and sordid history of forced labor, from the enslaved workers on sugar and other plantations to the forced prison labor that took hold and intensified with the end of Reconstruction. Beginning around 1875, one man in particular, a former enslaver named Edward H. Cunningham (1835–1912), made a fortune through the abuse of state prisoners, working them on his own lands and subcontracting them to others. He was regarded as "the principal founder and organizer of the extensive sugar industry in Texas in the area southwest of Houston," wrote historian Donald Walker. "He used hundreds of state prisoners to work the cane plantations that provided the raw material for his refinery at Sugarland." At convict leasing's peak, wrote Robert Perkinson, Cunningham presided over "some 2,300 convicts."[64] When the Texas legislature abolished the practice in 1910, Cunningham and his financial partners sold their land to the state, which opened the prison farm.

Life at Sugarland during Ledbetter's time (1920–1925) was not substantially different than it had been decades earlier. Prisoners "slept in squalid twenty-by-fifty-foot plank houses stuffed with double bunks," wrote Perkinson, describing conditions around 1910. "Up to fifty men jammed inside, sleeping on corn husk mattresses, relieving themselves in common buckets, and washing themselves in a trough of grimy water." There was minimal effort to protect them from cold, heat, or disease-carrying insects and vermin. They worked six days a week, sunup to sundown, which in the summer meant days as long as fifteen hours. "On the largest farms," Perkinson wrote, "the day began with a 'fast trot' to the fields, up to five miles away."[65] Between late May and late September, as humid temperatures climbed into the nineties and above, the sun beat down mercilessly on work gangs. "Go Down, Ol' Hannah," they sang, a holler into the abyss, a call for deliverance, a demand for justice.

> Go down ol' Hannah
> Don't you rise no more
> And if you do rise in the morning
> Set this world on fire.[66]

On January 18, 1921, nearly a year after Huddie Ledbetter was moved to Sugarland, the man who would unexpectedly change his fortunes took office as governor of Texas. The prison system that Pat M. Neff inherited included more than a dozen prison farms spread across the state, with land totaling more than 81,000 acres.[67] It was, according to a report in the April 1921 issue of *The Prison Journal*, "one of the most brutal penal systems in the world." The report's author, Houston attorney George W. Dixon, argued that the prison farms should be sold. "They are isolated and brutalities are carried on all over the system," he wrote. "Men have been beaten to death. Some are scarred from head to foot by the teeth of the dogs kept on these farms, and twenty-three men have been shot down by guards during the past two years. The present system is a disgrace to civilization."[68] That same year, "a coalition of women's organizations ... joined forces with a union-affiliated, left-leaning brain trust based in New York ... to conduct a sweeping 'scientific survey' of the state's penal institutions," wrote Robert Perkinson. On February 15, 1921, Neff authorized the group, the Texas Committee on Prisons and Prison Labor (CPPL) to conduct its investigation into conditions.[69] In 1924, the CPPL released its report, 400 pages that looked at prison management and facilities throughout Texas and made a "scientific study" of the physical and mental health of the state's nearly 4,000 prisoners, as well as a report on their education levels, employment, and issues such as parole and pardon.[70] Contrary to the view that outdoor labor resulted in strong, healthy individuals, the committee found that of "3811 examined, 3376 [nearly 89 percent] were affected with some sort of disease or defect..." Further, of 3,457 examined for mental health, "[l]ess than one-third of the inmates examined can be classified as normal." The 1920 federal census reported that 16 percent of Texans were Black and 84 percent were white.[71] The 1924 CPPL report put the Texas prison population at 46 percent Black, 43 percent white, and 11 percent Mexican. The prison farms, especially, were deemed a "complete failure." More than a third of the land, the committee reported, "is subject to overflow, and the rest does not make enough crops to pay on the investment, far less to keep the system going." The answer, the committee felt, was straightforward: Texas needed "a prison system new from start to finish."[72]

The reforms that the committee recommended, and what became of them, are beyond the scope of this book. What is relevant here is that as this investigation was under way, visitors to Sugarland were sometimes entertained by a prisoner known as Walter Boyd. Governor Neff was among these visitors, with records showing that he visited at least twice in 1923, again in March 1924, and again at the formal opening of Sugarland's new "Honor Farm," an experiment involving white prisoners, on September 29, 1924. This last visit was described by Ledbetter to Ken Britzius, a writer from Minneapolis, Minnesota, during a performing tour there in November 1948.[73] Knowing that Neff would be back at some point, he told Britzius, he made sure his prison whites were clean and crisply ironed. "Pat Neff came and there were four cars, all of them would be women, except for the chauffeurs," Ledbetter said. "And these women would have these little automatics in their pocketbooks; they didn't take no chances." Ledbetter told Britzius that he had an eight-piece band all set to go. "When we went up there that night, Governor Pat Neff and the women was sitting on the front porch." Neff "was sitting with his legs crossed and his arms folded. He wore these tall collars and a bow tie, looked a little like a priest, you know . . . I put my guitar on my shoulder, had my twelve-string Stella." His bandmates likely nodded silently as they went by the governor, but Neff singled Ledbetter out, demonstrating that he had heard him perform at least once before. According to Ledbetter, Neff greeted him: "How you doing?" "I'm just fine." "How're you feeling?" "Your honor, I feel all right." "Still dancing?" "I can dance all night."[74]

Ledbetter told Britzius that he sat "down near the piano player and the bass player" as they sang eight tunes, a few requested by the governor and some songs of their own selection. The program included "What a Friend We Have in Jesus," "Old Dan Tucker," "Down in the Valley," "Stack o' Dollars," and "Midnight Special." But Ledbetter also had a song none of the others knew he'd prepared. "I put Mary in it, Jesus's mother, you know," he said, as well as "inspiration from the Bible," roughly quoting Matthew 6:14–15: *For if ye forgive men their trespasses, your Heavenly Father will also forgive you. But if ye forgive not men their trespasses, neither will your Father forgive your trespasses.* As transcribed in the Lomaxes' book, the song's many stanzas included:

> Nineteen hundred and twenty-three
> De judge took my liberty 'way from me,
> Left my wife wringing her hands and cryin',
> "Lawd have mercy on de man of mine."
> Goodbye, Mary, oh, Mary.

Ledbetter then sang lines directly to the governor:

> I am your servant, compose this song,
> Please, Governor Neff, lemme go back home
> Please, Governor Neff, be good and kind,
> Have mercy on my great long time.
>
> Please, Governor Neff, be good and kind,
> Have mercy on my great long time.

> If I don't get a pardon, will you cut my time?
>
> Had you, Governor Neff, like you got me,
> I'd wake up in de mornin', an' I'd set you free.[75]

The likelihood of Neff pardoning anyone was slim. Born in Texas in 1871, Neff was four years younger than John Lomax. He had earned a law degree at the University of Texas and is described in the state archive as a "brilliant, merciless prosecutor [who] tried 422 defendants and won convictions in all but sixteen cases."[76] He ran for office on a progressive platform and "better treatment of prisoners," Robert Perkinson wrote, but then became "the first Texas governor to make hard-fisted, no-nonsense crime fighting a central part of his political identity." Neff also "radically curtailed executive clemency," according to Perkinson. "Whereas Neff's two predecessors had pardoned more than four thousand convicts between them, he extended clemency to just over two hundred during his two terms in office."[77] Yet on January 16, 1925, during his last day in office, Neff granted Ledbetter a full pardon, proclamation number 18141. Ledbetter walked out, a free man, on Wednesday January 21, 1925 – a day after his thirty-sixth birthday.

News of this unusual pardon reached readers of *The Marshall News Messenger*, in Harrison County, Texas, although it seems that no one connected "Walter Boyd" with Huddie Ledbetter. No image accompanied the page 7 article, headlined "Negro with Foghorn Voice Sings His Way To Official Pardon":

Houston, Jan. 23. – Walter Boyd is singing a new song. It is one of exultation, the shouting kind of singing.

Walter is a negro who has served eight years of a long term at Camp No. 3, of Imperial Prison Farm. He was on the entertainment program the day Pat Neff honor farm for white convicts was opened.

Visitors heard Walter sing in a voice of plaintive melody:

It I had you, governor,
    Where you got me,
First thing I'd do
    Be to set you free!

Now Walter is free. His name was among the 15 pardons issued by Governor Neff as one of the final acts of his four years in office.[78]

Governor Neff related the story in his book *The Battles of Peace*, published soon after he left office. "On one of the farms, during my administration, was a negro as black as a stack of black cats at midnight. I visited a number of times, during the four years, the farm where he worked, and on each visit he sang a song which was a petition for pardon set to music," Neff wrote. "In one verse he mentioned his wife; in another, his home; and I recall the third, closing with these words: '*I know my mother will faint and shout, When the train rolls up and I come stepping out.*'" The governor remembered that Ledbetter finished "with much negro pathos and in full confidence" by making the appeal: "*If I had the Governor where the Governor has me, I would, before morning, set the Governor free.*" In explaining the pardon, Neff wrote, "He had been in the penitentiary some seven years, and had proved himself to be a trustworthy convict."[79]

Huddie Ledbetter, now thirty-six years old, was starting over yet again.

CHAPTER 7

Northern Debut

As they reconciled outside the post office in Montgomery, Alabama on that rainy October day in 1934, both John Lomax and Huddie Ledbetter were focused on the long game: first Philadelphia, and then New York. But first, they had to finish the southern recording tour that Lomax had planned. Their final stop in Alabama was the 8,360-acre Atmore Prison Farm, now known as the Fountain Correctional Facility, where they recorded from October 30 to November 4, 1934. From there, they would take another break, with Ledbetter driving nearly 450 miles to Shreveport and Lomax continuing 330 miles from there to Austin. Ahead of them, at the end of December, lay the Modern Language Association (MLA) meeting.

While at Atmore, Lomax received an answer from MLA committee member Townsend Scudder III, a recent Ph.D. graduate of Yale University. The committee "welcomed your generous suggestion that your talented aborigine 'n[–]' sing for the guests at the M.L.A. smoker," Scudder wrote. In *Negro Folk Songs as Sung by Lead Belly*, Lomax as usual feigned to have played no role in the booking. "When the program committee heard of Lead Belly," he wrote, "I was asked to bring him along ... I was tempted to throw caution to the winds." He also claimed that he believed that after Atmore, "the adventure with [Ledbetter] had ended." Alan had recovered enough to travel, and Lomax said that he told Ledbetter there would be "no room" in the car for him. During the break in Austin, Lomax told readers, he received "almost daily letters" from Ledbetter in Shreveport, "repeating former promises of good behavior [and] begging that he be taken along."[1] This story, like the one in which Ledbetter unexpectedly appeared at Lomax's hotel in Marshall, Texas and stood "timidly" before him, is false. These revised narratives effectively painted Ledbetter as a supplicant dependent on Lomax's benevolence, rather than as a professional colleague. The truth is that by the time John Lomax was back in Austin, the Ledbetters were fully aware that Huddie would be heading north with Lomax. On Wednesday, November 7, 1934, they sent a letter to Lomax from Shreveport, acknowledging the plan. Martha, signing her name as Martha Ledbetter, told Lomax how happy she was to have Huddie home, just as she was sure that Mrs. Lomax was happy to have him home, and how she hoped that he and Ledbetter would make the trip to Philadelphia "as well as you made this one."[2] For his part, rather than writing to beg that he be brought along, Ledbetter had thoughts about how both he and Lomax might earn some money. "I am getting up all the songs I can for you," he wrote, and suggested they might make some records to sell at the MLA gathering. Whenever Lomax was ready to go, he was ready. In the meantime, he asked Lomax to send him a dollar, please.[3] There is no record of a response.

Lomax, back in Austin with the wife he'd barely seen since their marriage in July, used the time to begin generating buzz for the upcoming MLA presentations and to catch up on correspondence, most of it pertaining to *American Ballads and Folk Songs*, which had been published in October. Particularly vexing were the claims, occasionally valid, that songs contained in the book were already copyrighted, an issue that he and Macmillan worked quickly to address. Errors were almost inevitable in such a hefty book: 625 pages filled with works "COLLECTED AND COMPILED BY JOHN A. LOMAX, Honorable Consultant in American Folk Song and Curator of the Folk Song Archives of the Library of Congress, AND ALAN LOMAX." Even more so than his earlier books, *American Ballads and Folk Songs* was a vindication of Lomax's belief in the value of American folk music in all its diversity. It was also his chance, at age sixty-seven, to reclaim his place among the academics he had long admired and within a community in which, in his younger years, he had played a vital role.

For musicologists, a controversial aspect of *American Ballads and Folk Songs* (although a practice not unique to the Lomaxes) was their publication of a form that Lomax described as "the composite ballad – the stringing together of the best stanzas, no matter where found." He offered as an example the "Ballad of the Erie Canal," which included stanzas taken from individuals including a professor, a lawyer, and two cattlemen, in New York, Montana, Washington, Illinois, and "Rio Grande," along with additional material found as print sources in libraries. "Necessarily," the Lomaxes recognized, "the arrangement is ours."[4] Lomax acknowledged that moving an oral/aural tradition onto the page came at a cost: "Worse than thieves are ballad collectors," he confessed in his introduction, "for when they capture and imprison in cold type a folk song, at the same time they kill it. Its change and growth are not so likely to continue after a fixed model for comparison exists."[5] The range of songs is diverse, although the book was criticized for its absence of Native American material as well as material performed in other languages, notably including Spanish. Some critics felt the categories and chapter titles were random and confusing, from "Negro Bad Men" and "White Desperadoes" to "Cocaine and Whiskey" and "Songs of Childhood."

Anticipating criticism that too much space was given to "Negro folk songs," Lomax argued in the book that in his and Alan's judgment, "the Negro [has] created the most distinctive of folk songs – the most interesting, the most appealing, and the greatest in quantity."[6] The criticism they faced for these songs, however, focused on the prison songs and the way in which their inclusion in the book minimized the conditions under which they were created. In *New Masses*, a Marxist publication that attracted many of that era's top authors, reviewer Alan Calmer concluded that the book was "of importance not only in the field of folk-literature, but as first-hand evidence in revealing the revolutionary tradition of the proletariat." At the same time, he argued, the Lomaxes had not sufficiently acknowledged the ways in which "songs of Negro laborers ... are now used as speed up measures"; that the music "is now an overseer's whip to make his gang 'hustle.'" Nor did "Messrs. Lomax" sufficiently acknowledge music as resistance to oppression, he wrote.[7] Two weeks later, *New Masses* published a letter from activist Lawrence Gellert, who was then gathering material for his own book, *Negro Songs of Protest* (American Music League, 1936). Gellert wanted to "let the Lomaxes qualify themselves for the task they set out to accomplish," he wrote, and then quoted from a letter he attributed to Alan Lomax (identifying the recipient as "a friend"), which contained an extraordinarily racist description of Ledbetter before adding that the author was "thinking of bringing him to New York in January," where he could be his correspondent's "guest and could entertain [his] crowd."[8] On December 11, "Lew Ney," otherwise known as Luther Widen of Parnassus Press, wrote his own letter to *New Masses*, in which he revealed himself to be the recipient of the letter, sent not by Alan Lomax but by his father. Ney defended John Lomax as "a southerner with all of a southerner's prejudices" but also a person "nationally recognized as the most painstaking, conscientious literary collector of folksongs in all America." Ney, a Texan now living in Greenwich Village, publicly invited a broad range of activists, including Gellert, to come to his home and "break bread with Leadbelly when he comes north for the first time in his life next January." (Ney's letter was followed by a scathing reply from Gellert, which concluded, "I look for the complete liberation of all the Negro masses only under a Soviet America.")[9]

A month earlier, on November 8, Ney had sent a private letter to Ledbetter, inviting him to dinner and likely increasing the performer's hopes for a positive, respectful reception in the North. "Professor Lomax has told us about how beautifully you sing, and we are anxious to have an opportunity to hear you some time," he wrote. "We hereby extend to you a hearty invitation to have dinner with us when you are in this city, and are looking forward to the pleasure of hearing some of your songs."[10] Ney came to regret defending Lomax, however, claiming in an undated essay that Lomax had "soured" on him when he "suggested that the killer-singer would sit at my table as one of a score of guests and not be relegated to wait his turn at entertainment in my furnace room." It was the end of his thirty-year acquaintance with Lomax, Ney wrote, and he did not meet Ledbetter until years later.[11]

In early December 1934, a mechanic managed to squeeze a back seat into John Lomax's Ford V-8, making room – just barely – for himself and Alan, Huddie Ledbetter, the recording gear and luggage, and two guitars: Ledbetter's twelve-string and Alan's six-string, which Ledbetter was teaching him to play. They began to wind their way north via a route that would allow them to record in Georgia, South Carolina, and North Carolina before arriving in Washington, D.C. on Christmas Eve. From there, they would go to Philadelphia and the MLA gathering taking place December 28–29. On December 10, they reached their first stop, Atlanta, where John and Alan secured a room at The Atlantan Hotel, downtown. Its stationery boasted 312 rooms, 312 baths, and a radio in every room. Ledbetter, as usual, had to fend for himself, as the Atlantan did not agree to "admit Negroes" until January 1964, to avert planned civil rights protests.[12]

So far, the trip north was going well. "Leadbetter is a treasure thus far," Lomax reported to Ruby. "I could not ask for more considerate thoughtfulness." To Lomax, the break, and perhaps the threat of not traveling again together, had caused the change. "The days I left him out in the cold in Shreveport were certainly good for him," his letter continued, "just as I intended." Ledbetter was still doing nearly all of the driving, in addition to keeping the car in good running order and waking both father and son each morning with coffee. "Yes'sum," Lomax told his wife, "we are making progress in the department of personal relations." Uncharacteristically, he included Ledbetter in his sign off: "Alan sends love and Leadbelly, too!!"[13]

Unexpectedly, though, Lomax then found himself shut out of Georgia's state prisons. On Wednesday night, December 12, he began a letter of complaint to Ruby: "The trouble we have had in Georgia has been due to the fact that the hospitality of the Prison Board has been shamefully abused by writers from the North who have come here and written, after being the guests of these gentlemen, horrors and cruelties even worse than those practiced in the Dark Ages." Because of these writers, he complained, "It took me nearly three days to break down the opposition."[14] Primary among the northern writers to whom Lomax was likely referring was John L. Spivak, a "radical journalist and muckraking reporter"[15] from Connecticut, whose exposé of chain gangs in Georgia was published in 1932[16] and widely serialized.[17] Spivak's work was preceded, and overshadowed to some extent, by another 1932 exposé, the autobiography *I Am a Fugitive from a Georgia Chain Gang!*, written by Robert E. Burns, a white World War I veteran. Burns' book was adapted into a popular feature film, released that fall.

Despite the setback, and despite Alan ending up in bed for a few days with what a doctor thought might be a recurrence of malaria,[18] the group recorded more than two dozen songs in Georgia, working at the Bellwood Prison Farm in Atlanta and at the main penitentiary in Milledgeville. By Sunday night, writing from Milledgeville, Lomax declared that they were "through" in Georgia and heading out the next day for "an easy drive" to Columbia, the capital of South Carolina.[19] But here, too, Lomax had trouble gaining access, not because of exposés but because of a letter he had written that was sent, in error, to state prison officials. The story is important because of what it again reveals about the desperation of people caught up in the southern prison system. So far, Lomax had been focusing on *state* prisons in his travels throughout the South. Shortly before this last leg of the trip, "the idea occurred to [him] that prisoners in Federal penitentiaries might also know folk songs," he wrote in his autobiography. For that reason, he worked with the Library of Congress on a form letter to be sent out to federal facilities, describing the project and his search for what he called, in the letter, "made up" songs, "no matter how crude or vulgar they may be." He added, "The material I wish to secure is especially plentiful among Negro prisoners." Apparently, the letter was mistakenly sent to the Kirkland Institution in Columbia, South Carolina, a state prison. It found its way to trusties there, who spread its increasingly misunderstood message by word of mouth among the prisoners. By the time Lomax arrived, the incarcerated men believed that he had been sent by the federal government to "investigate the prison system," he wrote. "Any prisoner who had a complaint against the food or the brutalities of the guards, or thought he should be pardoned, [thought he] would be given a hearing." Corrections officials told Lomax that "[v]iolent altercations had occurred in the prison yard" about who could speak with Lomax first.[20] The Lomaxes simply moved on to South Carolina prison facilities in Camden and Boykin, where the letter had not been sent. From there, they spent a final three days recording at the State Penitentiary in Raleigh, North Carolina.

Christmas 1934 found Huddie Ledbetter, John Lomax, and Alan Lomax in Washington, D.C., joined by Lomax's older son, Johnny. John Lomax claimed he didn't have "money to spare" for Ruby to take the train and join him,[21] and instead insisted that his wife of five months bring his teenaged daughter, Bess, to spend Christmas in Lubbock with his daughter, Shirley, and her husband. For Ledbetter, who had spent the previous four Christmases incarcerated at Angola and was now far from family and friends, the holiday must have been especially lonely. Throughout his life, the time between Christmas and New Year's Day had been a special time, a lull in the agricultural cycle during which parties, music, good food, and good company prevailed. His mother, Sallie, would rejoice on Christmas morning, thanking the "good lord" that her son "had seen and smiled for so many Christmases," Ledbetter told Alan Lomax in 1940. He and his family would "go to church on Christmas Eve night and wait and see Christmas Day come." There would be a feast at Elizabeth Church, he said – "that's my mamas' and them's church" – and his father would join the other men in cutting down a big cedar tree.[22] Everyone put presents under the tree for the children, "[a]nd then when they call, you go up and get your present." Back at his parents' house, Christmas Day was when "a little jug" of wine would be brought out, and a white cloth spread over a table that was soon laden with food. His mother "had cakes, pies, chicken, and turkeys," he told Alan. "You see, we raised them there . . . . And we had sausages, pork sausages." Neighbors would come around, and the celebration would continue for days, with the table always heaping. "It goes on for a week that way," he said. "Christmas time takes a whole week, not just a day," and only ended when "New Year come." On New Year's Eve, they'd return to church, "and sing all night."[23] Now, here he was in Washington, D.C., without even Martha by his side.

The Lomaxes put a Christmas tree in Johnny's room and a few gifts were handed out, but the holiday celebrations were mostly overshadowed by the desire to begin introducing Ledbetter to a broader public. On Christmas Eve, he performed for guests at the home of Major Isaac Spalding, an Oklahoma native who would rise to the rank of general during World War II. On Christmas Day, Ledbetter performed for "two groups of newspaper people," Lomax wrote to Ruby. He and his sons "took Leadbelly to the zoo in the afternoon," and then – almost certainly without Ledbetter – "had a late dinner and went to see 'The Little Minister,'" starring twenty-seven-year-old Katharine Hepburn.[24]

The weather was mild – just under 50 degrees, with light rain – on Wednesday, December 26, as Huddie Ledbetter and John and Alan Lomax arrived in Philadelphia, Pennsylvania. Ledbetter pulled the Ford up to the Benjamin Franklin Hotel, where the MLA's fifty-first annual convention was being held. The hotel, which opened in 1923, was vast and grand, constructed of red brick and limestone, "18 stories high with 1220 rooms."[25] While the MLA did not have a whites-only policy, the hotel did. After leaving the Lomaxes, Ledbetter walked a mile farther to reach a rooming house at 1126 Pine Street.[26]

Lomax had arranged two "shows," as he called them.[27] The largest would be at 7:30 p.m. on Friday, December 28, followed the next morning by a smaller presentation. More than 1,000 people were in attendance at the MLA convention, and Lomax had worked hard to attract not only their attention but also that of the press and public, promoting Ledbetter as an "ex-convict" and using only his prison moniker, "Lead Belly." He later reported that it worked: "[T]he interest of the newspapers had been aroused by his queer name on the program of the Modern Language Association."[28]

That Huddie Ledbetter himself did not primarily use the prison name was not a consideration. In his recordings at Angola, he introduced himself repeatedly as "Huddie Ledbetter," sometimes adding "also known as Lead Belly." When speaking to a reporter for *The Philadelphia Independent*, a Black newspaper, on the morning of the first MLA event, he used his given name. But now, appearing before the largest audience of his life, he was introduced by the name – and identity – of John Lomax's choosing. The man Lomax introduced was not a multitalented dancer, singer, and musician whose deep repertoire allowed him to draw upon and transform the music that reflected the nation's diverse heritage; he was not a seasoned performer who had performed with Blind Lemon Jefferson and others whose names would be familiar to at least some of those in the audience; he was not even the essential assistant who had worked with Lomax long hours throughout the fall to enhance the archives of the Library of Congress. Instead, he was presented in terms of his race and imprisonment.

As a final straw, Lomax pulled out the clothing Ledbetter had been wearing when they met up at the hotel in Marshall, Texas, which he had insisted on packing away for safekeeping when they were in Little Rock. Up until this event, whether working among prisoners or performing in the classrooms of white college students in the South, Ledbetter had dressed well, albeit in used suits. There is a photograph of him from around this time, possibly in North Carolina, seated on a chair with his battered twelve-string guitar, painted green and held together with string.[29] His hair is dark and trim; he sports a bow tie, a starched white shirt with cufflinks, a vest, and dress pants. Now, before this well-heeled audience in Philadelphia, Lomax insisted that Ledbetter wear the denim overalls, work shirt, dusty shoes, and bandana that he'd worn to their meeting in Marshall, topped with a straw hat. Perhaps to assuage a disbelieving Ledbetter, Lomax promised that he could give the audience the full effect of a street busker, passing his hat as he cajoled people for tips, and that he could keep any of the money he gathered. Lomax himself was dressed with uncharacteristic "spiffiness," he told Ruby, adding that Alan "looked like a young prince."[30]

The Saturday night performance was scheduled to follow a ticket-only, semi-formal dinner for MLA members and members of the press. Ledbetter had not, of course, been invited, but was hidden in Lomax's room, waiting to

7.1 Huddie Ledbetter performing, c. November–December 1934. Image shared with the author by John Reynolds; use courtesy of the Lead Belly Estate, Murfreesboro, Tennessee.

be called upon. Up first on the schedule was a talk on "Elizabethan Ayres to the Virginals"; the second item was a sing-along with sea chanties. Finally, it was time for "Negro Folksongs and Ballads, presented by JOHN AND ALAN LOMAX with the assistance of a Negro Minstrel from Louisiana."[31] The crowd reacted to Ledbetter's appearance and performance as Lomax hoped they would. "His singing and playing while seated on the top center of the banquet table at the smoker before a staid and dignified professorial audience smacked of sensationalism," he crowed in *Negro Folk Songs as Sung by Lead Belly*.[32] At the end, Ledbetter passed the hat, performing the demeaning role expected of him. To Lomax, this part of the act "never failed to delight his audience …. Then he always became the smiling cajoling Southern darky minstrel extracting nickels from his 'White folks.' He would bow and thank each visitor with amusing comments, 'Bless Gawd, dat's a dime! Where is all de quarters? Thank you, boss!'"[33]

At nine on Saturday morning, both John and Alan were featured with Ledbetter in a presentation billed as "Comments on Negro Folksongs (illustrated with voice and guitar by Negro convict Leadbelly of Louisiana)." This is generally how the "shows" went for the next several weeks. As Lomax explained, "as a prelude to his playing, either Alan or I would tell the audience how and when and where we found him, while Lead Belly sat on the stage impassive, self-contained, seemingly uninterested." He added, "Many people could not understand his Negro vernacular, so that we usually explained each song before he played it, sometimes repeating in advance the principal stanzas." Once Martha Promise arrived in New York, Ledbetter did not enter until the Lomaxes' introductions were completed.[34]

It's impossible to know what Ledbetter thought about the shape of these "performances" or the need for the hat routine. He hadn't received a penny in income from John Lomax in the three months they had been working together. His hat collection from the two performances at the MLA netted him a welcome $47.50.[35] Spread out over the time between September 24 and December 29, 1934, it averaged about fifty cents a day.

The MLA debut was the first gust of a whirlwind to come. On the last day of 1934, the Lomaxes and Ledbetter drove under the Hudson River, traveling from New Jersey to New York through the Holland Tunnel, opened just seven years earlier. Ahead of them lay the skyscrapers of Manhattan, including the Woolworth Building, the Chrysler Building, the Metropolitan Life Tower, and – at 34th Street and Fifth Avenue – the 102-story Empire State Building, which opened in 1931 and for another forty years would be the tallest building in the world. More than 7 million people called New York City home in the mid-1930s. They lived in one of its five boroughs (The Bronx, Brooklyn, Queens, Staten Island, and Manhattan), getting around by bikes, cars, buses, taxis, and noisy subways that raced through underground tunnels and along elevated tracks. In his travels throughout the city, Ledbetter would cross the majestic Brooklyn Bridge, which was then celebrating its first half-century; the slightly newer Manhattan and Williamsburg Bridges; and perhaps, venturing farther north, the upper level of the new

George Washington Bridge. Some Manhattanites lived in fancy brown-stones or at large, ornate hotels such as the Waldorf Astoria. Many others suffered the cold in makeshift shacks that lined street after street, as the city endured the sixth year of global economic depression.

Alan and John were staying downtown, at an apartment at 181 Sullivan Street, just below Washington Square Park. It was owned by thirty-one-year-old Margaret Conklin, an editor at Macmillan, and she shared it with Mary Elizabeth Barnicle, a thirty-three-year-old American folklorist and a professor of English at nearby New York University.[36] Huddie Ledbetter, according to the Lomaxes, promptly dubbed the two women "Bonkel and Conkel,"[37] and the nicknames stuck. Ledbetter could not also stay at the apartment, and the Lomaxes claimed in the book that "No hotel or lodging house south of Harlem would take Lead Belly in with us." They seemed bemused that in Harlem, a neighborhood in northern Manhattan, "the Negro Y.M.C.A. would not take us in with Lead Belly."[38] The YMCA had been a central location during the Harlem Renaissance, an arts revolution launched in the aftermath of World War I. It had been a heady, complicated, rich decade, and the YMCA served as its "incubator," wrote journalist Sandra E. Garcia.[39] "The Y, which provided room and board for a few dollars, became a safe haven for artistic expression, a place to talk freely, away from the strictures of a country still run by Jim Crow laws, and a shared living room for some of the six million Black Americans who were moving from the South as part of the Great Migration," she wrote. Now, the Y seemed the "safest place," for Ledbetter, the Lomaxes reported, although they expressed concern about being "forced to separate, with him exposed to danger."[40] It was there that Ledbetter spent his first night in New York and the last night of 1934.

By New Year's Day, 1935, Ledbetter was ready to make his mark in the city. He began the day downtown at Margaret Conklin's apartment, performing for a gathering of people from New York University and Columbia University and collecting fourteen dollars in tips.[41] Afterward, he took the subway back up to Harlem, where a perusal of local newspapers would have given him a good sense of who was performing where. Wherever else he may have gone, Ledbetter ended up at the Harlem Opera House, about ten blocks south of the Y along Seventh Avenue. All that week, from Friday December 28 through Thursday, January 3, a twenty-seven-year-old headliner named Cab Calloway was playing there with his Cotton Club Orchestra. Calloway, already famous for songs including "Hi-De-Ho" and "Minnie the Moocher," many of which he had been seen performing on movie screens nationwide, was a native of Rochester, New York. He was a bandleader, singer, dancer, and more, and at this point in the 1930s, he was successfully bridging the waning days of vaudeville and the future of jazz-infused swing. Billboards for his show announced an "All-Star Supporting Cast of Revue Favorites," including Ada Ward, a singer; Nicodemus, a comic; the 5 Percolators; "Sandy, Apus and George"; and Alma Turner.[42] Calloway's orchestra included lots of brass and horns, along with a drummer, piano player, bass, and at least one guitar, sometimes more. Throughout the fall tour – and now, in Harlem – the show also featured talent contests. The dance contest was December 31 (Monday night), and the next night – the night that Huddie Ledbetter made his way there – the poster advertised "auditions." Both promised "liberal cash prizes."

Did Huddie Ledbetter audition? Did he sit in with Calloway? It seems possible, because at ten the next morning, hung over and apparently late for a meeting Lomax had arranged, he arrived at Conklin's apartment claiming that Calloway had "offered [him] a thousand dollars to sing for him," according to the Lomaxes' book. Lomax focused not on this news but on Ledbetter's condition: "a pitiable object – blear-eyed, loose-lipped, staggering," marveling that Ledbetter, "probably poisoned by a mixture of drinks," had been able to travel "the long distance from Harlem to our rooms near Washington Square without falling into the hands of the police." According to Lomax, Alan "silenced his wild talk and put him to bed."

While Ledbetter slept, Lomax conducted an interview with an unnamed reporter for *The Herald Tribune* that firmly established the Lomax narrative and caused irreparable damage to any chance Ledbetter had of establishing his own show business persona in the North. "Lomax Arrives with Leadbelly, Negro Minstrel," read the head-line. "Sweet Singer of the Swamplands Here to Do a Few Tunes between Homicides." The article announced that John Lomax, "tireless student and compiler of American folk songs," had arrived in New York with his son and a "walking, singing, fighting album of Negro Ballads named Lead Belly, self-acknowledged king of the twelve-string guitar." Lomax, the paper noted, was "Big Boss" and Alan was "Little Boss." For these two, the story continued – based solely on Lomax's word – "the Negro minstrel bears an undying affection which led him on September 1 to pledge them his life and services till death should part them. He has followed them everywhere as chauffeur, handyman, and ever-ready musician and has asked for nothing but the privilege to continue." It suggested that for a performer like Ledbetter, trouble was unavoidable: "Lead Belly's voice causes brown-skinned women to swoon and produces a violently inverse effect upon their husbands and lovers." After describing the "large scar which spans his neck from ear to ear," the piece noted that "Big Boss fears that in Harlem something catastrophic may happen when Lead Belly starts to sing."

Speaking with the reporter, John Lomax merged the two Angola encounters into one. He praised the singer's "repertoire of at least 500 songs which he knows by heart" and added, "Many of them he claims to have composed himself. There is no question as to his ability. He's better than any radio character I ever heard." Lomax implied, again, that the recording he brought to the governor had resulted in a "pardon" for Ledbetter, and that he'd been surprised to see Ledbetter appear before him "in a hotel in Texas." Lomax told the story of Ledbetter's job interview, complete with the request to inspect the knife. He said that Ledbetter "had been of great value to him on subsequent visits to the prisons" and talked about how well his performances had been received at the MLA. As at the MLA, there was no mention of Ledbetter's career as a performer. Instead, the article stated that after what the reporter believed would be upcoming shows at Yale and Harvard, "Mr. Lomax does not quite know what to do with him . . .. Lead Belly, he explained, was a 'natural,' who had no idea of money, law or ethics and who was possessed of virtually no self-restraint."[43]

With this article, published on January 3, the floodgates of national publicity opened. The "telephone jangled almost continuously," Lomax crowed in *Negro Folk Songs as Sung by Lead Belly*. "The term 'bad [n–]' only added to his attraction."[44] In a detailed letter to Ruby written on January 3, Lomax listed the "practical results so far" of his venture to New York with Ledbetter. This included *The Nation* requesting a 1,500-word article, an invitation to perform at the Rockefeller Foundation, and a luncheon the next day with the Texas-Exes, an independent alumni group of the University of Texas in which Lomax was very involved. *American Ballads and Folk Songs* was selling well, he reported, but there were still copyright challenges to be dealt with. Lomax seems to have picked up the letter and continued writing at a later point to report, "this n[–] has captured for a moment the imagination of New York. Just now two radio officials came in and talked $1000 a w[h]ack for a <u>fifteen</u> week engagement for me and Leadbelly!! Nothing done yet, but I'll give them 24 hours to sign. That would help the book, too. Hold your breath and <u>don't tell anyone</u>."[45]

By Friday, performance prospects were looking up. At a special luncheon held at the Hotel Montclair, the Texas-Exes invitation promised that "Alan Lomax" would be "bringing his colored chauffeur Lead Belly" to offer "some of the Louisiana prison songs which won him freedom by pardon of the Governor." Also featured: "John A. Lomax himself." Once again, Ledbetter performed before an influential, all-white crowd wearing "overalls with a blue hickory shirt over a yellow one."[46] The *Herald Tribune* admired the fact that as Ledbetter sang, "he tapped his left foot in single time and his right foot in double and triple beats. 'If you don't think that's hard,' Mr. Lomax pointed out, 'try it yourself.'"[47] From

7.2 Huddie Ledbetter performing in the outfit he wore at the MLA gathering. This photo taken at the Texas Exes meeting, January 4, 1935. J. Frank, photographer. Courtesy of the Lead Belly Estate, Murfreesboro, Tennessee.

there, Lomax and Ledbetter attended meetings at the Rockefeller Foundation and at the National Broadcasting Corporation (NBC), "where Leadbelly charmed their chief music man," Lomax told Ruby. He said that someone – unnamed – "shoved" a contract at him for "five years of Leadbelly, starting at $250 a week up to $500 a week." Saturday brought more of the same: "Huddie captured his crowd – an audience of 50 poets, artists, dilletantes, representatives of *Time, The New Yorker,* [and] three more radio men," Lomax wrote, adding that he had assigned Alan to do the introductions. By Sunday, though, Lomax was having doubts that the swirl of activity would lead to anything financially concrete. "Unless next week we sign some contract which means real money we will most probably journey back to Washington and put our records in shape for storage in the library," he wrote in the same letter. If all else failed, his priority would be hurrying out a book that he was discussing with Macmillan, then titled *Leadbelly and His Songs,* "in order to reap something from the current publicity. We ought to do that job in a month or so, near here, I think."[48]

The press juggernaut continued, as the news syndicates United Press and Associated Press shared stories nationally. Ledbetter was repeatedly described, as if such a term existed, as a "swamp Negro."[49] On the front page of *The Decatur* (Illinois) *Daily Review,* below a photograph of President Roosevelt, was the headline, "Sings His Way Out of Prisons." The subhead: "'Lead Belly' Makes Bayous Live; Plucks Swamp Noises, Splash of Alligator's Tail on Guitar." Like many of the articles, this one called attention to the long white scar on Ledbetter's neck (which he did not have in February 1918, but which was noted in June 1930). The presumption, which Ledbetter may have endorsed to avoid any sense that he had been in altercations with whites, was that the assailant was a Black man. *The Boston Globe,* for example, wrote, "His music does things to women, which their escorts do not like .... Hence, according to Lead Belly, this scar from ear to ear and the prison sentences." The paper also noted that Ledbetter had been performing "first at scheduled appearances" – those arranged by John Lomax – and later "in the nightclubs of Harlem whither he is drawn to the intense fear of Mr. Lomax."[50] While Lomax expressed his "fear" of Ledbetter's presence in Harlem as being about safety, it is evident that there were other reasons for his trepidation. Ledbetter was an independent artist. Even though people were coming to Lomax with contracts on

Ledbetter's behalf, there was no written agreement between the two men, and Ledbetter was free to accept other offers. At least in part for this reason, the Lomaxes would "whisk him off as soon as he [was] done playing (and passing his hat)," not making him accessible to reporters or entertainment industry professionals unless they themselves were present.[51] Additionally, Lomax was concerned that Ledbetter would adapt and develop his style to meet the tastes of northern audiences. In *The Brooklyn Daily Eagle*'s story, for example, he was quoted as noting that Ledbetter had adopted a new "striving for effect ... in his performances, a trick, evidently, that he picked up at Cab Calloway's on the first night of his stay here."[52] Given what he likely viewed as his own considerable investment in the performer, Lomax intended to see it pay off. Less than a week after their arrival in New York, he had a plan in place that would lock Ledbetter into a management contract, and at the same time get him far away from Harlem.

CHAPTER 8

Contracts

When Huddie Ledbetter considered building a career in the North, he didn't have in mind a move to Wilton, Connecticut, then a tiny, rural town, located more than fifty miles from New York City. Yet this was where John and Alan Lomax planned to move, excited by Margaret Conklin's offer to let them use her summer house for free. Their plan was to bring Ledbetter to Wilton, continue to record and transcribe his songs for the Macmillan book, tentatively titled *Lead Belly and His Songs*, and travel as needed into the city so that Ledbetter could also record in a commercial studio. Only 2,500 people lived in Wilton in 1935, and there were "noticeable stresses at Town Meetings between the 'old-timers' and the 'new people' as it changed from an agricultural community to one of commuters."[1] Conklin's place, at the corner of Belden Hill Road, was an old three-bedroom, one-bath farmhouse built around 1800.[2] The house had electricity, but not much else. Water had to be pumped from an outdoor well, and there was no telephone line.[3] Dishwashing was done by hand; clothing was scrubbed on an old-fashioned wash board, and cleaned clothes, sheets, table linen, and towels were hung on lines to dry. The closest significant Black community was ten miles away, in Norwalk.

To make the move more acceptable to Ledbetter, and conditional upon the signing of a management agreement between them, Lomax planned to wire for Martha, he told his wife Ruby on January 6, noting that the house would "keep Leadbelly and Martha busy making Alan and me comfortable." A bit later in the same letter, Lomax raised a concern that "for Leadbelly to escape [prosecution under] the Mason act he must marry Martha."[4] As he later corrected, he meant the Mann Act, the White-Slave Traffic Act of 1910.[5] These concerns masked what was likely Lomax's real purpose, which was to energize "interest in Ledbetter." They had yet to sign any contracts which meant "real money" and were waiting for "radio prospects." He expected that they could finish the book by February, and, in the meantime, he and Alan would "arrange a wedding affair that will again stir emotional New York."[6]

The management agreement the Lomax proffered to Ledbetter was dated Saturday, January 5, 1935, but the performer may not have seen it until Sunday or Monday. Lomax claimed the letter was crafted by a New York lawyer, but there is little evidence of this. The original, in the Lomax files at the University of Texas, is typed on what appears to be onion skin paper. It is written in the form of a letter from Huddie Ledbetter to John Lomax, engaging him as representative. While nearly all of it is typed, both the duration of the contract period and the percentage of monies to be earned by Lomax were left blank, apparently to be filled in later. When this information was added, in Lomax's handwriting, it was not initialed by Ledbetter. The address given for Lomax is simply "New York City," while no address, and no typewritten name, are given for Ledbetter. There is no indication of when the document was signed by Ledbetter or when it was "accepted and agreed to" by Lomax, and the signatures not witnessed.

"Dear Mr. Lomax," the agreement begins, "I engage you to represent me as my sole and exclusive manager, personal representative and advisor, and in consideration of your past services to me and of your agreeing so to represent me and to advise me regarding my interests in connection with any and all musical engagements, either in Radio, on the Stage, in Concert, on the Phonograph, in Private or Public Recitals, or in any other form." Lomax had few show business connections, no managerial experience, and a disdain for the types of commercial music and motion picture ventures into which Ledbetter was eager to expand. Despite that, this agreement gave him exclusive control over Ledbetter's career, in any venue or form, for "a term of" (*the word "five" is added by hand*) "years from the date hereof": from January 1935 until January 1940, when the singer would turn fifty-one and Lomax would be seventy-two. There were no provisions for how either party might be released from the contract. Ledbetter agreed to pay Lomax "for your said services and for your other services rendered and to be rendered to me the sum of" (*the word "fifty" was written in by hand*) "per centum of all moneys earned by me, either directly or indirectly, from all musical engagements during said term." Furthermore, "any and all moneys earned" by Ledbetter would be paid directly to Lomax, who was "hereby given the sole power and authority to receive such sums earned by me and to give receipts therefor in my name." From this income, Lomax was authorized to deduct his "commissions and any other moneys expended by you for me [Ledbetter] and the balance so remaining shall be used by you in my interests, as you may determine."

Lomax defended his right to payment on the grounds that he worked hard to arrange the performances, negotiate payment and accommodation, and arrange for travel. Further, he not only introduced Ledbetter but also explained the songs and their history to audiences. But, in an echo of sharecropping agreements, which put sole discretion over final accounting on the landowner, this contract gave Lomax complete control over gross income and allowed him alone to determine what funds could be deducted from Ledbetter's 50 percent before he was paid. That income, Ledbetter would learn, included the "hat money," that he had not previously been expected to share. Additionally, according to the contract, Ledbetter was "not free to accept any engagements" without Lomax's "written consent." The letter concluded, "Your acceptance of this employment, endorsed below, shall constitute a binding agreement between us," with a space for the signatures of both men. In the midst of a maelstrom of interest from the nation's most important media companies, the pressure on Ledbetter to do what it took to move forward – and bring his beloved Martha Promise north – was tremendous. This moment of attention might be fleeting. If Ledbetter signed, they would move to Wilton, Lomax would secure funds to bring Martha to Connecticut, and they could continue to pursue the show business offers. Ledbetter signed.

On Tuesday, January 8, 1935, Lomax told Ruby that he'd imposed an additional condition on the agreement, although it's not clear whether it was conveyed to Ledbetter or not. "If Leadbelly isn't drunk this morning I have permission [likely from Macmillan] to wire today money to bring Martha to him," he wrote. "So Alan and I will have two servants to look after us in a little wooded village." Before closing the letter, Lomax reported that Ledbetter had arrived at the apartment, and was "shouting happy over Martha's coming, to whom I am now arranging marriage as a reward for his sobriety this morning."[7]

Martha Promise (spelled "Primus" in older documents), a tall, slim woman with a dazzling smile, was at her job at the Excelsior Steam Laundry in Shreveport on January 8 when she received a rather

8.1 Huddie Ledbetter and Martha Promise Ledbetter, Wilton, Connecticut, February 1935. Library of Congress, Prints & Photographs Division, Lomax Collection, reproduction number LC-DIG-ppmsc-00660. Courtesy of the Lead Belly Estate, Murfreesboro, Tennessee.

odd proposal of marriage in the form of a telegram from John Lomax. He sent the wire via a Shreveport bookstore, the Hirsch & Leman Company, and the owner, Clarence "Red" Leman, delivered it in person.[8] Lomax, writing "in Lead Belly's name," as he put it, proposed marriage and said he'd be sending forty dollars to enable her to travel immediately to Connecticut. Promise, thirty-four years old, had not seen Ledbetter in five weeks, since he left for Philadelphia. It is unlikely they had even spoken by telephone in that interval, given the high costs then involved, both in owning a phone and in calling long distance. The timing of the proposal was also difficult, as Promise told Elizabeth Lomax. Her mother had just died and was buried "that Friday before," meaning the day after Christmas. On Promise's behalf, Hirsch & Leman wired to Lomax, in care of Macmillan: "Telegram and money received talked to Martha Primrose [*sic*] says impossible for her to leave before Thursday January 17th account of disposing house hold goods and getting affairs in readiness promised she would leave that day will wire you train and time leaving and time of arrival."[9] Keeping track of events with the book in mind, Lomax penciled a note on the telegraph, "Leadbelly wired in reply for her to come at once." The telegram that Ledbetter sent in reply is not in the files, and there are remarkably different versions of it quoted in the book and shared by the Lomaxes with reporters. The only line they have in common is a version of: "Martha Promise I wants you to come on to New York now . . .. I wants to marry you at once as you are my intended wife."

Martha Promise was about eight years old when she first met Huddie Ledbetter, who was then newly married to Aletha Henderson. Martha and her twin sister Mary were born around Shiloh, in the Caddo Lake region of Louisiana, in 1900,[10] the seventh and eighth living children of Sandy and Daisy Primus. Like Ledbetter, she had grown up farming, although her parents were renters, not owners. Her father, who died in 1919, "rented about forty or fifty acres on one place and forty or fifty on another," she told Elizabeth Lomax. "He was a good worker, and then had so many children to work it . . .. We just loved each other," she said. "We were just a close family." Her father loved music, and, one day, he "sent someone to tell [Huddie] to come down and play for us," she remembered, describing their first meeting. "We had a big house, and a big, big place covered with Bermuda grass," she said; her home was where neighborhood children gathered to play ball. From the porch, you could see the big pond for the cows; nearby were woods, "where we could play in the shade." Enthralled by Ledbetter, she remembered standing "right where I could see him, look in his face." She stayed "right there till the time came for him to go." And after that, she "just couldn't wait till he got back again," which he did, a month or two later.[11]

Their paths didn't cross again for "years," she told Elizabeth Lomax, "But my mind *stayed* on him. His face. It was just the wonderfullest face I ever looked at." Asked whether she might have fallen in love with him even as a child, she laughed and said, "I did. I'm sure," but added, "I never did know until I got big . . .. I didn't know whether it was the music or what. But after I got grown, I knew it wasn't the music. I knew that I was just crazy about him." Martha was in her teens when she next encountered Ledbetter, possibly while he was living in Bowie County as Walter Boyd. An old school friend of Martha and Mary's invited them to a birthday party "out in the country." Mary's husband decided they should go. "He said, 'Huddie's playing for this child's birthday, and so we'll go,'" Martha said. "Oh, Lord, I like to die. I just couldn't get myself together." She and her siblings hadn't been allowed to attend dances. "My daddy didn't think juke joints – square dances, we called them then – my daddy didn't allow his children to go because it wasn't a decent place, you know, people drinking and cursing. But we was grown then." Ledbetter failed to recognize Martha, but she recognized him. "I danced on by him, and he kind of caught me by the tail of the dress and said, 'When you finish the dance, I want to see you.'" Martha agreed to this, adding that to her, the dance couldn't finish soon enough. Ledbetter apparently felt the same. "He cut this piece short," she said. "Very short." She went back to see him, asking if he knew who she was. He said that he'd seen her dancing. She asked if he remembered Sandy Promise, her father, and "the two little twins?"

Ledbetter thought about it. "The little bitty things that were there?"

"I'm one of them," Martha answered, "Martha." Ledbetter couldn't believe it, Martha told Elizabeth Lomax. He said he had to play for another party after he left the birthday party and invited her to join him, but she still felt it was "against the rules" and declined. She didn't see him again until after he'd been released from prison in Texas. Ledbetter "was working in Mooringsport then, working at the Gulf Refinery." They stayed out late at a dance, and then he dropped her off at home, and then more years went by. "People would say, 'Lord, Huddie's gone back to the pen again,'" Martha remembered. "Just in a minute they'd all say, 'That couldn't have been Huddie! Somebody must have imposed on him or [been] doing something wrong. Huddie *never* bothers nobody.'" Martha's family "always thought he was just a sweet person," she said.[12]

Finally, after his release from Angola in August 1934, he went looking for her in Shreveport, and this time he stayed. Now, she considered the strange marriage proposal and decided to accept, telling Elizabeth Lomax that in retrospect, she was "kind of glad to get away." Her future husband, again through Lomax, sent a follow-up telegram: "Hurry up we are all waiting for you don't be frightened I'll be at the train steps waiting to kiss you just as soon as you arrive in New York."[13] Martha's change of heart was fortunate, because the Lomaxes had already told the press about her travels, putting their own spin on events, which as usual, the press did not question. On Thursday, January 10, 1935, one day before Martha left Shreveport, multiple New York newspapers published stories of her imminent arrival. The *Herald Tribune*'s piece was titled "Lead Belly Puts Songs Aside to Wed Tomorrow: Sweet Singer of the Swamp Grins All Over as 'Boss' Lomax Wires for Bride / She's Coming from South / Shreveport Laundress Will Help Keep Him in Check." It claimed that "[f]or years Lead Belly has been in love with Miss Promise, but his extralegal exploits with knife and fists invariably precluded wedlock." Now, with a contract from Macmillan for the book, "Mr. Lomax and his son, Alan are retiring to a house in Wilton" to help the singer "write his memoirs." It continued: "Feeling that they could use a female servant and that Lead Belly might be more tractable under the influence of a wife, they arranged for Martha's transportation to the North." The United Press was more specific about another of Lomax's concerns: "Marriage 'Cure' for Lead Belly," the headline read, "Advisor Seeks to Wean Pardoned Negro Tenor from Harlem Night Life."[14]

It is not difficult to imagine Martha Promise's reaction when she eventually read these articles. She was leaving a paying job at a steam laundry to come north and get married. She had never been asked, nor had she agreed, to work as an unpaid "servant." Not knowing what lay ahead, she left Shreveport at 5 p.m. on Friday, January 11, aboard an Illinois Central train. She would not arrive in New York, via Washington, D.C., until about forty-three hours later.[15] She was just three hours into her journey, and of course unable to listen, when the enormously popular radio show *The March of Time* aired live across the United States, with a story featuring her future husband.

The March of Time had aired weekly over the radio since 1931. On Friday evening, January 11, 1935, it featured six stories and an announcement that the program was expanding beyond radio: A new *The March of Time* newsreel-style film series would premiere in theaters in just three weeks. Then came the standard opening announcement: "The editors of TIME raise the curtain again on their new kind of reporting of the news – the re-enacting of memorable scenes from the news of the week – from *The March of TIME*!"[16] The brief radio story about "Lead Belly" built heavily on the January 3 *Herald Tribune* article. Ledbetter was recorded singing his own songs, but members of the show's stable of actors played the spoken roles: Ted de Corsia, a thirty-one-year-old white actor from Brooklyn, as "Leadbelly"; Bill Pringle as "Lomax"; Dwight

Weist as "Allen [*sic*] Lomax." Working alongside them in the studio were sound effects creators and an orchestra. The story opened with a re-enactment of Alan and John Lomax recording at the Louisiana State Penitentiary; "I'm making phonograph records of the songs you darkies sing for the Library of Congress," the actor playing John Lomax read. It included Ledbetter's plea to Louisiana's governor and recreated the fiction of Ledbetter surprising Lomax at a Texas hotel and pledging to work for him for the rest of his life. The narrator, dubbed the "Voice of Time" in the script, concluded the episode with:

> VOICE OF TIME: Thus John A. Lomax, ballad collector, acquires a follower. Bringing his protegee north, Mr. Lomax has him sing for the Modern Language Association in Philadelphia. This week before startled but interested Manhattan audiences Lead Belly sings his favorite tunes. Lovers of folk songs acclaim him one of the best ballad composers of his day, completely primitive and unspoiled by civilization. (SINGING UP TO FINISH.) 1935 MARCHES ON!

There is evidence that the Lomaxes had a chance to edit the script; "Carl Lomax," for example, was replaced in the typescript with a handwritten "John A. Lomax." It seems unlikely that anyone thought to give Ledbetter a chance to review it, and it's apparent that none of the all-white staff or cast of the show, the Lomaxes, or the network executives had a problem with the language used. Of course, Ledbetter must have noticed. But this world of mass entertainment was new to him as well, and at minimum, whatever Lomax was doing, it *was* gaining attention, book deals, and recording contracts.

The day before the program aired, John Lomax finalized the deal with Macmillan, not only for *Lead Belly and His Songs* but also for an autobiography of Lomax. Other offers were also still arriving. "Leadbelly at this moment is the most famous N[–] in the world and I the most notorious white man," a jubilant Lomax wrote to his wife. "What does that leave you? I have just <u>sold</u> him [Lomax underlined the word] for cash money to a party on Sunday, January 20 at which the Mayor of New York is the guest of honor." Once he'd finished his part of the penciled letter, Lomax handed it to Ledbetter. If he minded what Lomax wrote, there is no record of it. He added a note of his own to the housekeeper employed by Ruby, whom he'd met in the fall: "Miss Elnora Dear Girl

How are you This leaves me and my two bosses well. Hope you are well. By By Your friend Huddie Ledbetter."[17]

The arrival of Martha Promise offered the Lomaxes more opportunities for publicity. The press was waiting for her at New York City's Pennsylvania Station on Sunday, January 13, and drama ensued after she arrived early and waited for the Lomaxes and Ledbetter on one platform while they searched for her, reporters in tow, elsewhere. Ledbetter, the papers noted, was dressed in a sharp "double-breasted tan suit with red pin stripes, tan shirt with red tie, tan shoes and a white silk scarf."[18] After about forty minutes of searching, the two parties found each other. "That's my wife; that's my wife," the *Herald Tribune* reported Ledbetter calling out, as he "dashes to the waiting room and meets Mr. Lomax coming out with a tall, sweet-faced Negro woman with a brilliant smile and lustrous eyes. She and Lead Belly rush into each other's arms and kiss, while Mr. Lomax beams."[19] Martha said she was "nearly blinded" by the camera bulbs flashing as they raced to get everyone and all of the bags onto a Wilton-bound train. When the four of them finally settled into the carriage, Ledbetter was overcome with emotion. "Huddie was just so overjoyed," Martha said. "He just sat there and cried almost all the way back to Connecticut."[20] Lomax, who had witnessed the tears, commented to Ruby, "He is a strange combination of emotion and vacillation."[21]

Over the next several days, the media circus continued. "Lead Belly Sings the Blues When Bride-to-Be Misses Cue," read *The Brooklyn Daily Eagle*.[22] The *Herald Tribune* stated that "Lead Belly, erstwhile slayer, equally adept with knife or guitar, born in the Louisiana swamplands, is now tasting for the first time the sweet fruits of musical success as they drop from the richly laden branches of radio and stage." On January 14, a *Time* magazine profile began, "In Texas a black buck known as Lead Belly murdered a man," and described Ledbetter as being as "wild-eyed as ever" and a "hell-raising minstrel."[23] *The New Yorker* published a full-page poem about Ledbetter by William Rose Benet: "He was big and he was black and wondrous were his wrongs / But he had a memory that travelled back / Through at least five hundred songs."[24] Twenty-one-year-old reporter Winston Burnett, writing for *The Brooklyn Daily Eagle*, interviewed Lomax after a performance he and Ledbetter gave in the city. The reason Ledbetter was off limits to the press, Lomax told Burnett, was that he was concerned about the "effects of metropolitan life on the primitive character of his protégé's art" and that "[a]lready the pure n[–] in him shows signs of becoming corrupted." For this reason, Burnett explained, "One may shake hands, congratulate him, perhaps, but not flatter him or drop a word that might give him an inflated notion of his own importance." As if discussing an untamed animal, Burnett added: "The only two people who seem to have found the fine knack of subduing and diverting his illegal impulses are his wife-to-be and Mr. Lomax's son Alan."[25]

Reporters were again present on Sunday, January 20, as Martha Promise and Huddie Ledbetter were married at the house in Wilton.[26] The Ledbetters, new to the area, didn't know any clergy. They ended up being married by Rev. Samuel Weldon Overton, the pastor at the High Street African Methodist Episcopal Church in Norwalk.[27] Overton, *The Baltimore Sun* reported, had served for eighteen years as a missionary in the West African nation of Liberia. In the weeks that followed, the Ledbetters began to attend the church regularly, Martha said, and they got to know the Overtons well, along with other parishioners and the deacons. "They used to come out to see me and Huddie all the time. We got to be good friends with all of them."[28] It was decided that John would give Martha away and Alan would serve as best man. Mary Elizabeth Barnicle and Margaret Conklin, who arrived a day early to shop with Martha for a dress, were the bridesmaids. Martha chose a "black silk frock with brightly striped yoke and sleeves" and told a reporter that "she had bought it for $3, reduced from $12.95, in a Norwalk shop."[29] Ledbetter also had "a completely new outfit, from shoes to hat," including a "double-breasted cinnamon suit with red checks."[30] Both he and Martha wore white gloves. As per the new contract, the cost of the Ledbetters' outfits was added to expenses that would be deducted from Ledbetter's share of income. "Lomax paid for Huddie's clothes, to the tune of $18 for the suit, $2.95 for the hat, $1.75 for the shirt and tie, and $3 for the shoes," wrote Kip Lornell and Charles Wolfe. "On the nineteenth, Martha got her dress and Huddie got her ring; Lomax paid $3 for the dress and $5 for the ring. He even noted the white gloves for Huddie cost 25 cents."[31]

The ceremony itself went smoothly, although one reporter noted that Alan "dropped the ring at the crucial moment." Later, "[w]hen the ceremony was over and Lead Belly had saluted his bride, Mr. [John] Lomax gave his black minstrel and retainer a resounding whack on the neck and the party began."[32] Ledbetter picked up his battered guitar and sang for his bride:

> Loved you from the start, Honey
> Bless your little heart, Honey
> Every day would be so sunny,
> Honey, with you.[33]

He then went into a fast-paced, risqué tune, its lyrics quoted in *The Baltimore Sun*:

> A yellow-skinned woman keeps you worried all the time,
> A yellow-skinned woman makes a moon-eyed man go blind,
> But a dark-skinned woman makes a jack-rabbit hug a hound,
> And makes a dark-skinned preacher lay his Bible down.[34]

After that, Lead Belly showed why southern audiences had long praised his footwork, although Lomax did not allow it to be part of his act up north. He "laid down his guitar and went into a tap dance," a reporter wrote. "With a broomstick on his shoulder, he shuffled and slapped and clicked his glistening heels in the ineffable rhythms of an impromptu buck and wing." The assembled guests were thrilled. The party didn't last long, however. After some light refreshments, the wedding, which began shortly after noon (and coincidentally took place on Ledbetter's forty-sixth birthday), was over. At around 3:00 p.m., Ledbetter and Lomax left for the engagement Lomax had booked ten days earlier with the publisher of *The Brooklyn Daily Eagle*. Ledbetter graciously told reporters that he didn't mind working on his wedding day; he "liked the chance to express his happiness in song."[35]

Three days later, on January 23, Huddie Ledbetter and John Lomax braved a heavy snowstorm as they entered the studios of the American Record Corporation (ARC) at 1776 Broadway in New York, for Ledbetter's first-ever commercial recording. ARC was "then the dominant force in popular records."[36] Ledbetter was introduced to the company through thirty-year-old Woodward "Tex" Ritter, who had attended the Texas-Exes gathering on January 4. Ritter "had come under the influence of Lomax's *Cowboy Songs* while a student at the University of Texas in the 1920s,"[37] Lomax's biographer Nolan Porterfield wrote. Born in Texas, Ritter was making inroads as a country singer and actor, and he would

(a)

(b)

8.2(a) and (b) Wedding of Huddie and Martha Ledbetter at the house in Wilton, Connecticut, January 20, 1935. With them in the photos are John and Alan Lomax; Margaret Conklin; Mary Elizabeth Barnicle; deacons Leonard Brown, Maurice Podd, and Sol Nichols; and the Reverend Samuel Overton. The John Reynolds Collection, Smithsonian Institution's Center for Folklife and Cultural Heritage, Photographs: Box 3. Courtesy of the Lead Belly Estate, Murfreesboro, Tennessee.

8.3 Huddie and Martha Ledbetter at their wedding in Wilton, Connecticut, January 20, 1935. The John Reynolds Collection, Smithsonian Institution's Center for Folklife and Cultural Heritage, Photographs: Box 3. Courtesy of the Lead Belly Estate, Murfreesboro, Tennessee.

soon break into the movies. The deal that Lomax had made with ARC on behalf of Ledbetter was not bad for its time. They would record "40 songs on the cheap wax records that sell for 25 cents each," he told Ruby.[38] Initially, ARC offered Lomax the fairly standard payment of a half-cent per record,[39] but he'd managed to boost the payment "to 2 cents a record and a payment in advance to be charged against royalties, of $250.00."[40]

Ledbetter may have been especially excited because at ARC, he, like Ritter, would be working with producer Art Satherly, an Englishman who moved to the United States just prior to World War I. As the music recording industry took off in the post-war years, Satherly quickly gained a reputation as a pioneer in "hillbilly and race music."[41] In addition to Ritter, Satherly produced records for Roy Acuff, Ma Rainey, Blind Lemon Jefferson, Josh White, and Alberta Hunter. He also produced Gene Autry, a white Texan in his mid-twenties whose rapidly expanding career Ledbetter envied. Autry was "discovered at a Chicago radio station in 1934," wrote Ed Sullivan in *The Chicago Tribune*, adding that "[i]t was

Autry, his guitar, and his horse, Champ, that revolutionized westerns and proved to Hollywood there was gold in them thar prairies." Sullivan credited Autry's rise to a combination of talent and the good fortune to come to the attention of Satherly, who shaped Autry's identity and career as a singing cowboy.[42]

Ledbetter, who had herded cattle for Doc Waskom and broken horses for farmers in DeKalb, would have enjoyed being promoted as a singing cowboy, and he had a large repertoire of such material. Yet again, however, he faced limitations others placed upon him. On the basis of what Satherly recorded, wrote scholars Charles Wolfe and Kip Lornell, it was evident that the producer "saw Leadbelly's commercial value as that of a blues singer." The "first two days' work was full of classic blues," they reported, including a few songs recorded several years earlier by Blind Lemon Jefferson. Cowboy songs such as those Ledbetter had sung for the Lomaxes at Angola, including "The Western Cowboy," "Frankie and Albert," and "Ella Speed," were "[m]issing from these sessions." The only exception was "Old Chisholm Trail," recorded on the third day, a song that had appeared in *American Ballads and Folk Songs*. Otherwise, Satherly and his crew, "like so many commercial record producers," had "a simplistic perception of black folk music," Wolfe and Lornell wrote. "They divided folk and folklike music into two camps: Whites performed hillbilly and cowboy songs, while the black singers played blues and spirituals. A black man like Huddie, whose complicated repertoire ranged across these arbitrary lines, seemed problematic for them." Over the course of three days, January 23–25, Ledbetter recorded approximately forty songs for ARC, with two additional sessions in February and March. In January, he was still using the battered twelve-string he'd had with him at Angola. By the next session, on February 5, Lomax had found a used twelve-string Stella guitar in much better condition. Among the songs ARC recorded on February 5 was "Irene," noted Wolfe and Lornell, "but it was never issued."[43]

Back in Wilton, the labor of keeping the old farmhouse running in the middle of a New England winter fell entirely to Huddie and Martha Ledbetter. They "did all the work of the place, having quickly divided it between themselves – he the fire-maker, water-toter, washerman, car cleaner, snow shoveler, and dishwasher helper; she the cook, bed-maker, ironer, house-cleaner," Lomax cheerfully summarized in *Negro Folk Songs as*

Sung by Lead Belly, adding, "As a matter of fact there was little labor for two active strong people."[44] Alan, who celebrated his twentieth birthday on January 31, would, at times, sleep late unless he had an appointment in the city. Lomax himself was generally up early, he told his wife, busy with correspondence, scheduling performances, and writing his sections of the book. Lomax gave his son responsibility for writing the "autobiograph- ical" portion. "Alan made notes of his talk and songs, now and then recording new tunes," John Lomax wrote in the book, "while Martha, always serene and quiet, sat and listened." He noted that in Shreveport, Martha "had been a member of the Tri-State Jubilee Choir, and did not sing 'sinful' songs."[45] Both father and son complained when things at home did not go smoothly. On Sunday, January 27, John reported to Ruby that the previous day – the Saturday after three days of recording at ARC – the Ledbetters had driven to Norwalk to buy a winter coat and shoes for Martha and to pick up "groceries for tomorrow from Alan's list." The day ran late, however, and he and Alan "nearly starved" before the Ledbetters returned home. "Nothing to eat until after 8 o'clock," he grumbled. "The next time I'll have a definite understanding – with Martha."[46]

At the same time, Lomax recognized the precariousness of his situation with Ledbetter. Lomax believed the performer "would have been gone long ago" were it not for Martha and "the isolation" of Wilton. As it is, he wrote to Ruby, "we sit on a volcano."[47] Rather than view his own treatment of Ledbetter as problematic, Lomax blamed others. "Only his contact with outside influences brought troubles on us and on himself," he told readers of *Negro Folk Songs as Sung by Lead Belly.* To Lomax, these influences included the friends that Ledbetter and Martha had made in Norwalk, "with its Negro colony of two groups, one revolving around the Negro minister who mar- ried them, the other around Martha's hairdresser." To Lomax, the "Norwalk intimates flattered his vanity, furnished him drink, and, according to his own story, offered him contracts that would bring the money rolling in."[48] More likely, these friends simply expressed concern that the Ledbetters were being exploited, and wondered at the very negative por- trayal of Huddie Ledbetter being shared in the media. But as Lomax felt his own control of the performer slipping away, he doubled down on his personal demands, even amidst a busy performance schedule. "August 1 in stripes in Angola, La. Now a sought attraction in New York City. At times his vanity becomes annoying but, on the whole, I guess I shouldn't complain. He still looks after my shoes, helps me everywhere with my coat (Alan, too), helps Martha with the homemaking, does the washing, presses my suits, etc. etc." The man who until recently had been happily camping with his sons by the side of the road, now reported, "Our night requirement calls for my slippers, pajamas, and dressing gown to be hanging before the fire and a hot water bottle in my bed an hour ahead of the time I lie down .... I sleep in the only room not heated."[49] Finally, on Thursday, February 7, Lomax allowed the Ledbetters a day on their own in the city. Twenty-nine days had passed since the move to Wilton, and twenty-five since Martha's arrival. Yet Lomax was begrudging even about this break. "I fear for results, but we seem to have held the savages to the breaking point," Lomax wrote to Ruby. "It's rebellion or at least one free day."[50]

While both Martha and Huddie Ledbetter were likely writing letters to their families back home during this time, those letters aren't in the archives. It would be interesting to learn how they felt about the situation they faced and the compromises they were expected to make in the interest of Huddie Ledbetter's career. Their occasional notes to Ruby Lomax were upbeat and unrevealing. On January 27, Martha wrote to say that "Huddie and I and the Boss" were "doing fine and living happy," adding that she was "cooking and giving them a plenty to eat" and "they seems to like it mighty fine. I know it's making them mighty fat." (She added the word "smile" in parentheses.)[51] Huddie added a note, sending regards to Lomax's daughter, Bess Brown, and to the housekeeper, Elnora. "The Big Boss is in his room reading and singing. The Little Big Boss is gone in to New York." He noted that they were "making record[s] for to sell," adding that they would be released in three weeks.[52]

Of particular interest would be the Ledbetters' thoughts as filming began for *The March of Time* news program.[53] The crew arrived in Wilton on Friday, February 8, to begin three days of shooting. The Lomaxes had been paid $150 for their initial work on the script, with more to come later,[54] and the final version drew on the *Herald Tribune* article and the radio version of the story, "with some input ... from Messrs. [John Stuart] Martin and [Roy E.] Larsen of Time."[55] The filmed version featured Ledbetter and Lomax playing themselves. The crew shot exterior scenes of the Ford, with Ledbetter driving and Lomax in the passenger seat, pulling up to a gas station, where Ledbetter gets out and speaks with a white attendant. They also filmed the car pulling up to the house in Wilton, and Lomax waiting in the passenger seat for Ledbetter to get out, walk around the car, and open his door. On Saturday, many of the guests who attended the wedding three weeks earlier now re-enacted it, filming from 4:30 p.m. until 3:30 the following morning. Starting up again at noon on Sunday and working until 10:00 p.m.,[56] the crew filmed at a hotel in South Norwalk, re-enacting John Lomax's version of the meeting in Marshall, Texas. At some point, a few local men were asked to join Ledbetter in donning prison stripes for a scene at "Angola," filmed in a Connecticut garage. Soon after, Lomax traveled to Washington, D.C., where he was filmed at the Library of Congress.

The completed episode of *The March of Time*, three-and-a-half minutes long, is painful to watch, not only for its racism but also, less importantly, for the awkwardness of its re-enactments.[57] The segment opens with a title card, "Angola, La!" An off-screen narrator (Westbrook Van Voorhis) says, "To the Louisiana State Penitentiary goes John A. Lomax, Library of Congress curator, collector of American folk songs." Huddie Ledbetter, playing himself in prison stripes, plays his guitar as he sings "Goodnight,

8.4 Crew filming for *The March of Time*, Wilton, Connecticut, February 1935. Library of Congress, Prints & Photographs Division, Lomax Collection [LC-DIG-ppmsc-00631]. Use courtesy of the Lead Belly Estate, Murfreesboro, Tennessee.

Irene" to a group of young Black men, also in stripes. John Lomax, also playing himself, wears trousers and a white shirt with a dark fedora perched on his head as he sits, listening and fiddling with the dials on a recording machine. Ledbetter stops singing, and he and Lomax perform dialogue:

LOMAX: That's fine, Lead Belly. You're a fine songster. I've never heard so many good Negro songs.

LEDBETTER: Thank you sir, boss. I sure hope you send Governor O.K. Allen a record of that song I made up about him, because I believe he'll turn me loose.

LOMAX: Well, Lead Belly, I don't know this governor. You mustn't expect too much of me.

LEDBETTER: But Governor Pat Neff of Texas, he turned me loose when he heard the song that I made up about him.

LOMAX: So you were in the Texas penitentiary, too, Lead Belly?

LEDBETTER: Yeah, sir, it was 35 years for murder, but it wasn't my fault. A man was trying to cut my head off.

LOMAX: You're mighty bad, Lead Belly.

LEDBETTER: I believe Governor O.K. Allen, if you'll just send him a record of that song, I believe he'll turn me loose.

LOMAX: Lead Belly, I'll try it.

LEDBETTER: Thank you, sir, boss, thank you sir, thank you.

The scene changes, and a new title card reads: "Three months later, the travels of Curator Lomax take him to Marshall, Texas." This is the scene in which Lomax pretends that he is surprised by Ledbetter's visit. The first image is of Lomax in a hotel room, wearing round glasses, the fedora, a suit vest, and a long-sleeved shirt as he types at a table, with the bed in the foreground. It cuts to Ledbetter, in the overalls, shirt, and bandanna he'd worn to perform, carrying his guitar and a small sack as he stands before the hotel clerk, played by Alan.

CLERK (ALAN): Yes, Mr. John Lomax is staying here. He's in room 109.

LEDBETTER: Is that on the first floor?

CLERK: Yep –

Ledbetter turns and races up a staircase.

CLERK: Hey! Hold on a minute!

Ledbetter knocks on Lomax's door.

LOMAX: Come in!

LEDBETTER: Boss, here I is!

LOMAX: Lead Belly! What are you doing here?

LEDBETTER: No use to try and run me away, boss. I came here to be your man. I got to work for you the rest of my life. You got me out of that Louisiana pen.

LOMAX: I – you can't work for me. You're a mean boy. You killed two men.

LEDBETTER: Please sir, don't talk thataway, boss.

LOMAX: Have you got a pistol?

LEDBETTER: No sir, I got a knife.

LOMAX: Let me see it.

Lead Belly hands him a modest-looking knife. Lomax opens it.

LOMAX: What do you do with that thing?

LEDBETTER: I'll use it on somebody if they bother you, boss. Please boss, take me with you. You'll never have to tie your shoe..., shoestrings anymore, if you'll let me, as long as you keep me with you.

LOMAX: All right, Lead Belly, I'll try you.

In response, Ledbetter smiles, claps his hands, and stamps his feet as he moves closer to Lomax, who is still sitting at his desk, leaning back in his chair.

LEDBETTER: Thank you sir, boss, thank you. I'll drive you all over the United States and I'll sing all songs for you. You be my big boss and I'll be your man. Thank you sir, thank you, sir.

The film then shifts to an exterior of the farmhouse in Wilton, Connecticut, with snow on the ground. The narrator intones: "John Lomax does take the Louisiana Negro convict to be his man." It cuts to footage of Martha and Huddie in their wedding attire as Huddie plays for her and she smiles. "Takes him north to his home in Wilton, Connecticut, where Lead Belly's longtime sweetheart, Martha Promise, is brought up from the South for a jubilant wedding." From there, the story cuts to exteriors and interiors of the Library of Congress in Washington, D.C. Inside, we see John Lomax with Oliver Strunk and Herb Putnam, the Librarian of Congress (neither man is identified in the film). "Then hailed by the Library of Congress's Music Division as its greatest folk song find in twenty-five years, Lead Belly's songs go into the archives of the great national institution, along with the original copy of the Declaration of Independence." Throughout this last part, "Goodnight, Irene" is playing; it ends in a flourish as John Lomax supervises a folio being placed on a shelf.

If the filming of *The March of Time* made the Ledbetters' uncomfortable, the revised contract they were presented with during that busy weekend of production must have been shocking. At the bottom of the original onion skin document, dated January 5, 1935, John or Alan typed "Over." On the reverse side, they typed: "Supplement to the herewith contract: For one dollar and other valuable considerations, including the services of Alan Lomax, I hereby agree that the division of the net receipts from music engagements" (*in the top margin, John Lomax handwrote, "or from other sources," circling the words and inserting them*) "during said above expenses shall be one third to me and two thirds to John A. Lomax." Underneath, the word "Signed" was followed by Ledbetter's signature, this time with the additional typed notation of "Wilton, Connecticut" and "February 9, 1935." Below to the left, there were two spaces for "Witnesses," to be signed by Martha Ledbetter and Alan Lomax. No consideration was made for the non-performance-related work still expected of Ledbetter, nor was any payment built in for the labor and insight of Martha Ledbetter. Instead, for the next five years, Huddie Ledbetter had apparently agreed to accept as payment just one-third of his total performing income, minus whatever John Lomax, at his sole discretion, deducted for both Martha's and Huddie's expenses.

Not surprisingly, tension between Ledbetter and Lomax intensified. On a letter dated February 11 (but possibly written on Sunday, February 10, at the end of the last day of *The March of Time* filming), John Lomax sent Ruby a bitter litany of complaints. "He is an unbelievable combination of a brute, a pest; a shuffling servant and a supreme egomaniac; a liar incarnate, a hypocrite, a willing worker (he does all our washing, builds the fires, keeps them going, pumps and brings in all the water); he is totally devoid of any sense of gratitude; he seems devoted to Martha; he confessedly cares for me only because I am 'the money man'; he seems fond of Alan," Lomax wrote. When Ledbetter was pleasant, it was because he wanted "something that he shouldn't have." The performer was "an amazing mixture of craft, guile, cunning, deceit, ingratitude, suspicion, fawning, hypocrisy, and at times a charming companion and entertainer. In one sense he has no more character than a rattlesnake."[58]

One can only imagine the letter that Huddie Ledbetter might have written.

CHAPTER 9

1930: *The State of Louisiana v. Huddie Ledbetter*

All through February 1935, between public performances, another recording session at the American Record Corporation, and planning for an upcoming road trip, John and Alan Lomax worked to capture Huddie Ledbetter's music and stories for the Macmillan book, still titled *Lead Belly and His Songs*. The Lomaxes had known Ledbetter for just over eighteen months, since their first encounter at the Louisiana State Penitentiary in July 1933, and John Lomax had been working with him for four months, since the reunion in Marshall, Texas, at the end of September 1934. They had been living together in the Wilton home since January 9, 1935, escaping and at the same time fueling a continued storm of press attention. Yet none of the reporters, editors, radio and television producers, or recording executives thought to investigate the facts behind the story of Ledbetter as told by John and Alan Lomax, and even by Ledbetter himself. For the Lomaxes' part, even as their research revealed inaccuracies (notably including information that Ledbetter had not been pardoned in Louisiana),[1] they did little to change the narrative. Perhaps most surprising, given how recent the events were, is that no one investigated the circumstances that led to Ledbetter's incarceration at Angola between 1930 and 1934 – although Ledbetter might have been as relieved about this as anyone, because research would have revealed that he *had* been in an altercation with a white man, and he was nearly lynched because of it.

Wednesday, January 15, 1930, the day of Huddie Ledbetter's arrest in Mooringsport, Louisiana, was gray and cold. Prohibition, enacted a decade earlier (January 17, 1920), would remain in effect until late 1933. The United States stock market had crashed the previous October. Ledbetter's birthday was less than a week away; he'd be forty-one years old. Five years had passed since he was pardoned by Texas Governor Pat Neff, in January 1925. Leaving the Houston area, he returned to the region of Caddo Lake, where he continued to perform, as before, at parties and dances and for local white merchants and landowners. "People, when they heard he was playing some- where, they would always go," Liz Choyce told Monty and Marsha Brown. Her husband Leonard, with whom she lived and worked on the Jeter farm, agreed. "He'd have a big crowd," Leonard said. "He was the one they used to follow, Mister Huddie."[2] Winner Lane, born in Leigh, Texas in 1914, told an interviewer that Ledbetter "was one of the danciest men I ever knew. When he got out of the Huntsville pen [1925] he come to our house near Latex [east of Leigh on the Texas–Louisiana line] and Mamma made supper for him. I was a very young girl. After supper, Hud[d]ie taught me to dance. Everything from buck-timing to waltzing. That night we danced round and we danced square."[3] Booker T. Washington, born around 1903 and named after the famous educator and political advisor, lived in Mooringsport and met Ledbetter at a dance in 1926. "It was at Red Chester's place out on the lake – Kool Point," he remembered. Kool Point was "on the bank of Caddo Lake west of Oil City, where several nights a week there was live entertainment."[4] Ledbetter played all around the area, Washington said: Vivian, Oil City, Shreveport, Blanchard, Leigh, Karnack. "He would get out a chair and put his hat on the chair. That hat would be full sometimes," Washington said. "Sometimes $30 or $40." Both Washington and Ledbetter worked in the oil industry; Washington drove a truck, and Ledbetter was a maintenance worker. They would drink together, Washington remem- bered: "bourbon." Washington sometimes made whiskey and sometimes got it from others, traveling across the border to Texas where "the law wasn't so strict." Once, Washington's father barbequed a pig to sell at a ball game. He sent for Ledbetter, and Ledbetter brought "a gang up with him to my daddy's house. Played that guitar and sold that meat out," Washington said. "Sold out in about thirty minutes. Broke that porch down! So many people. If people heard that Huddie was going to play, they'd come if they had to walk. People come around dancing. Huddie was free-hearted, really good." Washington added, "He was 'for real' famous."

Nearly three years after his release from Sugarland, Ledbetter had a daughter with Mary Elizabeth "Lizzie" Pugh, from Mooringsport.[5] Pugh was twenty-three (and Ledbetter thirty-eight) when she gave birth to Jessie Mae Ledbetter on September 19, 1927. Pugh had known Ledbetter "most all my days," she told Kip Lornell in 1991;[6] her stepfather was Azzie Pugh, one of Ledbetter's maternal cousins.[7] She said she had run into Ledbetter at a dance he was playing at after his release from Sugarland, and, despite her mother's disapproval, they dated some. In time, she married Wilbert Carey and took his last name, but her daughter Jessie Mae continued to use the name Ledbetter. According to her mother, Jessie Mae corresponded a bit with Huddie, and he suggested she come to California while he was there in the mid-1940s (she would have been about eighteen) to be his secretary, although that didn't happen.[8]

At some point during the five years between 1925 and 1930, Ledbetter lived with a woman named Era Washington (no relation to Booker T.), and she is named as his wife on his Louisiana State Penitentiary record, although the relationship ended before he was released. If Alan Lomax's notes (allegedly quoting Ledbetter) are true, it was a tempestuous relationship. "She was a nice, pretty woman an' I loved her," Ledbetter is quoted as saying, adding that she was jealous of his performing, "drinkin' good whiskey" and "foolin' wid de wimmens and gals and havin' a good time." He claimed she was angry enough at one point to break his "twelve string box."[9]

Also during these years, and perhaps surprisingly, Huddie Ledbetter doesn't seem to have pursued or been pursued by talent scouts for the now-burgeoning recording industry. These were important years for Black musicians, especially those from the South, who were drawn north by record producers in Chicago, New York, and elsewhere, and joined the Great Migration that began around 1910 as Black southerners fled the South in search of safety and opportunity. In August 1920, three months after Ledbetter was transferred from Shaw to Sugarland, songwriter Perry Bradford "convinced ... a white executive at Okeh records ... to let Mamie Smith record Bradford's composition 'Crazy Blues,'" reported Adam Gussow. Smith was "the first black woman to record a secular song for commercial consumption" and "the first black superstar," he wrote, noting that "75,000 copies were distributed to Harlem record shops alone within four weeks after the November release." Within a year, hundreds of thousands of copies sold nationwide as "[w]ord quickly spread, helped in part by an informal record-distribution network of black Pullman-car porters."[10]

Many of the people Ledbetter had known and performed with now had contracts, including twenty-nine-year-old Bessie Smith, who signed with

Columbia Records in 1923, and thirty-seven-year-old Ma Rainey, who began to record for Paramount that same year.[11] In 1925, Blind Lemon Jefferson was auditioned by a Dallas talent scout, using "a portable machine that had been set up in the rug department of a local furniture store,"[12] and he, too, was signed by Paramount. By 1929, the company had released more than forty records by him. Now, Jefferson was gone; he died of an apparent heart attack in a Chicago snowstorm in December 1929, at the age of thirty-six.

Beyond the growth of the recording industry, technological innovation brought tremendous change to the business of entertainment overall. Radio broadcasting took root in the late 1920s, and, by 1930, roughly 12 million households (about 40 percent of the US population) owned radios,[13] with programming that featured music, sermons, drama, and even westerns, giving rise to the careers of singing cowboys including "Tex" Ritter and Gene Autry. Motion pictures now featured synchronous sound recording; federal census records for 1930 reported that 80 million people attended the cinema each week, roughly 65 percent of the population.

But Huddie Ledbetter may have had personal reasons for not pursuing a show business career between 1925 and 1930. He had endured and witnessed untold suffering and horror while incarcerated in Texas. He had also experienced significant loss: at some point while he was at Sugarland, his father died.[14] His family never regained their thirty acres of farmland, nor did they return to live on the balance of the property. In December 1924, Sallie Ledbetter, now a widow in her early seventies, began selling off the remaining 38.5 acres, transferring about ten acres for a nominal price to her daughter Australia Carr.[15] Those ten acres changed hands a couple of times before being sold in 1928 to Ledbetter's cousin, Queenie Davidson, and her husband Early. In December 1928, Sallie and Huddie Ledbetter together sold another twelve acres to the Davidsons. In October and November 1929, the remaining acreage was conveyed by Sallie and Huddie to Australia, who, Sallie noted, "has had the responsibility of my care and support for many years." That land, too, soon changed hands, meaning that, by January 1930, the Ledbetters owned none of their 68.5 acres.[16] Huddie's half-brother, Alonzo Batts, died in Shreveport in July 1929; he was only in his mid-fifties. Their mother, Sallie, now suffering from cancer, was living with and being taken care of by Australia Carr, in Marshall, Texas. Still, Ledbetter had family and friends and was performing regularly throughout the region, and he was employed. He was coming home from work, dinner bucket in hand, on that fateful Wednesday in January 1930 when his world, once again, collapsed.

To John and Alan Lomax, the arrest of forty-one-year-old Huddie Ledbetter was all but inevitable. "These years around Mooringsport were violent and bloody," they wrote. "Without the protection of some powerful white man, no Negro could stay out of jail long in northwestern Louisiana and go the pace that Lead Belly went during the years he lived in Mooringsport. Trouble came down on him soon enough."[17] In fact, the evidence suggests that Huddie Ledbetter was sent to Angola *because* of "some powerful white man." It was late afternoon, and an all-white Salvation Army band was gathered on the porch of Croom's general store, by the railroad tracks. These bands often relied on brass instruments to aid in worship and draw loud attention to their message of evangelical Christianity. Members included women as well as men; one of the most active members of the area's Salvation Army was a cornet-playing teenager, cadet Bernice Lyon, and both Captain and Mrs. Albert V. Walker were in charge of the Shreveport chapter.[18] Ledbetter stopped to listen. He would have recognized at least one of the players, Dick Ellett, a white man four years his junior who was born and raised in Mooringsport.[19] Tall and fair, Ellett worked on behalf of the Lucey Manufacturing Company, with stints drilling oil wells on the islands of Sumatra and Java[20] before serving in the military in World War I. The Ledbetter and Ellett families knew each other. In 1900, seven-year-old Dick Ellett lived in Shreveport's Ward 3 with his family, close to where eleven-year-old Edmon Ledbetter, son of Wesley's brother Bob, lived with his family.[21] In the 1920 census, Dick Ellet's older siblings – Tom, Hetty, and Louis, as well as Louis' wife (all of them white) – shared a home just three doors away from Huddie Ledbetter's parents, Wes and Sallie, and Sallie's younger granddaughter.

Perhaps, as the Salvation Army band played tunes such as "Onward, Christian Solders" and "Nearer, My God, to Thee," Ledbetter moved his feet to the rhythm. Maybe he sang along. Maybe he had been drinking, as press and court records suggest. Maybe it was just his audacity, as a Black man, to stand amid a crowd of whites as he listened and responded to the music. Whatever it was, something about his behavior attracted attention, violence broke out, and Ledbetter was arrested. "The trouble with the negro started when he, while in an alleged intoxicated condition, was disrespectful to a Salvation Army meeting that was in progress on a Mooringsport street," reported *The Shreveport Journal.* "According to reports, Ledbetter insisted upon doing a dance during the service, which aroused a group which included Elliott [*sic*]. In a scuffle which followed, Ledbetter drew a knife and slashed Elliott's arm." Ellett had suffered "a severe gash in the arm and hand," the paper reported, and he was taken to a local hospital.[22] *The Shreveport Times* added that "Elliott's condition was said not to be critical by hospital attendants Wednesday night."[23] Huddie Ledbetter, who "incurred a gash on top of his head," was arrested without being treated and brought to the Mooringsport jail. A day later, newspapers reported that "[a] charge of assault to murder was filed . . . against Huddie Ledbetter, 42, negro, for an assault with a knife upon Dick Elliott, 36, white man, at Mooringsport late Wednesday afternoon."[24]

In the Lomaxes' book, this altercation is not between Huddie Ledbetter and a white man, but between him and a group of Black men, a falsehood Ledbetter repeated throughout his life. The Lomaxes wrote that Ledbetter was on his way home from work with his dinner bucket in hand when he was jumped by a Black "gang" who demanded whiskey. He told them that all he had was "mule" – moonshine – but they wouldn't believe him. Ledbetter said he grabbed one of the men and "beg[a]n to put my knife to him, *Whop! Whop! Whop!* 'Goddamn you black bastard, you'll fool wid me, will you?'" One by one as the men approached, he cut them. "Putty soon they was six ob 'em runnin' down de street wid blood jus' gushin' out," the Lomaxes wrote. They ended this story with Ledbetter being arrested, adding that after a night in the "calaboose," Ledbetter said that Sheriff Tom Hughes (in fact, it was deputies) "carried me down to de Shreveport jail an' kep' me there till I come to be tried."[25]

Changing the race of the victim was a strategic choice both for Ledbetter and for the Lomaxes, based on the understanding that if white audiences, not just in the South but nationwide, knew that Ledbetter had knifed a white man, even in self-defense, they would have been repelled. In fact, as noted, *all* of the violent encounters the Lomaxes ascribed to Ledbetter in the book – and there are many – pit him "against his own people," as if those alleged victims counted less. Years later, white record producer Frederic Ramsey, Jr., with whom Ledbetter spent time during the last decade of his life, argued that the "miracle" of Ledbetter's survival in the "feudalistic"

South and its "larger pattern of 'new slavery'" could be attributed to one thing: "He never challenged a white man. All of his convictions and all his sentences were for assault, or assault with intent to kill – but never against a white person. He wouldn't have lived to be tried if he had."[26]

Ledbetter almost didn't live to be tried. On the night of the arrest, a white mob came to the Mooringsport jail intent on lynching him. Caddo Parish, Louisiana, which encompasses both Mooringsport and Shreveport, ranked third in southern counties with the highest number of reported lynching victims in the years between 1877 and 1950: forty-eight.[27] Nearly 550 people in Louisiana, and more than 4,000 in Southern states overall, were lynched during this same period, often with minor, false, or no reasons given. In a 1935 article in *The Nation*, authors Carlton Beals and Abel Plenn examined Louisiana's record of lynching in 1933, citing the parishes in which the murders occurred: "January, Fell Jenkins, a Negro (Aycock), charged with trespassing, beaten to death; three Negro fishermen (Tavernia), no charge, hacked to death; February, Robert Richardson (Baton Rouge), charged with annoying a white woman, unnamed, shot; Nelson Nash (Ringgold), no charge, hanged. Skip six months: September, John White, charged with attacking a white woman, shot; October, Freddy Moore (Labadieville), charged with murder to which a white man later confessed, tortured and hanged."

Huddie Ledbetter's life was spared. According to *The Shreveport Times*, "only the prompt response of the sheriff's office for help saved the negro from mob violence at the hands of a band of men who stormed the Mooringsport jail Wednesday night." A pair of officers held the mob "at bay," the article continued, "until Bert Stone and A.C. Collins, deputy sheriff, arrived to carry him to the jail in Shreveport."[28] Waiting for him at the jail was Sheriff Thomas R. Hughes, a tall, fifty-two-year-old former cotton dealer. Hughes is featured in Ledbetter's song "Fannin Street," also known as "Mr. Tom Hughes' Town," but he was not yet sheriff when city leaders voted to establish the red-light district in 1903. Hughes was elected in 1916, probably after Ledbetter was living in Bowie County as Walter Boyd, and he was in office when the city decided to close the red-light district in 1917. According to a 1928 report by Maude Hearn O'Pry, a member of the Daughters of the Confederacy,[29] Hughes was a "popular member of various branches of the Masonic order," a group in which Dick Ellett – Ledbetter's alleged victim – was also active, as well as numerous other fraternal orders.

Hughes would gain fame the following May, 1934, for his role in setting up an ambush that led to the deaths of white outlaws Bonnie Parker and Clyde Barrow. Hughes was not present at the scene, but for a time kept as a trophy the glasses Parker had been wearing.[30]

Ledbetter's "The Shreveport Jail" seems a direct lament about what happened next.

> Oh, the sheriff, he will 'rest you,
> Bound you over in jail
> Can't get nobody,
> To go your bail.

On February 7, 1930, roughly three weeks after his arrest, Ledbetter was brought before a grand jury in the District Court for the First Judicial District, State of Louisiana.[31] The district attorney was Lawrence Crain "Lal" Blanchard, Sr., a graduate of Tulane University School of Law and a "member of a family long prominent in political and social affairs of Louisiana."[32] In court, Ledbetter listened as Blanchard presented the charges: that Huddie Ledbetter "In and upon Dick Ellet, feloniously did make an assault, with the intent then and there, him, the said Dick Ellet, willfully, feloniously, and of his malice aforethought to kill and murder."[33] The grand jury indicted him. A trial date was set for February 18, 1930, and Ledbetter was returned to the Shreveport jail. Built to hold up to 350 prisoners, the jail occupied the top two floors[34] of the eight-story Caddo Parish Courthouse, a "white limestone and concrete structure" that opened just two years earlier, in 1928.[35] Entering it from Texas Street, visitors (and prisoners) passed by a Confederate Veterans Reunion Monument, placed in 1906;[36] the gallows were on the top floor.

Four days later, on February 11, 1930, Sallie Ledbetter died. Her son was not permitted to attend her funeral and burial at the Shiloh Baptist Church in Mooringsport.[37] Instead, the following Tuesday, February 18, he faced Judge Thornton Fletcher "T.F." Bell, in *State of Louisiana v. Huddie Ledbetter*, docket number 28640,[38] on the charge of assault to murder.

> There sets de judge,
> I like to forgot,
> De damnedes' rascal
> De state ever picked out.

Judge Bell, in his fifties, was born and raised in Shreveport and was a public-school classmate of Sheriff Hughes.[39] He had served on the bench since 1912, when he was appointed to complete the unexpired term of his enormously popular father, Col. Thomas Fletcher Bell, upon the older man's death. Like the district attorney, Lal Blanchard, and Blanchard's brother, Frank, Judge Bell was a graduate of Tulane University School of Law. In a not-so-strange twist, given the web of power and influence among the planter class throughout the South, Frank Blanchard shared office space and sometimes legal cases with James T. Jeter, an attorney with family ties to the plantation the Ledbetters fled decades earlier.

Louisiana had a tiered jury system, one that minimized the power of any Black individuals who happened to make their way into the jury pool, as discussed by historian Thomas Aiello in his book *Jim Crow's Last Stand*. By law, he wrote, "[c]ases in which the punishment **may** be at hard labor shall be tried by a jury of five, all of whom must concur to render a verdict; cases in which the punishment **is necessarily** at hard labor, by a jury of twelve, nine of whom concurring may render a verdict; cases in which the punishment may be capital, by a jury of twelve, all of whom must concur to render a verdict."[40] (Emphasis added.). Ledbetter faced a jury of just five people, all of them white men, drawn "from the regular criminal Venire."[41] (It was unusual at the time for white women in Louisiana to ask to be registered for jury duty, although legally they could.) Prosecuting the case on behalf of the state was Aubry Mackay Pyburn, the Assistant District Attorney. Defending Ledbetter was E.B. Herndon of the law firm of Herndon & Herndon, most likely working pro bono.

> Send for your lawyer
> Come down to yo' cell
> He'll swear he can clear you
> In spite of all hell.
>
> Git some o' your money,
> Come back for de res'
> Tell you to plead guilty,
> For he knows it is bes'.

It is not clear which Mr. Herndon defended Ledbetter, whether it was Edward Beverly Herndon, Sr., eighty-one years old (former mayor of Shreveport, 1890) or his fifty-one-year-old son, Edward Beverly Herndon,

Jr. The elder Herndon was still practicing law and was in his office when he was stricken with a heart attack in late August 1930, dying soon after.[42] (Honorary pallbearers at Herndon's funeral included Sheriff Thomas Hughes and Attorney L.C. Blanchard.)[43] Full trial records have not been found, but it was reported that a verdict was reached "a few minutes after the completion of the testimony."[44] The court minutes stated that "after hearing the evidence, the argument of the Counsel and the Charge of the Court, the Jury retired to their room in charge of the Sheriff to consider their verdict and returning into open Court, through their foreman, upon their oath, do say, 'We, the jury find the defendant guilty as charged.'"

What had actually occurred? Unpublished draft material from *Negro Folk Songs as Sung by Lead Belly* strongly suggests that Ledbetter's prosecution was steered by a powerful white man determined to get him convicted. Almost certainly written by Alan Lomax, this section begins with a paragraph that was typed and then crossed out: "~~L.B., in describing his 'killin's' and the 'killin's' he has seen, takes a fierce pleasure in them, like a little boy who recites the tale of some bloody Western to his parents. He told me about the trouble that sent him to the Louisiana penitentiary for ten years for "sault 'tepmpt to murder,' in some such way as this~~ –."[45] The rest of the typed story includes a Mister Jim, whose last name, "Candy" or perhaps "Gandy," is then crossed out multiple times and replaced, in Alan's handwriting, with "Currie Tilly" and "Mr. Tilly." (In other manuscript pages, "Currie" is typed in.) "I was comin' on home from work one day wid my dinner bucket in my hand when I met up wid Mister *Currie Tilly* [material in italics is handwritten] an' a gang o' his n[–]s down on the street, drinkin'," the draft reads. "Mister *Tilly* owned a big lot of land near Mooringsport an' worked his n[–]s hard an' never give them not one nickle, besides feedin' an' givin' them the clo's on their backs." This was the man who got him into the trouble he "rode" to the penitentiary, Ledbetter apparently told Alan.

The Currie family had been prominent in the area for generations, as had the Tillinghasts, Moorings, and Crooms, and members of these families often held civic roles. Born in 1890,[46] Edwin Tillinghast Currie was just a year younger than Huddie Ledbetter, and his family's large plantation, just outside Mooringsport, was adjacent to that of the Jeters. Ledbetter and Currie were "always friendly," Ledbetter told Alan Lomax; they'd "been raised up right together." Currie's 1917 draft registration card (he didn't serve) described him as a farmer and constable, tall and stout.[47] In later years, Ledbetter sang and played for Currie and his wife "when they would get to drinkin', and I thought me an' him was friends." At the time of Ledbetter's arrest in 1930, Currie was serving as the Caddo Parish deputy sheriff under Sheriff Tom Hughes.[48] He lived with his wife and two small children on Front Street in Mooringsport,[49] and was a member of the Scottish Rite, a fraternal organization.

Currie was "always" drinking with his Black workers, Ledbetter was quoted as saying, adding that, to him, these workers seemed crazy: "workin' for him year in an' year out an' never getting' nothin' out o' it," Alan Lomax typed. According to Ledbetter, Currie was drinking and "was pretty well loaded dat day." It was Currie, and not a "gang" of Black workers, who called out to him, demanding whiskey. He told Currie that he didn't have whiskey, just some mule – "which it is a mixtry of alcher-rub an' water," Alan typed, purportedly quoting Ledbetter. "I give him that. He smelled but wouldn' drink it an' I walked on away from there." This is when Ledbetter was jumped by workers at Currie's instigation, and they also demanded whiskey; "I s'pose he had put 'em on me to have some fun, but he didn' have much fun dat day," Ledbetter says. He turned around and told the workers, "Didn' you hear me tell Mister Currie Tilly I ain' had no whiskey?" And then the story continues, in a version of what's in the book, until "Mister Tilly" caught Ledbetter by the collar and held him roughly – "but he didn' hit me an' I didn' hurt him." A penciled note from Alan follows, and the writing instrument and handwriting suggest that this note was made at the same time the name was amended in the typescript: "Later, as L.B. grew to confide in me more, he added in retelling this story: 'Yes, he did, too. He did hit me. Had a pair o' brass knuckles on his hand ….'" Ledbetter pointed to the scar across his upper lip, and says he showed the injury in court and told them about Currie hitting him, adding, "an' it made him pow'ful mad."[50] Ledbetter stressed, in telling this story, that he didn't hurt Currie, even though he was still holding his knife in his right hand. According to Ledbetter, another sheriff caught Ledbetter by the arm, and he was dragged to the jail.

The Lomaxes could not have invented "Tilly Currie." Before she married, Liz Choyce lived on "Mr. Currie Tilly's" place, "not too far from off the Jeter place. Over across the road," she remembered, decades later. "He had a big plantation."[51] It is believable that Currie would have had the power to order his workers to jump Ledbetter. In this telling of events, it is not clear how Dick Ellett became involved. He seems to have been injured in the melee, but was not the target. Was Ledbetter even the person whose knife wounded him?

In the unpublished manuscript, Ledbetter states that Currie ensured that he would be found guilty. He said that at trial, "them white people o' Mister ~~Jim's~~ *Tilly's* said so many bad things a[g]ainst me I didn' have a chance."[52] Interestingly, the newspaper accounts of the skirmish changed after the trial, suggesting that the testimony might also have been tainted. For the first time, newspapers noted not only that "Ledbetter had resented the efforts of white men to prevent him from dancing," but added a twist: "Ledbetter ... after quarreling with the men, went away and returned with a knife."[53] In other words, he left the scene and returned with a weapon, suggesting premeditation. The newspapers don't report, as Ledbetter told Alan, that "Mister Tilly" fixed the trial. "It was Mister *Currie Tilly* what got it in for me 'cause I had cut his n[–]s so they couldn' work, that sent me to Angola," Ledbetter says in the unused draft, with the name handwritten in. "Didn' a n[–] 'pear 'gainst me. All was white people swearing what they'd been told to swear."[54]

Martha Promise also told a version of the story that suggested Ledbetter had been set up. "One time he didn't do nothin'," she told Elizabeth Lomax. "A white man that he had played with from a chile grabbed him. He was drunk or somethin, an wanted to say xxxx [crossed out in typed pages] hello to Huddie. Peoples thought they were fighting," Martha said, and "they never gave him a chance to say anything. They railroaded him."[55]

A week after the one-day trial, Judge Bell decreed Ledbetter's sentence: "imprisonment in the State Penitentiary, at Baton Rouge, Louisiana, at Hard Labor, for a period of not less than Six (6) nor more than Ten (10) years, subject to the commutation provided by law."[56]

> Oh, de judge he will sentence you,
> Clerk will write it down,
> You can bet yo' bottom dollar,
> You Angola-bound.[57]

CHAPTER 10

The End of the Road

Given their growing enmity, the relationship between Huddie Ledbetter and John Lomax was bound to end badly and inequitably. Despite all of the time they spent together, Lomax could not see Ledbetter beyond the racist identities he assigned to him. Ledbetter, having deferred to Lomax as a pragmatic choice, now increasingly – and particularly due to the isolation of Wilton, Connecticut – found himself imprisoned by the dual, demeaning roles of servant and primitive artifact, each of which was sharply contradicted by the enthusiastic response his performances elicited from audiences. To make matters worse, John and Alan Lomax had begun writing to people for information about Ledbetter's past, from prison administrators to family members, including Margaret Coleman and her daughter Arthur Mae, both of whom worked as maids in Dallas and shared a home there.[1] Still, in the middle of February 1935, the two men continued to try to make the alliance work, holding out hope that their investment in time and effort would pay off. The entertainment industry whirlwind that had greeted their arrival in New York had waned,[2] but Art Satherly of the American Record Corporation was about to test the market with his first release of two "Lead Belly" records. The first had "Packin' Trunk Blues" on one side and "Honey, I'm All Out and Down" on the other; the second paired "Four Day Worry Blues"[3] with "New Black Snake Moan."[4] In addition, *The March of Time* "newsreel" would be released in theaters nationwide on March 7. In the meantime, to keep money coming in, John Lomax decided that he and Ledbetter would return to the performing circuit he knew best: academia.

On March 3, they loaded the car and left Wilton for a 1,000-mile, ten-day journey through upstate New York: Albany to Rochester, then Buffalo, and then back to Albany, where they would be joined by Martha and Alan.

From there, all four would travel to Cambridge, Massachusetts, where Lomax planned a triumphant return to Harvard University, his graduate alma mater. The trip was a disaster, however, with the growing estrangement between the men made worse by bitter winds, heavy snow, and ice. After spending Sunday night, March 3, in Albany, New York, they traveled to Rochester for their first performance, planned for Monday, March 4. No one was there to greet them, however; some correspondence had been missed, and that night's performance had to be delayed until Tuesday. In the meantime, Lomax and Ledbetter "were put up (to [Ledbetter's] great discomfort) in one of the student dormitories, his room opening into mine," Lomax reported to his wife, Ruby.[5]

By the end of Tuesday, John Lomax was lamenting that he had "lost control" of "his" man. At breakfast, because "he had proved to be so angelic," Lomax "allowed him to take the car for a short drive into the Negro section," he wrote.[6] When Ledbetter wasn't back by noon – even though there was nothing on the schedule until that night – Lomax seems to have panicked. He had a student drive him around, searching for Ledbetter, and then went to a police station to report "a lost car with a Negro driver"[7] to a force that would not employ its first Black officer until 1947.[8] Soon, the make, model, and plate number of Lomax's car were "flashed over the city,"[9] sparking reporters' interest. As Lomax told the story in *Negro Folk Songs as Sung by Lead Belly*, he waited at the station until about 6:00 p.m. and then returned to campus, planning to do the concert on his own. The car was in front of the dormitory, however, and Ledbetter was in his room with a friend; Lomax claimed they were both "half drunk."[10] In the book, he deemed the friend a "penniless black tramp" and claimed that Ledbetter, "holding in his two hands a big ham bone," had "said to his companion between bites, 'Dis is de best piece of n[–] ham I'se eat since I left Louisiana.'"[11] If Ledbetter *did* say these words, he was likely mocking the older white man who thought it appropriate to scold him – in front of another adult, no less – as if he were a child. This was not the first time Ledbetter's mockery was reported by Lomax as if to confirm his view of Ledbetter's character. For example, among unpublished material in the files is a short essay by Lomax, "Lead Belly and the Gulf." In it, Lomax waxed poetic: "The highway runs for miles among groves of live oak and scattering pines" before the Gulf of Mexico appears suddenly into view, "a scene of surpassing beauty." Having previously claimed that he could find "no little feeling for beauty" in Ledbetter,[12] Lomax now reported that Ledbetter's response to the vast expanse of water was to say, "Dis is sho de biggest river I ever seen."[13] Ledbetter, who spent much of his life around the 25,400-acre Caddo Lake, had also surely seen the Gulf of Mexico before. The mockery may have served as a defense against Lomax's constant assessment and negative judgment of Ledbetter and the ways in which he shared those assessments publicly, as he did that night at the University of Rochester, their first big public performance of the trip.

A crowd of about 200 people listened as Lomax told them that Ledbetter had spent twelve years in prison, "killed two men," and "cut several more to ribbons." Lomax added that, in his view, Ledbetter was "an artist and a poet," and also "primitive and savage," someone who "lives only in the present with never a thought for yesterday or tomorrow."[14] The University of Rochester was not segregated, although the number of Black students was small, and an indication that the audience was receptive to Lomax's portrayal of Ledbetter comes through an account of the visit by white sophomore Reed McBane. Writing in the student newspaper, *The Campus*, he began the article by describing the day's search for the car and driver, quoting a figure of speech in use at the time: "There's a n[–] in the woodpile somewhere." He continued, "Perhaps the chocolate colored jailbreaker was cutting himself a few throats down on Front Street, or maybe bagging a few policemen in the heart of Rochester with his trusty six shooter." With all of this, McBane enjoyed the concert: "For more than an hour these wild songs of the free, fiery ex-convict held the audience enthralled," he reported.[15] Lomax was more sanguine, telling Ruby that they "got through after a fashion."[16]

But Lomax wasn't done punishing Ledbetter, who announced after the concert "that he was taking his friend back to town where they had been invited to a party." Lomax told Ruby that he "objected" and "almost begged him to spare himself." Still, Ledbetter ignored him. He went off with the friend (he did not take Lomax's car) and later told Lomax that he returned at 1:30 the next morning.[17] Writing about the incident soon after in *Negro Folk Songs as Sung by Lead Belly*, Lomax added details: "He picked up his guitar and hat and left me, declaring ... that I wasn't treating him right, that he was going back to a birthday celebration, that he never broke engagements, that he would keep his promises to his own color." To Lomax, the small rebellion was calamitous: "I had told Lead Belly he must not go. For the first time, he had flatly disobeyed me. I had lost Lead Belly."[18] To Ruby, he vowed that this was his "last journey with Lead Belly . . . unless I let him drive me home [to Austin] which at the present writing I think unlikely."[19]

On Wednesday morning, the pair made their sullen way from Rochester to Buffalo, about eighty miles west, where the alliance reached its actual breaking point. They had performances scheduled from Wednesday through Saturday nights, March 6–9, 1935. Lomax had arranged a room for Ledbetter at Buffalo's "Negro YMCA" on Michigan Avenue, but he moved himself to a room on William Street,[20] closer to the city's music scene and the Colored Musicians Club.[21] After Wednesday night's performance at the University of Buffalo, for which Lomax was paid $100,[22] Ledbetter refused to turn over the hat money. On Thursday morning, as "one of the worst blizzards of the year rage[d],"[23] the pair had a more low-key recital. Lomax "talked ballads to the students of the Buffalo State Teachers College" and Ledbetter sang a couple of songs, receiving some payment from the dean. Lomax wanted the singer to hand over this money and the previous night's hat collection, arguing that he was "trying to help" Ledbetter and that he "made only a few requests of him, and those for his protection in a strange country." Ledbetter, he wrote, "silenced me by declaring resentfully that he knew exactly how to take care of himself." Lomax would later claim that in this moment, he realized that he had "failed" to "help" Ledbetter, and "never again advised him."[24] In a second letter to Ruby on Thursday, Lomax said that he'd begun to contemplate canceling the remaining engagements, and that he was looking forward to that "day of reckoning" when he would "be quit" of the performer.[25]

Events reached a head on Friday. Lomax was working in Buffalo's Grosvenor Library when Ledbetter appeared and, in Lomax's telling, demanded ten dollars. Lomax refused, and when Ledbetter persisted, Lomax became frightened. Having worked hard to convince audiences and the press that the man he'd been living and working closely with for nearly six months was a ruthless killer who would cut a man "to ribbons," he now convinced himself that his own life was at risk. "He looked dangerous," Lomax told readers of *Negro Folk Songs as Sung by Lead Belly*.

"He started towards me threateningly." The standoff ended when Judge Louis B. Hart, a white man about two years younger than Lomax and president of the Board of Trustees of the library, walked in and supported Lomax's assertion that Ledbetter would only waste any money he was given.[26] Ledbetter left without incident, and he showed up as promised at 5:00 p.m. for a Friday afternoon classroom presentation, and at 9:00 p.m. on Saturday for their last show in Buffalo, at the Buffalo Club.[27] "He was a pitiable figure straining to get tones from a throat split and shattered from a wild orgie [sic] the night before with his 'own color,'" Lomax told his wife.[28] In the book, he wrote that "Detective Stegeman, a special officer assigned to Judge Louis Hart, visited [Ledbetter] twice" on Saturday; he told Ruby that "[f]or the last 24 hours in Buffalo," Ledbetter was "under arrest."[29] He worried that Ruby would think him "hard," and defended his actions: "[W]hen faced with death I found myself wishing strongly to live for Bess Brown and for you." He said he would "always regret that I have wasted my time on a person in whom gratitude or appreciation can find no place," adding that he was "terribly disappointed, for I could have grown really fond of him."[30]

What Ledbetter did during the day on Saturday, before that night's show at the Buffalo Club, is unknown. It's possible, however, that he or friends in the area saw *The March of Time* newsreel, including his story; it opened at the Great Lakes theater on Main Street in Buffalo that day. The feature it accompanied was *The Little Colonel*, starring six-year-old Shirley Temple and fifty-six-year-old Bill "Bojangles" Robinson in a post-Civil War drama about a young white woman whose father, a Kentucky colonel, forbids her to marry a Yankee. *The Buffalo News* reviewer wrote, "Kindly old Southern mammies, happy colored children, and a puppy dog figure in the joys and sorrows of the story, while through most of its length there is a soft musical accompaniment of Southern airs" including "Dixie." Robinson, "[t]hat nonpareil of tap dancers ... plays the part of a faithful old family retainer," he wrote, and he praised the scene of Robinson and Temple dancing on a staircase.[31] Admission for the first three shows of the day (before 6:00 p.m.) was only twenty-five cents. (Lomax, too, was aware that *The March of Time* had been released, but, by that time, his antipathy toward Ledbetter was such that he vowed to Ruby, "I shall not see it now or ever."[32])

Sunday found them heading back toward Albany, where Alan and Martha were due to arrive by bus at around 7:00 p.m. On the way up, Lomax had stayed overnight in Albany at the home of Harold Thompson, a professor of English literature at the New York State College for Teachers (now the University at Albany) who had helped to arrange the northern tour. He and his wife, Jean, had hosted Lomax and Ledbetter for dinner, after which Ledbetter "gave us a concert, singing right merrily and strongly," Lomax told Ruby.[33] But Ledbetter slept elsewhere,[34] at Lomax's insistence (not the Thompsons'). Thompson's daughter, Katy, remembered that her father found a Black doctor on Spring Street, within walking distance of the campus, who agreed to let him stay.[35] Now, both Martha and Huddie Ledbetter stayed with the doctor, while Lomax and Alan were guests of the Thompsons. On Monday morning, Ledbetter (accompanied by Alan alone) performed at the Albany Academy for Girls, attended by eleven-year-old Katy. "He did a marvelous concert," she said, decades later. "They had never seen anything like it . . .. I think it was when he started to sing 'When I was a little boy' ["Ha-Ha Thisaway"], it hit them. They all started to dance, and he was thrilled to pieces."[36] But Lomax was still on edge, and at that night's concert at the college, he became visibly upset when Ledbetter took out his knife to play "bottleneck" style, interpreting the technique as a personal threat. John "began fidgeting," Katy Thompson DePorte remembered. "You could tell that something was wrong." Whatever words were exchanged, by the time everyone arrived at a post-show party at the Thompson home, Ledbetter refused to engage with the guests. To DePorte's delight, he "just sat with me in the breakfast nook and sang to me," she said. "That made John livid." In a note sent to Ruby the following morning, Lomax didn't offer details, except to say, "Yesterday Hoodie [*sic*], despite Martha, turned berserk again." He was determined that the Ledbetters would return to Shreveport, and he had told Alan, who seemed "somewhat cut up at my decision to part company,"[37] Lomax told his wife, adding, "Poor Martha!"

Still, Lomax was not going to give up the two performances that were most important to him, those he had planned for Harvard University on Wednesday, March 13. There would be one in the afternoon at Emerson Hall, and one in the evening at Leverett House. Both exceeded his expectations. Ledbetter "held them all, from Prof. George Lyman

Kittredge to the lowliest freshman, spellbound with his primitive chants and his unique harmony," reported *The Boston Globe*, referencing Lomax's former mentor. Ledbetter "was introduced by John A. Lomax, Harvard, 1907, collector of early American ballads, to whose service the troubadour has devoted his life since Lomax maneuvered his release from the Louisiana Prison at Angola last [s]ummer." The reporter added, "Gone are the wanderings with guitar and knife …. Today he is the chauffeur, servant and handyman of Mr. Lomax." At each of his two Harvard appearances, the *Globe* reported, "he played and sang for more than a[n] hour, filling the halls with his powerful hoarse voice and the vibrant music of his guitar." The contrasting beats of his left and right feet "are a musical education in themselves … an impossible feat of muscular coordination."[38] Reporters for the student newspaper, the *Harvard Crimson*, were also enthusiastic. Ledbetter "brought to a crowded Leverett House Dining Room a new negro music, a music of the negro as a man apart from his religion, simple and natural," they wrote. Surprisingly, Ledbetter also broke out some old dance routines: "With the same perfection of rhythm he danced his interpretation of a duck hunt and of stylish ladies walking down the street."[39]

John Lomax felt vindicated. "Staid New England broke down its reserve and cheered and cheered as long as they could see the two performers," he told Ruby, referring to himself and Ledbetter.[40] A celebratory dinner was held following the two performances, with Alan and John Lomax as guests of honor.[41] Huddie and Martha Ledbetter were not invited.

On Tuesday, March 26, nine days after their return to Wilton, John and Alan Lomax brought Huddie and Martha Ledbetter to the Greyhound station at New York's Port Authority for the two-day bus trip back to Shreveport. "I think the main reason I feel about Huddie as I do is that he frightened me," Lomax explained to his wife. "The humiliation of that will be lasting." Now, though, "I no longer have any fear," he said. "[H]is attempts to gain my favor only sicken me."[42] Before the Ledbetters left, there was one final recording session at the American Record Corporation, on Monday, March 25, even though Ledbetter's other records were not selling well.[43] This time, ARC recorded five songs: "Yellow Jacket," "T.B. Woman Blues," "Pig Meat Papa," "Bull Cow," and "My Baby Quit Me."

According to Charles Wolfe and Kip Lornell, Lomax's ledgers revealed that he and Ledbetter "had managed to take in about $1,550" from their northern performances, the recording sessions, radio appearance, and *The March of Time* radio production and film newsreel, "an impressive amount by Depression standards." Initially, half of that money, minus expenses, would have gone to Ledbetter, but since the February contract revision, he was due only a third. In the end, after John Lomax's deductions for expenses, Ledbetter's share was $298.94, roughly 20 percent.[44] Counting just the time just since their arrival in New York, the amount came to about $3.56 per day, and as noted, did not compensate Ledbetter for his services driving and maintaining the car or both of the Ledbetters for their labor at the Wilton house. Still, records suggest that the Ledbetters held out hope that their relationship with the Lomaxes – if not John, then Alan – might be salvageable, if they could just negotiate better terms. As soon as they arrived in Shreveport, they both sent notes to the Lomaxes with best wishes. Ledbetter said that people were after him "to play at the Strain theater,"[45] probably a reference to Shreveport's ten-year-old Strand Theatre, an air-conditioned, 2,500-seat opera house that featured live performances as well as movie screenings.[46] If John didn't want to take "care of the money," maybe Alan could. Ledbetter also wanted to play in Dallas, where he and Martha were headed to visit his daughter, Arthur Mae.[47]

Lomax did not reply. Instead, he reprinted Ledbetter's letter in *Negro Folk Songs as Sung by Lead Belly*, saying it evidenced "a complete reversal of [Ledbetter's] attitude" rather than what it seems to be, a good faith effort to find a mutually satisfactory way to move forward. Back in Shreveport, meanwhile, the Ledbetters' good wishes were tempered by the discovery that John Lomax's need to control was ongoing. Having rounded the amount due Ledbetter to $300, he gave the couple half of that amount in cash at the Greyhound station and then handed them an envelope containing three $50 checks drawn on The Republic Bank of Dallas. But, as they discovered a few days after they arrived in Shreveport, the checks could not yet be cashed: Lomax had post-dated them, tying up their money until May 1, June 1, and July 19. On April 4, the Ledbetters sent a telegram via Western Union to Lomax in Wilton, calmly pointing out the error: "We have checks post dated must have money on same answer by western union what to do. Huddie and Martha Ledbetter."[48]

Rather than respond to the Ledbetters, Lomax contacted the authorities. Just a month earlier, he had been told in writing that

Ledbetter's early "good time" release was provisional: Should he again be convicted by the state of Louisiana, he would have to serve a balance of nearly six years before beginning the new sentence.[49] Knowing this, Lomax still sent a telegram to Sheriff Tom Hughes, a handwritten draft of which remains in the files: "Huddie Ledbetter ~~inquire~~ address Excelsior Laundry ~~threatening my life telegram~~ threatens my life for giving him and Martha Ledbetter post dated checks," it reads. "This I did ~~because he has no money sense~~ after explaining to ~~his wife~~ her that it was for her protection. Please see Ledbetter and if you think best ~~I~~ will ~~arrange to~~ put cash into your hands or his as you suggest. Answer ~~my expense~~ collect.[50]

Hughes had likely known Ledbetter since he returned to the Mooringsport–Oil City area after his Texas pardon in 1925, and he was closely involved in the events surrounding the 1930 altercation with Dick Ellett. In September 1934, just two days after Ledbetter and Lomax met up at the hotel in Marshall, Texas and headed out together, a concerned Hughes wrote to Angola prison manager R.L. Himes to confirm a report he had heard. Was it true that "Hughie" Ledbetter, who was "sent up for the assault to murder of Mr. Dick Ellett, a splendid white citizen of Mooringsport," had been paroled? "This negro committed an unprovoked assault on Mr. Ellett with a pocketknife and cut him up pretty badly," Hughes wrote, adding that "he was convicted and sentenced to six to ten years." Himes replied that, yes, Ledbetter was out, but that he had not been paroled. "Hughie Ledbetter was on our records as Huddie Ledbetter, No. 19469," Himes told Hughes, and then explained the good time allowance under which Ledbetter had been released.[51] Given Hughes' interest in Ledbetter, it is likely he also followed some of the news reports about his northern performances. Now, John Lomax was trying to involve him in what should have been a private matter between himself and Ledbetter.

Fortunately, Hughes did not rise to the bait, but instead turned the matter of the post-dated checks over to William Shade "W.S." Johnson, a white attorney in his mid-forties. Johnson spoke to Ledbetter and then wrote to Lomax, stating that Ledbetter told him the money was his, "which you collected for him in his rounds for singing and playing, and should have been given to him after each performance." Johnson noted that Ledbetter was badly in need of the funds, and on the basis of what

Ledbetter had said, "I think he is entitled to his money now." He asked Lomax to send him (Johnson) a check for $150, upon which he would return the three original checks.[52] It's not clear why Hughes then got involved, but, two days later, he sent a telegram to Lomax, in care of Macmillan: "Huddie Ledbetter and wife hold three checks totalling one hundred fifty dollars wire me this amount and will have their attorney mail you receipt and checks advise." On April 10, 1935, the Commercial National Bank of Shreveport received the amount and the sheriff signed for it.[53]

Lomax's actions troubled Martha and Huddie Ledbetter, who grew concerned that they would not be treated fairly when it came to future income. On April 16, attorney Johnson wrote on their behalf to ARC, introducing himself as "an attorney for Huddie Ledbetter, a colored man, who has made some forty records for your Company." He wanted to know "in what manner the royalty receipts are being paid at this time, or will be paid in the future," and asked that the Ledbetters receive the payment directly in care of the attorney's office.[54] Art Satherly of ARC forwarded Johnson's letter to Lomax's address in Austin, saying that direct payment to the Ledbetters was not possible because ARC's contract was solely with Lomax. ARC "has an agreement with you and we can only recognize you regarding Huddie Ledbetter," Satherly explained. "We cannot make separate payments when royalties become due."[55] Alan Lomax checked in with Satherly, curious about how the two records were selling and which would next be released. Satherly answered that they were "giving the first two records a chance to do something before we make additional releases." He reminded Alan that ARC could not make payments directly to Ledbetter "unless we receive [notarized] written authority from your father allowing us to pay royalties to this party and also how much."[56]

Lomax's telegram to Sheriff Hughes also meant the Ledbetters had to leave Shreveport. Hughes "told Huddie he expected he'd better leave, because if it was going to have to be trouble all the time, he'd rather for him to go," Martha told Elizabeth Lomax.[57] She left her job at the steam laundry, where they'd been happy to have her back, and they relocated to Dallas for "almost the balance of that year," Martha said, staying with Huddie's younger sister, Australia Carr. There, they contacted another lawyer, Edward S. Pearce, from the Dallas firm of Earl M. Deterly.

Pearce wrote on their behalf to Lomax on May 7, 1935. Ledbetter, he said, felt that "he was due some money from the use of his pictures in the various theatres and picture shows over the country, and that there is now being printed song books to be sold, containing his songs." Notably, his client "does not want to throw any monkey wrenches into the machinery" but is "at a loss" to explain the reasons for the post-dated checks and therefore "somewhat" skeptical about financial matters overall. Pearce asked for detailed information from Lomax and told him that he was also contacting Macmillan and *The March of Time*. He signed off with the assurance "that Mr. Ledbetter does not want to jeopardize any prospects of making something out of this venture and also that he expects an equitable settlement all the way through."[58]

Meanwhile, George Platt Brett, Jr., the forty-one-year-old president of The Macmillan Company, was annoyed by the entire situation. He wrote to Lomax to complain that Pearce, Ledbetter's lawyer, "serves notice on us that you will restrain us from publishing your book until you have made your peace with Ledbetter." Brett said that he had warned of this happening and been assured that all "documents outlining the arrangement between yourself and Ledbetter" were secured. Now, Brett said, he needed "a photostat copy . . . so that we may know where we are at."[59] On May 20, Lomax sent Brett a first full draft of the book, soon to be renamed *Negro Folk Songs as Sung by Lead Belly*; he and Alan had moved out of the Wilton farmhouse within days of the Ledbetters' departure, and they finished the book while holed up in adjoining rooms at the Hotel Earle in Greenwich Village. On May 21, Lomax sent Brett "a certified copy of my contract with Huddie Ledbetter, drawn by a good New York lawyer" – a copy of the management agreement dated January 5 and revised February 9.[60] Executives at Macmillan reviewed the agreement and weren't satisfied. They drafted up a new letter from Ledbetter that authorized Lomax to act on his behalf with Macmillan, but it was never executed.

Throughout this period, the Ledbetters continued to be conciliatory. On May 22, writing from Dallas, Martha and Huddie each wrote to Lomax, thanking him for resolving the post-dated check issue and sending their best wishes to Mrs. Lomax, Miss Bess, and Elnora, the housekeeper. "Tell all of them hello and don't forget us," Martha wrote, before also asking after "Mr. Allen" and "Mr. Johnnie." Ledbetter resorted to the subservient tone that had previously worked, addressing his note (written below Martha's) to

"Mr. John A. Lomax Dear Boss" and continuing, "How glad we was to get a letter from our Big Boss." After also asking about the family and Elnora, he wrote: "Boss we have a lots money to make but I could not tell the peoples anything until I see you." He asked Lomax to let him know if he was heading to Dallas; otherwise, Ledbetter would "love to come to Austin and play for the new Governor Hon. Mr. Allred." He had some new songs that he knew Lomax would like, and added that if Lomax wanted to continue performing, he was "ready to go any time."[61] By then, the Ledbetters were likely broke. They had lived briefly on Martha's salary of four dollars per week in Shreveport, but they were now in Dallas. The need to pay lawyers in addition to meeting daily expenses may have been what prompted Martha to write (on behalf of her husband) to Lomax on June 3, asking what he might pay to buy out Huddie's third of potential income from the ARC recordings; they changed their minds later, withdrawing this possibility.[62]

The Ledbetters then met with another Dallas-based lawyer, Joseph Utay, "one-time Texas A&M football star," whom Lomax had known "a long time ago," according to biographer Nolan Porterfield.[63] Utay wrote to Lomax to try to sort through all of it: Macmillan, the ARC contract, and *The March of Time* proceeds.[64] Like the lawyers at Macmillan, Utay had reservations about "the contract dated January 5, 1935, and supplement dated February 9, 1935, purported to be executed by Huddie Ledbetter and Martha Ledbetter." His clients, he said, "emphatically deny that they executed the instruments and that they at any time made any agreement with you," and that, furthermore, "they would not have executed a contract for five years, nor would they have been willing to give you either fifty per cent of the moneys earned by Huddie Ledbetter or sixty-six and two-thirds per cent." He said that Huddie felt the one-third share was "wholly unfair and unreasonable," and reported that Ledbetter's proposed settlement was that *Lomax* accept one-third of the income earned "while in the East." This would mean that Lomax owed Ledbetter a balance of $661.77. If Lomax was not willing to pay that amount, Utay wrote, Ledbetter would "institute suit for the collection of same." Further, the contracts that Lomax had made with Macmillan and ARC would need to be reviewed and approved by Ledbetter to ensure that the terms were satisfactory. In closing, he reiterated: "Unless this matter is adjusted in the next thirty days, Ledbetter will proceed to institute suit in this matter."[65]

And so it continued, as any hope of getting the book out in time to cash in on the publicity of early 1935 faded. Returning on July 23 after "a week's holiday," a clearly annoyed George Brett warned Lomax that unless the matter was resolved soon, "the fall and Christmas sale is to be ruined." It was all a mess, and Lomax blamed Ledbetter. On August 28, he wrote to Austin-based attorney Edward Crane, a personal friend and member of the Texas-Exes, seeking his help. "I fancy [Utay] has lost any control he may have had over Ledbetter; or he may want some money as he goes along," he told Crane.[66] In this and subsequent letters, Lomax went back and forth on what concessions he was willing to make. Finally, on September 12, 1935, Crane told Lomax that his "alliance with Ledbetter" was "at an end."[67] There were a couple of agreements entered into that day. The typescript of one, from Dallas, Texas, dated September 12, 1935, is signed by Huddie Ledbetter and witnessed by Joe Utay and Edward Crane. This one-page typed document (with no handwritten amendments) gave John A. Lomax "full and complete release and acquittance" of Ledbetter from any "action, claim and demand against him and Alan Lomax" that he has or had "asserted against them" arising from the contracts dated January 5 and February 9, 1935. Per separate instrument, Ledbetter did "hereby assign, grant and transfer unconditionally . . . all publication and other rights" to the Macmillan book. In addition, he did "hereby assign, grant and transfer unconditionally to John A. Lomax . . . one-third . . . of all the rights, royalties and revenues that have accrued or may hereafter accrue" under the contract between Lomax and ARC. For the sum of $250 and the one-third division as stated of revenue from the recordings made at ARC, "each party" was "hereby released from any and all obligations assumed under the prior contract and amendment."[68]

The "separate instrument" regarding the contract with Macmillan was also signed on September 12, 1935. Huddie Ledbetter granted to Lomax "the words and music of all his Songs *to be printed in a book entitled 'Lead Belly and his Songs,' about 75 in number* [italicized words written in by hand], together with all abridgements thereof and selections therefrom, and the sole right to arrange for the publication of the aforesaid material in book form or otherwise." Ledbetter guaranteed that he (Ledbetter) was the "sole owner" of this material and had "full power and authority" to make the contract. He also agreed to take sole responsibility for clearing any rights and paying any expenses should they prove to be already copy-righted, a proposition Lomax knew from experience to be potentially time-consuming and costly. In exchange for these concessions, Lomax would pay to Ledbetter $250.00 "in full payment for all publication and other rights in the aforesaid material."[69] With that, each party was "hereby released from any and all obligations assumed thereunder by him." The agreement was signed by Huddie Ledbetter and John Lomax, and wit-nessed by attorneys Edward Crane and Joe Utay, along with Elnora Leavison and J. Jacqueline C. Eckert.[70]

Three months later, writing from Dallas and in bad financial straits, exacerbated with Christmas approaching, Ledbetter wrote to Lomax, asking for help. "I would love for you and me and Martha to make a trip again," he told Lomax; all he wanted was for Lomax to give him his money "every time" so that he could manage it on his own. "Me and Martha are not mad at you," he wrote. "I believe if we go, we will make more money this time than we made before."[71] He was curious about ARC royalties, as he hadn't received any, and noted that he was working for a filling station. Lomax's response is not in the file, but Ledbetter acknowledged it in a conciliatory letter he sent on December 23: "Boss, I was not talking to make you mad at me," he wrote. He had just wanted some information about the money they'd made. "Don't think about that," he urged. "Come on and let's go and we can make two times as much this time." This letter is more urgent than the last; he and Martha were ready to go but they had some bills due, and Ledbetter wanted Lomax to help with them.[72]

Negro Folk Songs as Sung by Lead Belly was not released until November 1936, its title changed by Macmillan. The book's cover and frontispiece featured a photograph of a barefoot Ledbetter playing his guitar and singing in denim overalls, seated atop sacks of grain.[73] Reviewers once again repeated the Lomax narrative, apparently because this is how the book was promoted. Macmillan's "announcement" of the book, quoted by a reporter, described Ledbetter as "a double mur'derer [who] has sung his way to pardons in the Texas and Louisiana penitentiaries." His throat, it said, "has been cut from ear to ear and his left cheek slashed open in barrelhouse brawls."[74] Reviewers were quick to describe Ledbetter's life as "lurid,"[75] and Ledbetter himself as a man "[w]ith the strength of a gorilla and the appetite – for women – of a Solomon."[76] They repeated the Lomaxes' introductory statement that Ledbetter "was the type known as 'killer,' [who] had had

10.1 Book jacket, *Negro Folk Songs as Sung by Lead Belly*. Alan Lomax Collection, Manuscripts, *Negro Folk Songs as Sung by Lead Belly* (AFC 2004/04), American Folklife Center, Library of Congress, 1935. Ledbetter photograph by Otto F. Hesse; use courtesy of the Lead Belly Estate, Murfreesboro, Tennessee.

a career of violence the record of which is a black epic of horrifics."[77] James Weldon Johnson, a noted African American author, lyricist ("Lift Every Voice and Sing"), and civil rights activist, wrote a lengthy review in the *New York Herald Tribune* in which he made an effort to put some positive spin on the book's promotion of Black music: "This book is further verification of the fact that Negro American folk music is the basic material of American popular music," he wrote.[78] African American journalist Floyd J. Calvin, writing in the *New York Amsterdam News*, strongly disagreed with Johnson. "'Strutting Genius' is the encomium plastered on 'Lead Belly,' illiterate Negro singer of the Louisiana delta, by James Weldon Johnson, our No. 1 critic." Calvin was critical that Johnson's review included the book's cover photo "of the 'Genius' – a man past 40 – in bare feet," and even more critical at this prominent attention paid to "an avowed murderer." To Calvin, the book was a way of "'packing' public opinion against the Negro . . .. There are ever so many Negroes of even literary achievements who never get their pictures in the Sunday newspapers, not to mention the 'book' sections."[79]

Huddie and Martha Ledbetter were not given a chance to review the manuscript, including "Lead Belly Tells His Story." Now that it was out, they "just didn't like it," Martha told Elizabeth Lomax. "What was wrote and how it was wrote." In a long, somewhat autobiographical and philosophical essay, perhaps intended as liner notes, in the collection of Moses Asch, the founder of Folkways Records, and addressed "To whom it may concern," dated May 22, 1947, Huddie Ledbetter wrote, "There is a book [written] about my life and i don't think nothing of that book." His handwriting is difficult to read in parts, but it seems to state that the book was in no way a biography of his life, "because Lomax did not [w]rite nothing like i told him." He said he planned to write his own book, which he envisioned titling, "We Shall Walk through the Vall[e]y in Peace." After that, he wanted to write a children's book, titled "Ha Ha Thisaway," after the song.[80] Among the topics Ledbetter's essay touched upon was his call for peace and his criticism of those who used the N-word, although it doesn't specifically mention the Lomax book. (In the Lomax book, the word appears fifty-seven times in the first sixty-four pages (Part I), often as if spoken by Ledbetter or used by Ledbetter to quote others, including white people.) Years later, Martha's niece, Tiny Robinson, denied that he used the word, and it does not appear in letters written by him. "The sound of that word irritated him," Robinson wrote, adding that "any Negro recognized" it as a very serious putdown. "The word" leaves a "bigger wound than any weapon you can use on the battle front."[81]

The Macmillan contract had to be modified one final time, in 1937. Trying to build his own career, Ledbetter discovered that, under the existing agreement, the copyright to the entire book, including the forty-eight songs it contained, was held by The Macmillan Company. Unless Macmillan gave permission, he could neither record the songs nor perform them on the radio. He retained Sol Perlow, a white attorney in

New York, and again threatened a lawsuit. As summarized by Macmillan's president to John Lomax, Perlow was claiming in part that the September 12, 1935 contract "was signed under duress."[82] It took until November 16, 1937 to secure the final signatures on a new agreement, in which John Lomax, Alan Lomax, and The Macmillan Company agreed to "permit and authorize" Ledbetter to use "any of the songs or other material contained" in the book. In addition, for five dollars each from John and Alan, Ledbetter agreed to "forever" discharge them from any claims against the book, "or from any other cause whatever."[83] Huddie Ledbetter was free to perform his own songs.

Epilogue

Huddie Ledbetter died at Bellevue Hospital in New York on December 6, 1949, at the age of sixty. By then, and increasingly over the previous decade, press coverage of him, including in college newspapers, had become more respectful, as reflected in an announcement of his death. "'Lead Belly,' Who Won International Fame as Interpreter of Negro Folk Songs, Is Dead," reported *The New York Times*, accompanying the write-up with a photograph of Ledbetter in a formal suit and bowtie.[1] Alan Lomax, who remained in touch with the performer despite his father's admonishments, produced a memorial concert, "Take This Hammer," held at New York's Town Hall on January 28, 1950. At the program's start, Alan announced that this would be the first public memorial to an American folksinger. "Lead Belly came before all the rest of us," he said, "busting open the doors for us all with his clarion voice, his tiger stride, his merry heart, and his booming twelve string guitar." Because "so many people" had "wanted to sing for Lead Belly – for he touched everyone with his fire," Alan said, they'd had to impose time limits. The program was broken into ballads and folk songs, blues, and then jazz and ragtime, followed by a recording of Ledbetter, introduction of family members, and the screening of a short film of people performing Ledbetter's music, including Woody Guthrie, Brownie McGhee, W.C. Handy, Count Basie, Harold Thompson, and Dizzy Gillespie.[2]

Attendees shared stories of the Huddie Ledbetter they knew, building a portrait different from the one spun by the Lomaxes fifteen years earlier. In the years that followed, they would continue to share these stories. "Lead Belly was the man," Brownie McGhee told Kip Lornell in

1989. "The [folk] music that existed in New York at the time, Lead Belly brought it with him." Like many of Ledbetter's friends, he said he'd never seen him drunk. "I would not want to know a better person," McGhee said. "Was he a murderer? He was a self-defense man. I have gone to bat for him," he added, "because if you can't say why it happened, just don't say it." In contrast to the myths being perpetuated, McGhee said, "He loved children and he loved people, and most of all he loved himself."[3] By many accounts, Ledbetter did not start trouble and would try to stop it. At the same time, he was not a pushover, and he met aggression with aggression. "He never tried to interfere with any one unless they would give him a cause," Margaret Coleman, mother of two of his daughters, wrote in 1935. "Then he would try to defend himself. Through all of his troubles he has always been a boy to regain the same friendship with his enemies."[4] "As far as him being a *mean* man, he wasn't. He was gentle," Martha Ledbetter explained in the 1950s. "But he just wouldn't stand for nobody to punch him in the face. He was strong and he could win fights – oh, Lord – very easy."[5] In 1955, author and longtime family friend John Reynolds asked Ledbetter's cousin, Edmon Ledbetter, then in his late sixties, if Ledbetter had a bad temper. "Oh, he had a quick temper, all right," he said Edmon responded, "but if you didn't make him angry he wouldn't bother you. He was very kindly with my family, especially the children. He had such a sweet smile. He even smiled when he was angry. Sometimes you couldn't tell."[6]

The Ledbetters had not remained in Shreveport for long, but returned to New York City in March 1936. The Lomax narrative had permanently changed the way audiences, promoters, and the press perceived Huddie Ledbetter. When he and Martha returned, they were greeted with familiar-sounding headlines. "'Ain't It a Pity?' But Lead Belly Jingles into City," announced the *Herald Tribune*, adding, "Ebon, Shufflin' Anthology of Swampland Folksong Inhales Gin, Exhales Rhyme."[7] On Friday, April 3, 1936, Ledbetter began a week-long engagement that for other Black performers might have been a career-making break: He was the "special added attraction" at the Apollo Theatre on 125th Street in Harlem. Open to integrated audiences for just two years and under new ownership since 1935, the Apollo was becoming "the premiere showplace for live, theatrical entertainment in Harlem."[8] The show in which Ledbetter performed was spectacular, with a cast of sixty-five people.

There was a chorus of "fourteen Harperettes and fourteen white girls," reported the *New York Amsterdam News*. "The comedy situations ... will be in the hands of Pigmeat, Mason and Hawley .... The music will be rendered by Willie "Lion" Smith and his band."[9] One of the advertisements included a flattering publicity photo of a handsome Ledbetter in jacket and bowtie, holding his guitar and looking off camera. But the rest of the images, like the headlines, were sensational, with captions including A TEXAS JURY SENTENCED HIM FOR MURDER – THE GOVERNOR PARDONED HIM and KILLER PARDONED! Under the direction of the Apollo's co-owner, Frank Schiffman, a white man from Rochester, Ledbetter did not appear on stage in a suit and tie; he performed in prison stripes and was pardoned two times a day by an ersatz governor of Texas, played by Monte Hawley, a light-skinned Black actor. The show was poorly attended and poorly reviewed.[10]

Coincidentally, on the same day in April that the *New York Amsterdam News* ran a notice about Ledbetter's upcoming show, "Ex-Convict Is Apollo's Star,"[11] *Time* magazine ran its own story: "After Lead Belly, Ironhead." After beginning with a brief paragraph about Ledbetter and the pardon songs, the article continued, "Researcher Lomax again made news with another singing convict."[12] John Lomax, "[t]rading on his passing acquaintance with Texas governor James Allred," had managed to get James "Iron Head" Baker paroled "in his care for four months, with the understanding that he would provide employment for Iron Head during that time."[13] Baker, in his early fifties, had been incarcerated at Sugarland since 1927, and was serving a life sentence on a charge of habitual burglary.[14] The paroled man would only serve as "go-between with black musicians and demonstrating the kinds of songs Lomax was looking for," Nolan Porterfield wrote; there was no plan to build toward a singing career.[15] Baker did not drive and never learned, "despite Lomax's comical efforts to teach him."[16] By early June, Lomax had ended the arrangement, and, because Baker needed employment to stay out of prison, Bess and Alan "appealed to a friend of the family to find him a job on a farm."[17] Baker's furlough was revoked the following summer, after he was convicted of burglary.[18] He died in 1944, while still incarcerated in Texas.[19]

The publicity surrounding Huddie Ledbetter and his criminal past caught up with him again on March 5, 1939. Now fifty years old, he was charged with felonious assault, accused of using a knife against another Black man, Henry Burgess.[20] According to the grand jury minutes, a group of about eight people had gathered at the Ledbetters' apartment on the lower East Side. Around 10:00 p.m., Martha left to go to a party, but her husband stayed behind. "He was supposed to play next day," Martha told Elizabeth Lomax, "And he said, 'Well, if I go out now, I'll probably get hoarse.'" Two of the guests, Henry Burgess and Anna McCrimmon, had long disliked each other and were fighting when Martha left. She told Burgess to leave, which he did, but he returned. McCrimmon testified that Burgess "hauled off and hit me in my stomach with his fist and that is when I fell down on the couch and the next thing I knew is when the window was broken out." She hadn't seen a knife and didn't know how Burgess was cut. "[A]fter he hit me in my stomach, the next I hear and the next I seen was Mr. Burgess standing up right by the window with a chair in his hand . . .. He had knocked the window out then."[21]

Although his arrest record lists Ledbetter as a "laborer,"[22] in court when he was asked what he did for a living, Ledbetter said that he was "a musician, song composer and a dancer." He had played at the Savoy, on the Labor Stage Theatre, and at other places. He hadn't gone to the uptown party with Martha because he had to work the following night. He was asleep when he heard McCrimmon cry out, and when he told Burgess to leave, Burgess came after him with a chair and a knife; Ledbetter insisted that it was Burgess who was armed. The two men struggled, and both were injured. The prosecutor then asked about Ledbetter's 1918 and 1930 convictions. Ledbetter told the pardon stories and (falsely) said that both crimes involved guns, not knives. He said that he hadn't owned a knife for six or seven months, but that he'd had one in the past, which he used as he played his guitar. After Ledbetter was excused as a witness, the prosecutor offered into evidence the records of Ledbetter's prior convictions.[23] The grand jury indicted him for assault in the second degree and for carrying and possessing a dangerous weapon (a knife) after prior conviction.[24]

Alan Lomax paid Ledbetter's fifty-dollar bail,[25] and he, Mary Elizabeth Barnicle, and other friends held benefits to raise money for his defense.

Alan also "set up . . . a commercial record deal with a new company called Musicraft, with the advance to go to legal fees," scholars Charles Wolfe and Kip Lornell wrote.[26] In addition, supporters hoped for leniency after Ledbetter, awaiting trial, happened upon a robbery at a bodega. "Leadbelly moved up behind the bandit, tackled him, and held him until a policeman arrived."[27] Nothing helped. In the files at Cornell University is a two-page handwritten memo to assistant prosecutor Milton Schilback, written by deputy assistant district attorney Nathaniel Kaplan one day after the grand jury hearing. It summarized the grand jury testimony and dismissed McCrimmon's credibility. It also inaccurately summarized Ledbetter's prison record: "Def. committed of manslaughter (with a gun) in Texas in 1917 & was sentenced to 30 yrs in jail but was paroled at the end of 7½ yrs because he wrote a song about the Gov. of Texas," the note read. "In 1930 def. convicted of assault with intent to murder in the State of Louisiana & received a 10 yr. sentence but served only 4 years because he wrote a song about the Gov. of Louisiana & was paroled." This inaccuracy is emphasized in a note in the margins of the first page: "Mr. Schilback: Do not let this [defendant] sing his way out of this indictment."[28] The case went to trial on May 4, 1939, in the Court of General Sessions.[29] The judge was fifty-five-year-old George Donnellan, a "rather short, stout man with thin white hair"[30] born in New York City. The jury convicted Ledbetter of assault but recommended clemency.[31] "No," Judge Donnellan said, according to the United Press. "Every time he gets drunk he wants to fight somebody. One year."[32] Sentenced on May 15, Ledbetter was received at Rikers on May 20, 1939, and released six months later, on November 20.[33]

Before and especially after his release from Rikers, Huddie Ledbetter continued to build a life and career, finding welcome among folk musicians as well as social and political activists of the late 1930s and 1940s. He appeared regularly in clubs, on stage, and on the radio. He also returned to recording studios, where he made records on his own and with a range of other musicians. In the 1940s, he spent a couple of years in Hollywood, hoping to break into the movies, although it never happened. While his dreams of becoming the next Gene Autry were never realized, Ledbetter was a role model and mentor to a generation of younger performers, many of them about Alan Lomax's age, including

Pete Seeger (1919–2004), Josh White (1914–1969), Woody Guthrie (1912–1967), and Brownie McGhee (1915–1996). Authors Kip Lornell and Charles Wolfe quoted Woody Guthrie's description of staying with the Ledbetters at their walk-up apartment on East 10th Street in New York; "three little rooms painted a sooty sky blue," Guthrie wrote. "I watched him set after breakfast, look down eastwards out of his window, read *The Daily News, The Daily Mirror* and *The Daily Worker*. I listened as he tuned up his Twelve String Stella and eased his fingers up and down along the neck in the same way that the library and museum clerk touched the frame of the best painting in their gallery." Guthrie, the authors wrote, was "especially fascinated with the gentle side of Leadbelly."[34]

In 1941, after she graduated from high school, Martha's niece, Queen "Tiny" Love, a daughter of Martha's twin sister Mary, moved to New York. She moved into the same lower East Side apartment building as her aunt and uncle, one floor below. "She had known Leadbelly when she was a child in Louisiana," wrote Wolfe and Lornell, "and now took an interest in his work in New York," managing his career during the latter half of the 1940s. She reviewed contracts, helped to set up dates, reminded others of "overdue royalty payments," and "read the royalty statements closely," they said. In 1945, Love, now married, had a son, Alvin Singh,[35] upon whom the Ledbetters doted. (Robinson is Tiny's last name from a later marriage.) She also met Arthur Mae Ledbetter, who remained in contact with her father. "I took her around New York," Robinson remembered. "She was his size, had the high cheek bones . . . . She [was] very warm, kind and sweet just as her father was."[36]

In May 1949, Ledbetter traveled outside the United States for the first time in his life, performing a series of concerts in Paris, France.[37] For several months, his health had been declining, and he needed a wheelchair to get around. On June 15 of the same year, he gave an hour-long concert at the University of Texas in Austin, the alma mater and former employer of John Lomax, who had died the previous year, on January 26, 1948, at the age of eighty. Ledbetter began the concert with "Goodnight, Irene," which he called his "theme song." For an hour, he kept the audience, including children, enthralled and often laughing as he performed a range of material, including "Go Down, Ol' Hannah" and "Rock Island Line." The audience knew the words to many of them, and, at his invitation, they sang along. He closed the concert with two spirituals performed with Martha: "Old Ship of Zion" and "I Will Be So Glad When I Get Home."[38] The performance was bittersweet: Doctors in Paris had diagnosed him with amyotrophic lateral sclerosis (ALS), and this would prove to be his last concert.

Despite his profound significance on America's musical landscape, Huddie Ledbetter never achieved commercial success, and he and Martha at times sought public relief. The 1950 census, enumerated in April, just months after her husband's death, found Martha working as a "folder" at a New York laundry.[39] That July, just seven months after Ledbetter's death, a recording of "Goodnight, Irene" was released commercially. It was performed by The Weavers, a young white quartet: Pete Seeger, Lee Hays, Fred Hellerman, and Ronnie Gilbert, "all old friends of Huddie's." The song was the first break-out hit of the modern folk music movement, selling "more than a million recordings" and "250,000 sheet [music] copies in the first 20 days of its publication."[40] Other artists rushed to cover it, including Frank Sinatra.

The song's runaway success fueled discussion of copyright involving traditional materials in general, and, given the hardships Martha Ledbetter was facing, the Ledbetter material in particular. Alan Lomax's view, wrote biographer John Szwed, "was that the folklorist who recorded a song in the field was obliged to ensure that the singer was paid for his work but should also have a share of the royalties in consideration for his or her role as a collector if the record was ever sold commercially." Considering the sheer amount of effort his father and he had expended over many decades and the cultural and historical value of their collection, the argument has merit. According to the Library of Congress, "The entire body of material collected by Alan and John A. Lomax at the American Folklife Center encompasses more than 100 collections and includes 700 linear feet of manuscripts, 10,000 sound recordings, 6,000 graphic images, and 6,000 moving images."[41] And, as scholar Lizzy Cooper Davis noted, prior to the runaway success of The Weavers' "Goodnight, Irene," the copyrighting of "material collected in the field" by folklorists – including, she noted, "Zora Neale Hurston, Carl Sandburg, Cecil Sharp, and Lawrence Gellert" – had not previously been of significant concern. Now, however, "when such copyrights began to hold the promise of significant returns, both Lomax's copyright defenses and the folk field's critiques of them grew louder." According to Davis, Pete Seeger "helped negotiate an agreement between [The Weavers'] managers and Martha Ledbetter and Alan Lomax, who represented Huddie and John's estates respectively."[42] In addition, in part due to the efforts of Alan Lomax, attention was paid to the rest of the Ledbetter repertoire, and additional rights were accorded to Martha. When she died in 1968, the Ledbetter estate passed to her niece, Tiny Robinson, who was also the executrix. The Lead Belly Foundation and the Lead Belly Archive are now operated by Robinson's grandchildren.

Acknowledgments

There is a lengthy list of people and institutions to who I am indebted for their help in making this book a reality. Thank you to Cecelia Cancellaro, whose encouragement, expertise, and guidance made a world of difference; I remain honored that she chose to bring this book to Cambridge University Press. Thanks also to Lisa Carter, Steven Holt, and Victoria Phillips. Thank you to the National Endowment for the Humanities (NEH), which awarded me a 2021–2022 Public Scholars grant that supported a large stretch of research and writing. (Any views, findings, conclusions, or recommendations expressed in this publication do not necessarily reflect those of the NEH.) Thank you to my sister, Susan M. Bernard, for not only commenting on multiple drafts of the book but also being in my corner 24/7. Thank you also to Richard Hamm, University at Albany; Mary Ellen Curtin, American University; Gustavus Stadler, Haverford College; Talitha LeFlouria, University of Texas at Austin, and others for their very insightful comments on the book proposal, chapters, and especially full drafts. Any errors, of course, are mine.

Important research for this project builds on work conducted independently over many decades by several people to whom I am indebted. This includes Judge Joni Haldeman, who conducted roughly sixty oral histories, mostly with very elderly people, in the area of DeKalb, Texas, searching for answers to the mystery of "Walter Boyd" and the truth of Huddie Ledbetter's early life. With thanks to a generous grant from the Summerlee Foundation, I was able to digitize and transcribe a lot of this material (because of a 1999 tornado, some of it was in rough shape and the transcripts had been lost), in preparation for its donation to the Portal to Texas History. Joni and her husband Charles welcomed my friend Joel

Scheraga and me to DeKalb in 2019 and we spent two days with Joni at the wheel of her large pickup as she plowed across rough fields and down county roads, sharing local history. Through Joni, we enjoyed the hospitality of Kyle Barrett and David Thomas, and a visit to the Williams House Museum in DeKalb. She continued to share tips and stories in the months afterward, despite illness. I regret that she did not live to see the final product to which she contributed so much.

Thank you also to musicians Monty and Marsha Brown, who welcomed Joel and me to the Mooringsport–Shreveport area and drove us to local museums, historic sites, and other locations, including the Mooringsport Mini Museum and the hauntingly beautiful Caddo Lake. Monty Brown completed his master's thesis on Huddie Ledbetter in 1989, and in the decades since he and Marsha wrote a series of blog posts about Ledbetter, much of it built on oral histories that they, too, conducted with elderly people in the early 1990s. The Browns generously shared their bundle of research with me, and their years of work were enormously helpful and deeply appreciated.

I am also indebted to the late Sean F. Killeen, a former executive director of Cornell University's Einaudi Center for International Studies and founder of the Lead Belly Society, which published *The Lead Belly Letter*. Killeen spent two decades compiling extensive research about the performer, and his legacy, the Sean F. Killeen Lead Belly research collection, 1885–2002, housed in the Division of Rare and Manuscript Collections at Cornell University, proved to be a treasure trove of material. Thank you to Natalie Kelsey and her colleagues for helping to make the visit to Cornell so productive.

Thank you to attorney Michael E. Warwick of Marshall, Texas, who generously pulled records and expertly guided me through the Ledbetters' land transactions as well as Huddie Ledbetter's 1915 criminal files. Thank you to Marianne Fisher-Giorlando, Professor of Criminal Justice emerita at Grambling State University and currently Chair of the Education Committee for the Louisiana State Penitentiary Museum Foundation Board, who has been a generous and valuable source of information and support, and to Natalie J. Ring, a professor of history at the University of Texas at Dallas, for introducing us. Special thanks to Todd Harvey and John Fenn at the American Folklife Center, Library of Congress; to Aryn Glazier, Caitlin Brenner, Marisa Jefferson, and everyone at the Dolph Briscoe Center for American History at the University of Texas at Austin; and to Jeff Place and his staff at the Smithsonian Center for Folklife & Cultural Heritage. Thank you to Francis Abbott, Executive Director of the State of Louisiana Board of Pardons and Parole, for granting permission to search records held in the Louisiana State Archives; thanks also to librarian John Fowler and to Louisiana State University graduate student Peyton E. Jeffcoat for her assistance with them. Thank you to John Reynolds, a longtime Ledbetter family friend and a New York-based blues scholar, collector, and Lead Belly archivist, who was also generous in sharing research. He and Tiny Robinson, Martha's and Huddie's niece and the executor of the estate, are the authors of *Lead Belly: A Life in Pictures* (Göttingen: Steidl, 2008), an elegant book about to be re-released. Thanks also to Jonas Wettre, formerly with Steidl and now a freelance designer based in Sweden, for his help.

A very special thanks to Huddie Ledbetter's heirs, Terika Singh Dean, licensing manager at The Lead Belly Estate; Alvin Singh, historical curator of the Lead Belly Archives; and Tanya Singh, Director of the Lead Belly Foundation, for their encouragement, for permitting me access to certain Ledbetter recordings at the American Folklife Center, and for their assistance with photographic materials; also to Nathan Salsburg at the Association for Cultural Equity for permission to use the photographs of John A. Lomax. I am also grateful to the staff at TRO Essex Music Group, especially Sarah Smith, Courtney Cloud, and Nora Sheridan, and to Robert Meitus of Meitus Gelbert Rose, representing Global Jukebox, for their help in securing permission to include song lyrics in these pages.

Work on this book builds on a career's worth of involvement in a broad range of film and writing projects, for which I thank colleagues and friends from Blackside, Inc., Filmmakers Collaborative, The 9th Floor, Steeplechase Films, Twin Cities PBS, and elsewhere. I also want to acknowledge the support of the National Endowment for the Humanities for many of the film projects on which I've worked over the years; as they note, "Democracy demands wisdom." Thank you in particular to Jeff Hardwick, Mac Ruppel, and David Weinstein, Division of Public Programs; Adam Wolfson, Acting Chairman; and Karen Little, Office of Grant Management. Thank you also to Catherine Allan, Kyle Bass, Douglas A. Blackmon, Deborah Brevoort, Ric Burns, Julie Casper Roth, Robin Espinola, Frederick Keith Fiddmont, Gary Garrison, Denise A. Greene, Gregg Henry, Dante James, Susan Kim, Rena

Kosersky, Maggie Mancinelli-Cahill, Daphne McWilliams, Michelle Phillip, Sam Pollard, Judy Richardson, Tracy Heather Strain, Sean Wilentz, and countless others.

Special thanks to the University at Albany, State University of New York, which has been my academic home since 2008, for its support, including a fellowship from the university's Institute for History and Public Engagement, a Faculty Research Award, and an approved sabbatical for the final push on the book. I'm grateful to the current and former deans of the College of Arts and Sciences, Jeanette Altarriba and Edelgard Wulfert, for their encouragement and support. I also can't say enough positive things about my extraordinary colleagues in the Department of History: Mitch Aso, Carl Bon Tempo, Robin Campbell, Alexander Dawson, Richard Fogarty, Federica Francesconi, Kori Graves, David Hochfelder, Ryan Irwin, Maeve Kane, Nadieszda Kizenko, Dmitry Korobeynikov, Susan McCormick, Patrick Nold, Christopher Pastore, Kendra Smith-Howard, Michael Taylor, Laura Wittern-Keller, and Gerald Zahavi. Big thanks also to Jamie Winn, Irene Andrea, and Erika Dockey; to M.A. program graduates Sheri Sarnoff and Hannah Swezey; Ph.D. student Tina Peabody; and subject librarian Jesús Alonso-Regalado. Thanks also to Amy Murrell Taylor, University of Kentucky; and Susan Gauss, University of Massachusetts Boston.

Lastly, I am beyond grateful to my family for their support over the years I've spent researching and writing this book. To my mother Kathleen, my five siblings, their spouses, ten brilliant and inspiring niblings, and Joel, my thanks and love.

Notes

Abbreviations

AFC	American Folklife Center, Library of Congress
American Ballads	John A. Lomax and Alan Lomax, *American Ballads and Folk Songs*. New York: The Macmillan Company, 1934
Ballad Hunter	John A. Lomax, *Adventures of a Ballad Hunter*. New York: The Macmillan Company, 1947
Briscoe	Dolph Briscoe Center for American History, University of Texas at Austin
HL	Huddie Ledbetter
JAL	John A. Lomax
Killeen	Sean F. Killeen Lead Belly research collection, Cornell University
LSU	Louisiana State University (Shreveport or Baton Rouge)
NFS	John A. Lomax and Alan Lomax, *Negro Folk Songs as Sung by Lead Belly*. New York: The Macmillan Company, 1936
RTL	Ruby Terrill Lomax

Introduction

1. For more on convict leasing and its aftermath, see also Mark T. Carleton, *Politics and Punishment: The History of the Louisiana State Penal System*. Baton Rouge: Louisiana State University Press, 1984; Mary Ellen Curtin, *Black Prisoners and Their World, Alabama, 1865–1900*. Charlottesville: University of Virginia Press, 2023; Pete Daniel, *The Shadow of Slavery: Peonage in the South, 1901–1969*. Champaign: University of Illinois Press, 1990; Risa L. Goluboff, *The Lost Promise of Civil Rights*. Cambridge, MA: Harvard University Press, 2010; Talitha L. LeFlouria, *Chained in Silence: Black Women and Convict Labor in the New South*. Chapel Hill: University of North Carolina Press, 2016; Alex Lichtenstein, *Twice the Work of Free Labor: The Political Economy of Convict Labor in the New South*. London: Verso, 1996; Matthew J. Mancini, *One Dies, Get Another: Convict Leasing in the American South, 1866–1928*. Columbia, SC:

University of South Carolina Press, 1996; and Robert Perkinson, *Texas Tough: The Rise of America's Prison Empire*. New York: Picador, 2010.

2. *NFS*, 3.

3. *NFS*, x.

4. Charles Wolfe and Kip Lornell, *The Life and Legend of Leadbelly*. New York: Da Capo Press, 1992, 160.

5. Nolan Porterfield, *Last Cavalier: The Life and Times of John A. Lomax*. Chicago: University of Illinois Press, 1996, 345–346.

6. John Szwed, *Alan Lomax: The Man Who Recorded the World*. New York: Viking, Penguin Group, 2010, 69.

7. Ellen Harold and Dom Fleming, "Huddie Ledbetter (Lead Belly)," Association for Cultural Equity, www.culturalequity.org/alan-lomax/friends/ ledbetter. They wrote: "The book is noteworthy as the first in-depth autobiographical account of a folk singer from his/her point of view. Lead Belly's story as told by himself, his songs, and his explanations of them are transcribed faithfully and constitute a valuable historical document."

8. AFC 1933/001: Writings, books, "Notes on the Songs of Huddie Ledbetter" (6/7), John A. Lomax and Alan Lomax papers. United States, 1907–1969. Manuscript/Mixed Material. www.loc.gov/item/afc1933001_ms442.

9. The second edition of *The Midnight Special* was issued by Edmond G. Addeo in 2009 (Bloomington, Indiana, AuthorHouse). See Adam Boretz, "Self-Publishing: A Second Life for Leadbelly Novel," *Publishers Weekly*, July 8, 2011.

10. Edmond Addeo interview with Kip Lornell, July 4, 1990. Addeo also described the creative liberties taken in his article, "The Message of Leadbelly's Fate," *The San Francisco Examiner*, November 28, 1971, 17.

11. See, for example, "Leadbelly," Roger Ebert, *Chicago Sun-Times*, April 15, 1976. www.rogerebert.com/reviews/leadbelly-1976.

12. Bullock Museum, Austin, Texas, in describing an item in their artifact gallery (a 78 rpm Lead Belly recording of "Grey Goose").

13. The Louisiana Music Hall of Fame, "LeadBelly," https://louisianamusichallof fame.org/leadbelly.

14. "Lead Belly," website of the Rock and Roll Hall of Fame, June 11, 2019. Accessed via Internet Archive's Way Back Machine. https://web.archive.org/web/201906 11184604/https://www.rockhall.com/inductees/lead-belly.

15. Hazel V. Carby, *Race Men*. Cambridge, MA: Harvard University Press, 1998, 103.

16. Disc 1 SF 40068 Last Sessions, September 27, 1948. Preface to "Yes, I Was Standing in the Bottom."

Chapter 1 Encounter at Angola

1. Louisiana State Penitentiary Records, 1866–1963, database with images, FamilySearch. Correctional institution records, Convict records vol. 32

no. 19451–20100 (records in reverse order) 1930, image 703 of 720; Louisiana State Archives, Baton Rouge.

2. *Ballad Hunter*, 121.
3. *NFS*, ix.
4. "Goodnight, Irene." See music credits (in Selected Sources) for details.
5. "Angola Blues (So Doggone Soon)." See music credits for details.
6. AFC 1940/018, June–July 1933, Angola, La. Disc numbers AFS 116 and 119–121a.
7. Charles Wolfe and Kip Lornell, *The Life and Legend of Leadbelly*. New York: Da Capo Press, 1992, 115.
8. Nolan Porterfield, *Last Cavalier: The Life and Times of John A. Lomax*. Chicago: University of Illinois Press, 1996, 297.
9. *NFS*, 31.
10. *Ballad Hunter*, 121. As far-fetched as it may seem, John Lomax actually did get a prisoner paroled to him in 1935, as discussed in the epilogue. See also Porterfield, *Last Cavalier*, 375.
11. *NFS*, 31.
12. *NFS*, 32.
13. Porterfield, *Last Cavalier*, 300, quoting a letter from JAL to RTL, July 21, 1933, Briscoe. John Lomax did not copyright the song at that point; it was included in *Negro Folk Songs as Sung by Lead Belly*, published in 1936.
14. Stephanie L. Perrault, Roger T. Saucier, Thurston H.G. Hahn III, Dayna Lee, Joanne Ryan, and Chris Sperling, *Cultural Resources Survey, Testing, and Exploratory Trenching for the Louisiana State Penitentiary Levee Enlargement Project, West Feliciana Parish, Louisiana*. Final report, prepared for New Orleans District Army Corps of Engineers. Baton Rouge: Coastal Environments, Inc., 2001, 84. https://archive.org/details/DTIC_AD A387997. For additional information, visit the website of the Louisiana State Prison Museum & Cultural Center, www.angolamuseum.org.
15. In 2023, Louisiana's population was roughly 62 percent white and 33 percent Black, but 64 percent of those incarcerated there are Black, and 34 percent white. See Hassan Kanu, "Louisiana's Over-incarceration Is Part of a Deeply Rooted Pattern." Reuters, February 1, 2023, www.reuters.com/legal/govern ment/louisianas-over-incarceration-is-part-deeply-rooted-pattern-2023-02-01.
16. *1930 Census: Volume 3. Population, Reports by States*. United States Census Bureau, Washington, D.C., 1932, www.census.gov/library/publications/ 1932/dec/1930a-vol-03-population.html.
17. Patrick A. Langan, "Race of Prisoners Admitted to State and Federal Institutions, 1926–86." US Department of Justice, May 1991. Table 7, "Sentenced prisoners admitted to State and Federal Institutions, by race, 1930," 14. www.ojp.gov/pdffiles1/nij/125618.pdf.

18. Louisiana State Penitentiary, Baton Rouge, Louisiana, *Report to His Excellency, the Honorable O.K. Allen, Governor of Louisiana, and to the Honorable Senators and Representatives of the General Assembly of the State of Louisiana*, May 1932, 13. This report (following those of 1867, 1869, etc.) is available via Google Books; excerpts are also in Box 12, folder 2, Killeen. The total number incarcerated at Angola, measured each April 1, rose annually from 1928 (1,792) to 1932 (2,884); by May 16, 1932 the total was 2,950. (Louisiana also has other state and federal prison facilities, as well as local and parish jails.)

19. *Report to His Excellency*, May 1932, 4.

20. For more on Franklin, see Joshua Rothman, *The Ledger and the Chain: How Domestic Slave Traders Shaped America*. New York: Basic Books, 2021. Angola, Panola, and Loango were names Franklin gave to "three new plantations" in the 1840s, according to Rothman. "There is no evidence" for the claim that "Angola" is a reference "to a place of origin of those he enslaved on the property," Rothman, *The Ledger and the Chain*, 303.

21. Rothman, *The Ledger and the Chain*, 309–310.

22. While the terms "farm" and "plantation" both apply to sites of agricultural labor and housing for owners and workers, "plantation" tends to also mean crops sold domestically and, at times, internationally.

23. Jack Temple Kirby, "Black and White in the Rural South, 1915–1954." *Agricultural History*, July 1984, 58.4, Symposium on the History of Rural Life in America: 411–422; this quote p. 412. For more on sharecropping specifically in West Feliciana Parish, Louisiana, see Perrault et al., *Cultural Resources Survey*, Chapter 3.

24. See, for example, Isabel Wilkerson, *The Warmth of Other Suns: The Epic Story of America's Great Migration*. New York: Vintage Books, 2010.

25. See National Archives, "Milestone Documents," www.archives.gov/milestone-documents/13th-amendment.

26. Matthew J. Mancini, *One Dies, Get Another: Convict Leasing in the American South, 1866–1928*. Columbia, SC: University of South Carolina Press, 1996, 2–3.

27. Eric Foner, *Reconstruction: America's Unfinished Revolution, 1863–1877*. New York: Harper & Row, 1988, 276.

28. National Archives, www.archives.gov/milestone-documents/14th-amendment; National Archives, www.archives.gov/milestone-documents/15th-amendment.

29. Eric Foner, *Reconstruction*; Encyclopedia Britannica, www.britannica.com/event/Reconstruction-United-States-history.

30. Eric Foner, *The Second Founding: How the Civil War and Reconstruction Remade the Constitution*. New York: W.W. Norton & Company, 2019, 126.

31. Eric Foner, "Rooted in Reconstruction: The First Wave of Black Congressmen," *The Nation*, October 15, 2008. www.thenation.com/article/archive/rooted-reconstruction-first-wave-black-congressmen.

32. Hon. E.B. Kruttschnitt, president of the convention, in Official Journal of the Proceedings of the Constitutional Convention of the State of Louisiana held in New Orleans, Tuesday February 8, 1898, New Orleans. Printed by H.J., 371, 381. https://catalog.hathitrust .org/Record/001143970Hearsey, Convention Printer, 1898.

33. David W. Blight, "Lincoln Would Not Recognize His Own Party," *The New York Times*, July 23, 2019, www.nytimes.com/2019/07/23/opinion/lincoln-repub lican-party-trump.html. See also Kevin M. Kruse, "The Southern Strategy," in Kevin Kruse and Julian E. Zelizer, *Myth America: Historians Take On the Biggest Legends and Lies about Our Past.* New York: Basic Books, 2023, Chapter 12.

34. Mark T. Carleton, *Politics and Punishment: The History of the Louisiana State Penal System.* Baton Rouge: Louisiana State University Press, 1971, 20. Carleton's book also offers detailed information about the factors that led the state to end leasing and resume control over state prisoners.

35. Joanne Ryan and Stephanie L. Perrault, "Angola: Plantation to Penitentiary," US Army Corps of Engineers, 2007. www.crt.state.la.us/Assets/OCD/archaeology/ discoverarchaeology/virtual-books/PDFs/Angola_Pop.pdf.

36. Alabama was the last state to end the practice, in 1928, although vestiges of the convict lease system remained elsewhere until 1933, according to Carleton, *Politics and Punishment*, 83.

37. Ryan and Perrault, "Angola," 10.

38. Carleton, *Politics and Punishment*, 83.

39. Carleton, *Politics and Punishment*, 109.

40. Carleton, *Politics and Punishment*, 112, 118, 120.

41. Associated Press, "Salaries Are Raised, Materials Bought without Bids Asked: Senate Investigation Committee Says Long Has Appointed Law Student as Warden and He Gives Little Time to Duties – Financial Affairs in Bad State – Favoritism Charged – Rice Farm Contract Held Illegal," *Weekly Town Talk*, Alexandria, Rapides Parish, La., July 12, 1930, 11.

42. Carlton Beals and Abel Plenn, "Louisiana's Black Utopia," *The Nation*, October 30, 1935, 503–505.

43. Associated Press, "Louisiana Prison Quiet after Riot," *Greeley (Colorado) Daily Tribune*, August 27, 1930, 2.

44. The nickname was due to his fiscal discipline while serving as business manager at Louisiana State University. See "Himes Named Manager of Pen.," *The Weekly Town Talk*, Alexandria, Rapids Parish, La., April 25, 1931, 5.

45. *Baton Rouge Morning Advocate*, May 16, 1932, quoted in Carleton, *Politics and Punishment*, 126.

46. Anthony J. Badger, "Huey Long and the New Deal," in Stephen Baskerville and Ralph Willett (eds.), *Nothing Else to Fear: New Perspectives on America in the Thirties.* Manchester: Manchester University Press, 1985, 73.

47. In fact, 194 convicts managed to escape between 1931 and 1936, according to the *Biennial Report of the Louisiana State Penitentiary* (Baton Rouge, 1934–40), cited in Carleton, *Politics and Punishment*, 132.
48. B.L. Krebs, "Blood Took Penitentiary 'Out of Red,' Records Show," *The Times Picayune New Orleans States*, Section 2, May 11, 1941, 4–5.
49. *NFS*, 24.
50. 1930; Census Place: Police Jury Ward 6, East Baton Rouge, Louisiana; Page: 5A; Enumeration District: 0028; FHL microfilm: 2340527; he is mentioned as a captain in charge of Camp E at Angola in *The Shreveport Times*, November 11, 1914, 1.
51. Krebs, "Blood Took Penitentiary 'Out of Red,' Records Show," 5.
52. Elizabeth Wisner, *Public Welfare Administration in Louisiana*. Social Service Monographs, No. 11. Chicago: University of Chicago Press, 1930. Information is from June 30, 1929, 176. See also Paul W. Garrett and Austin H. MacCormick (eds.), *Handbook of American Prisons and Reformatories*. New York: National Society of Penal Information, 1929, 391.
53. *Report to His Excellency*, May 1932, 7.
54. Ledbetter's "Louisiana State Penitentiary Prison Record," dated June 27, 1934, can be found in Box 12, folder 5, Killeen. It notes "Punishment: Nov. 21/31 – 10 Lashes – Laziness; June 27/32 – 15 Lashes – Impudence." Then: "He was placed on the Eligible List May 1/30 as waiter at 'F,' then as Tailor at Road Camp no. 5, and is now Free Man's waiter at 'A.'"
55. "Louisiana State Penitentiary with Objective of Building Men Is Now Living on Its Own Income," *State Times Morning Advocate*, May 16, 1932, 61.
56. Louisiana State Penitentiary, Death Report, page 6. The men were all buried at "Johnson's Cemetery near Jackson, La."
57. Carleton, *Politics and Punishment*, 112.
58. Krebs, "Blood Took Penitentiary 'Out of Red,' Records Show," 5.
59. 1930; Census Place: Police Jury Ward 7, West Feliciana, Louisiana; Page: 3A; Enumeration District: 0008; FHL microfilm: 2340561.
60. Krebs, "Blood Took Penitentiary 'Out of Red,' Records Show," 4.
61. *NFS*, 31; also JAL to Himes, June 20, 1934, Box 12, folder 4, Killeen.
62. Himes to JAL, June 21, 1934, Box 12, folder 4, Killeen.
63. John Szwed, *Alan Lomax: The Man Who Recorded the World*. New York: Viking, Penguin Group, 2010, 43.
64. Wolfe and Lornell, *The Life and Legend of Leadbelly*, 113.
65. Alan Lomax to Carl Engel, Library of Congress, July 30, 1933. John A. Lomax and Alan Lomax papers. United States, 1933. Manuscript/Mixed Material. AFC193301_ms006.
66. *Ballad Hunter*, 121.

67. Mary Miles Loveless, "The Life and Times of Curt Ward," *Memphis Magazine*, June 2018, 101–109.
68. *Ballad Hunter*, 121.
69. Alan Lomax, "'Sinful' Songs of the Southern Negro: Experiences Collecting Secular Folk-Music." *Southwest Review* 19, no. 2 (1934), 115.
70. Szwed, *Alan Lomax*, 46; also Lomax, "'Sinful' Songs of the Southern Negro," 108–109.
71. Lomax, "'Sinful' Songs of the Southern Negro," 107.
72. Pete Daniel, *The Shadow of Slavery: Peonage in the South 1901–1969*. Chicago: University of Illinois Press, 1972, ix–x. The Department of Justice addressed "Involuntary Servitude, Slavery, and Peonage" in December 1941, with its issuance of Circular #3591; see National Archives, www.archives.gov/resear ch/investigations/fbi/classifications/050-slavery.html.
73. John Szwed, quoting Szwed, *Alan Lomax*, in Judith L. Graubart and Alice V. Graubart (eds.), *Decade of Destiny*. Chicago: Contemporary Books, 1978, 311.
74. *American Ballads*, xxvii. For a discussion of petitions to the federal government, see Risa L. Goluboff, *The Lost Promise of Civil Rights*. Cambridge, MA: Harvard University Press, 2007.
75. Porterfield, *Last Cavalier*, 306.
76. John A. Lomax, "'Sinful Songs' of the Southern Negro." *The Musical Quarterly*, 20, no. 2 (April 1934), 181.
77. *Ballad Hunter*, 128–129. This material is also available in a letter from JAL to Mr. F. P. Keppel, Carnegie Corporation, November 6, 1935, in the records of The Macmillan Company records, New York Public Library.
78. Porterfield, *Last Cavalier*, 314–315.
79. "Prisoner Asks His Freedom in Poetic Epistle," *The Shreveport Journal*, October 9, 1931, 17.
80. "Poetical Pardon Appeal Is Barred by Technicality," *The Times-Picayune*, October 10, 24.
81. Louisiana State Archives, "Pardons: 1879–1940," accession number P1988-143, box 51, location 8951.
82. *The Shreveport Times*, July 28, 1933, 13.
83. Himes to HL, December 6, 1933, Box 12, folder 4, Killeen.
84. HL to Himes, December 8, 1933, Box 12, folder 4, Killeen. In addition to being typed, the style of writing and punctuation suggests that he worked with someone else on the letter.
85. John F. Ard, Captain Camp B, to Warden, Texas State Pen., May 9, 1930. Box 12, folder 3, Killeen.
86. J.W. Denton, Chief Clerk, Criminal Record Department, to Captain John F. Ard, May 22, 1930. Box 12, folder 3, Killeen.

87. Himes to HL, December 15, 1933. Box 12, folder 3, Killeen. A poor photo-copy of "Walter Boyd's" fingerprints, likely provided in 1939 to the FBI, can also be found in the Killeen archive, Box 4, folder 2, "FBI Records and Correspondence."

88. HL to Himes, March 2, 1934. Box 12, folder 4, Killeen.

89. Himes to HL, March 13, 1934. Photocopy in files of Monty and Marsha Brown.

90. HL to Himes, April 2, 1934. Box 12, folder 4, Killean.

91. Himes to JAL, June 21, 1934. Box 12, folder 4, Killeen. Himes to Bureau of Records & Identification, June 21, 1934, Box 12, folder 4, Killeen.

92. W.M. Thompson, Chief, Texas Prison System, to Himes, June 25, 1934. Box 12, folder 12, Killeen.

93. "Texas Prison System Certificate of Conduct," in AFC 1933/001, Writings, books, "Notes on the Songs of Huddie Ledbetter," 5/7-oversized, John A. Lomax and Alan Lomax papers. United States. Manuscript/Mixed Material. www.loc.gov/item/afc1933001_ms441os.

94. Box 12, folder 5, Killeen. These changes also made their way to Ledbetter's record cited previously, Louisiana State Penitentiary Records, 1866–1963, data-base with images, FamilySearch. Correctional institution records, Convict records vol. 32 no. 19451–20100 (records in reverse order) 1930, image 703 of 720; Louisiana State Archives, Baton Rouge. On the top left, where "Aliases" included the typed notation "As Walter Boyd – Texas State Pen. – Murder," someone handwrote, "Pardoned." To the right, at the top of the page and in the middle, the typed notation "2nd Termer" was crossed out.

95. *NFS*, 32.

96. American Folklife Center, Library of Congress, AFC 1935/002, AFS121–126.

97. This may be poetic license. Weather records suggest that the rainy days were July 17–18, 1933, during the Lomaxes' first visit to Angola.

98. *NFS*, 31–32.

99. See, for example, "358 Convicts Given Reprieves by Governor Allen Thursday," which notes that this increased "to 658 the number of prisoners cited for release on recommendation of Penitentiary Manager R.L. Himes." *The Shreveport Times*, September 30, 1932, 1.

100. "Governor O.K. Allen." See music credits for details. Recording, American Folklife Center, AFS 124B. Ledbetter follows the song with a message: "Now this song is composed by Huddie Ledbetter, on Angola, Camp A, under Capt. Reaux, resident of Mooringsport, king of the 12-string guitar." For a guide, see Nicholas Fournier, Todd Harvey, Bertram Lyons, and Nathan Salsburg, *Lomax Family Audio Recordings*, 1908–1991. American Folklife Center, Library of Congress.

101. *NFS*, 32

102. *NFS*, 33. The letter from Himes to JAL, February 15, 1935, begins "Huddie Ledbetter was not pardoned in Louisiana, but was released by operation of the 'good-time' laws. Note attached certificate." Briscoe.
103. *NFS*, 34, 53.
104. Marianne Fisher-Giorlando and Chris Turner-Neal, "Angola: Fact and Fiction," *64 Parishes*, https://64parishes.org/angola-fact-and-fiction. A copy of the signed commutation is in Box 12, folder 5, Killeen.
105. Act no. 311, House Bill No. 316, "AN ACT Providing for the commutation of sentence for good behavior of the convicts in the penitentiary and in the parish prisons of the State." *Acts Passed by the Legislature of the State of Louisiana at the Regular Session, begun and held in the city of Baton Rouge on the tenth day of May, 1926. Published by authority of the state.* Ramires-Jones Printing Co., Baton Rouge, LA, 1926. Hathi Trust: https://babel.hathitrust.org/cgi/pt?id=osu.32437123304947&view=1up&seq=599&q1=311.
106. R.L. Himes to Sheriff T.R. Hughes, September 28, 1934. Box 16, folder 5, Killeen.
107. Himes to JAL, February 15, 1935. Box 12, folder 3, Killeen. This is a photocopy of material from the papers of Mary Elizabeth Barnicle Cadle, Schlesinger Library, Radcliffe College, Cadle 79-M149, folder 102.
108. JAL to RTL, September 24, 1934, written on stationery of The Marshall, in Marshall, Texas, one of three hotels within the Marshall-Pethybridge Hotel Companies. Briscoe.

Chapter 2 Two Men from Texas

1. Louisiana State Penitentiary Disbursement Records, P1981-451, location 12967. Louisiana State Archives, Baton Rouge.
2. HL to JAL, July 20, 1934, Briscoe; photocopy also in Brown file. "Looking to get out every day / i hope that the record is in the governors hands / i hope you will find out just when is he going to let me go / my time is already past / the warden say he was going to see bout my time / if you want to you can com[e] back after me / if not you find out when they are going to turn me out and send me a tick[et] / send it to Mr. Himes and he will bring it and give it to [me] there / if not i will com[e] on to Austin / i wont stop no where I won't go by home ... (etc.)." *Slashes added where sentences might break.*
3. HL to JAL, August 10, 1934, Briscoe.
4. HL to JAL, September 4, 1934, Briscoe. (Lomax noted: "ans'd 9/6/1934.")
5. When he was admitted to Angola in 1930, Huddie Ledbetter named "Era Ledbetter" (Era Washington) as his wife. There is no evidence that they were married.
6. Martha Promise Ledbetter, interviewed by Elizabeth H.G. Lomax, 1950s, in Alan Lomax collection (AFC 2004/004), folder 17.07.09. This is a transcript of

the interview; the audio may no longer be available. https://crowd.loc.gov/ campaigns/alan-lomax/new-york-city-1950s.

7. Porterfield, *Last Cavalier*, 329.

8. HL to JAL, September 12, 1934, Briscoe.

9. JAL to HL, handwritten draft of telegram, undated, Briscoe.

10. JAL to RTL, September 23, 1934, Briscoe.

11. There is debate over whether his birth was in 1885 or 1888, but 1889 is the year on his 1936 Connecticut driver's license, his World War II registration card, his US Social Security card, his US passport (issued May 3, 1949), and his death certificate. The majority of these also give the date as January 20.

12. Census records give varying dates for their ages. Wesley Ledbetter is listed as ten years old in the 1870 census (Ward 1, Caddo, Louisiana; Roll: M593_508; Page: 299B). In the 1880 census, Wesley is twenty-three, Sallie is twenty, and her son Alonzo Batts is six (3rd Ward, Caddo, Louisiana; Roll: 449; Page: 211B; Enumeration District: 014). In the 1900 census, Wesley's birthdate is given as February 1855, and Sallie's as May 1853 (Justice Precinct 2, Harrison, Texas; Roll: 1643; Page: 5; Enumeration District: 0041). In the 1920 census, Wesley is listed as sixty-six years old and Sallie as fifty-two, which is impossible (Police Jury Ward 3, Caddo, Louisiana; Roll: T625_607; Page: 5B; Enumeration District: 39). Sallie Ledbetter's grave lists her birthdate as May 1859, so that is the date chosen for her, and I'm using 1858 for Wesley Ledbetter.

13. Queen Esther (Pugh) Davidson to Joni Haldeman. Joe Batts married Cora, and they had three children, Arthur, Percy, and "Little Joe."

14. Photocopy of marriage document, Box 4, folder 14, "Government Records," Killeen.

15. 1880; Census Place: 3rd Ward, Caddo, Louisiana; Roll: 449; Family History Film: 1254449; Page: 211B; Enumeration District: 014; Image: 0188.

16. Copy of document in Box 4, folder 14, Killeen. Witnessed by three people, including Joe Batts.

17. 1880 US Federal Census; 3rd Ward, Caddo, Louisiana; Roll: 449; Page: 211A; Enumeration District: 014; 1900; Census Place: Police Jury Ward 3, Caddo, Louisiana; Page: 10; Enumeration District: 0030; FHL microfilm: 1240559.

18. Queenie Davidson to Joni Haldeman.

19. Texas, US, Death Certificates, 1903–1982. In some census reports and oral histories this is written as the similar sounding "Bridge," "Burch," and "Bridges."

20. Allen and Barbara/Barbary Pugh are in the Freedmen's Bureau Records and reported at that point to have three small children. Looking at the 1870 census (1870; Census Place: Ward 1, Caddo, Louisiana; Roll: M593_508; Page: 300B), that would be Sallie's younger half-brothers Kemp, Jim, and Jackson, with George born c. 1865. The National Archives in Washington, D.C.; Washington, D.C.;

Records of the Field Offices for the State of Louisiana, Bureau of Refugees, Freedmen, and Abandoned Lands, 1863–1872; NARA Series Number: M1905; NARA Reel Number: 41; NARA Record Group Number: 105; NARA Record Group Name: Records of the Bureau of Refugees, Freedmen, and Abandoned Lands, 1861–1880; Collection Title: United States Freedmen's Bureau Labor Contracts Indenture and Apprenticeship Records 1865–1872.

21. William N. Jeter, 1870; Census Place: Ward 1, Caddo, Louisiana; Roll: M593_508; Page: 303B.

22. Monty and Marsha Brown, "Leadbelly." For several years, beginning in 2007, the Browns created a blog about Huddie Ledbetter, which can currently be found online beginning at https://leadbellyhuddie .blogspot.com/2007/09, but is no longer being maintained. Excerpt from Chapter 1, "Jeter Plantation." Huddie Ledbetter was also the subject of Monty (Phillip G.M.) Brown's M.A. thesis at Northwestern State University of Louisiana, 1989.

23. Bureau of Land Management, General Land Office Records, 1776–2015; Washington, D.C., USA, Federal Land Patents, State Volumes, certificate 16954, October 1, 1860; these are searchable records. Additional information can be found at the University of Chicago Library.

24. The correct spelling is Sims, although it is sometimes written as "Simms." He appears in the 1900 census for Harrison County (1900; Census Place: Justice Precinct 2, Harrison, Texas; Roll: 1643; Page: 5; Enumeration District: 0041), listed as having been born in 1838 in North Carolina; married for thirty-nine years to Jane, born in 1840, also in North Carolina. They had two living children and a number of adopted children. This identity is confirmed by Jane, listed as a widow in the 1910 census (1910; Census Place: Leigh, Harrison, Texas; Roll: T624_1561; Page: 10b; Enumeration District: 0035; FHL microfilm: 1375574). Sims is described in the 1870 and 1880 census records as "mulatto" (partially white), as were his children; his wife Jane is "Black" (Year: 1870; Census Place: Ward 1, Caddo, Louisiana; Roll: M593_508; Page: 301A; Year: 1880; Census Place: 3rd Ward, Caddo, Louisiana; Roll: 449; Page: 213A; Enumeration District: 014).

25. 1870; Census Place: Ward 1, Caddo, Louisiana; Roll: M593_508; Page: 303B. The Ledbetters are also in Ward 1 in 1870; both the Sims and the Ledbetters are in Ward 3 in 1880.

26. "History of Shiloh, 124 Years Old," 1996 anniversary program. Box 5, folder 9, Killeen.

27. "Henry Simms Dead," *The Marshall Messenger*, June 18, 1907, 1.

28. Box 12, folder 12, Killeen. "Four promissory notes bearing date of July 1st, 1897 – of Sixty dollars each bearing Interest at 10 pr-ct from date.// One note $60 due on

1st day of January 1898" (and then the same for 1899, 1900, and 1901 – this was written after the first two notes had been paid).

29. *NFS*, 3.

30. Arthur Mae Ledbetter and Margaret Coleman to Alan Lomax, March 23, 1935. AFC 1933/001, Writings, books, "Notes on the Songs of Huddie Ledbetter," 3/7, John A. Lomax and Alan Lomax papers. United States, 1907–1969. Manuscript/Mixed Material. www.loc.gov/item/afc1933001_ms439.

31. Deed Records of Harrison County, Texas, vol. 54, pages 521 and 587.

32. Jas Obrecht, "Lead Belly: King of the 12-String Blues." *Guitar Player* 30, no. 8 (August 1996). Obrecht notes, "Most of this article's Lead Belly quotes were transcribed from his 78s."

33. Irene Batts Campbell to Monty and Marsha Brown.

34. Viola Batts Daniels to Monty and Marsha Brown.

35. Claudia Alta "Lady Bird" Taylor Johnson (1912–2007) was born in Karnack, Texas, in Harrison County.

36. Mark Odintz, "Taylor, Thomas Jefferson II (1874–1960)." www.tshaonline.or g/handbook/entries/taylor-thomas-jefferson-ii.

37. Jan Jarboe Russell, *Lady Bird: A Biography of Mrs. Johnson.* New York: Taylor Trade Publishing, 1999, 27.

38. Irene Batts Campbell to Monty and Marsha Brown.

39. Her birth year is clearly written out in the 1900 census, enumerated in June; her age is given as ten (1900; Census Place: Justice Precinct 2, Harrison, Texas; Roll: 1643; Page: 5B; Enumeration District: 0041; FHL microfilm: 1241643).

40. Arthur Mae Ledbetter and Margaret Coleman to Alan Lomax, March 23, 1935. AFC 1933/001, Writings, books, "Notes on the Songs of Huddie Ledbetter," 3/7.

41. Kemp and Sallie were both the children of Allen Pugh, but Sallie was the daughter of Louise Birch or Bridge. The genealogy is unclear because, on Sallie's death certificate, Australia Carr wrote "Louise Birch." Queen Esther Pugh Davidson, Sallie's niece, remembered that "Uncle Ed and Aunt Ann Bridges" were somehow related to Huddie through Aunt Sallie, who was "an outside child." The 1870 census finds Louisa Bridges, born around 1836, married to Edward Bridges, born around 1824 (1870; Census Place: Ward 1, Caddo, Louisiana; Roll: M593_508; Page: 323A). If this is correct, Sallie had half-siblings on the Bridges side. The 1870 census for Shreveport (Ward 1) shows younger siblings Julius, Leona, Maria, and Henrietta, ages ten, nine, seven, and infant.

42. Viola Batts Daniels to Monty and Marsha Brown.

43. John Reynolds, notes on a conversation with Edmon Ledbetter, summer 1955. Box 5, folder 10, Killeen.

44. Irene Campbell, interview with Wyatt Moore.

45. Wolfe and Lornell, *The Life and Legend of Leadbelly*, 16.

46. Wolfe and Lornell, *The Life and Legend of Leadbelly*, 17.
47. John Cowley, "Take a Whiff on Me," *Blues & Rhythm*, No. 59, March–April 1991, 16–20; also No. 60, May 1991, 18–21.
48. Viola Batts Daniels to Monty and Marsha Brown.
49. J.L. Wilson, "Kinfolk Remember Their 'Leadbelly,'" *The Shreveport Times*, October 20, 1974, 118.
50. Arthur Mae Ledbetter and Margaret Coleman to Alan Lomax, March 23, 1935. AFC 1933/001, Writings, books, "Notes on the Songs of Huddie Ledbetter," 3/7.
51. John Reynolds, notes on a conversation with Edmon Ledbetter, summer 1955. Box 5, folder 10, Killeen.
52. Pinkie Ledbetter Williams to Kip Lornell.
53. Monty and Marsha Brown, preface to their interview with Pinkie Ledbetter Williams.
54. 1920; Census Place: Justice Precinct 2, Harrison, Texas; Roll: T625_1815; Page: 13B; Enumeration District: 48. Interview with Wyatt Moore, Box 5, folder 9, Killeen, with Aunt Mary Patterson and Irene Campbell present. Mary Patterson's older sister married Huddie's half-brother, Alonzo Batts.
55. Viola Batts Daniels to Monty and Marsha Brown.
56. Moses Asch and Alan Lomax, *The Leadbelly Songbook*. New York: Oak Publications, 1962, Foreword, 5.
57. *Ballad Hunter*, 1.
58. John Nova Lomax, "Wrestling With My Confederate Texas Heritage," *Texas Monthly*, April 16, 2015. He is quoting from a memoir by James Lomax (father of John A. Lomax), dictated to James' wife, Susan Cooper Lomax.
59. The history and landownership records for other Lomax siblings were not researched for this book.
60. 1860; Census Place: Richland, Holmes, Mississippi; Roll: M653_582; Page: 806; Family History Library Film: 803582.
61. Porterfield, *Last Cavalier*, 12–13.
62. *Ballad Hunter*, 22.
63. Alonzo Cooper, August 29, 1843–August 1, 1902. Father Charles Hooks Cooper (1809–1879); mother Ann Elizabeth Smith (1820–1867). In the 1850 census, Charles is a wealthy planter in Lowndes, Mississippi (1850; Census Place: Lowndes, Mississippi; Roll: M432_376; Page: 89A; Image: 182). Alonzo: 1900 census, living in District 0011, Justice Precinct 08, Bosque, Texas. He's a stock raiser; his oldest son is a cattle dealer.
64. Division of Diversity and Community Engagement website, University of Texas at Austin, https://diversity.utexas.edu/integration/timeline. The site mentions *Sweatt v. Painter*, a 1950 US Supreme Court decision that said qualified Black students had to be admitted to graduate study in public universities.

65. Porterfield, *Last Cavalier*, 50–51.
66. Porterfield, *Last Cavalier*, 258–259.
67. The Lomax children: Shirley (August 7, 1905), John (June 14, 1907), Alan (January 31, 1915), and Bess (January 21, 1921).
68. *Ballad Hunter*, 106.
69. Porterfield, *Last Cavalier*, 268–269.
70. *Ballad Hunter*, 106.
71. *Ballad Hunter*, 108.
72. *NFS*, 29.
73. JAL to RTL, "Wednesday" (September 26, 1934), Briscoe.
74. Queen Davidson to Monty and Marsha Brown.
75. JAL to RTL, September 26, 1934, Briscoe.
76. Paul Laurence Dunbar, "We Wear the Mask" (1909), in *The Complete Poems of Paul Laurence Dunbar*. New York: Dodd, Mead & Company, 1945, 112–113.
77. T.L. Hughes to R.L. Himes, September 26, 1934. Box 16, folder 5, Killeen.
78. *NFS*, 30.

Chapter 3 On the Road

1. JAL to RTL, September 26, 1934, Briscoe.
2. Nolan Porterfield, *Last Cavalier: The Life and Times of John A. Lomax*. Chicago: University of Illinois Press, 1996, 333.
3. See, for example, JAL to RTL, October 2, 1934, Briscoe.
4. JAL to RTL, September 24, 1934, Briscoe.
5. *NFS*, 29.
6. Viola Batts Daniels to Monty and Marsha Brown.
7. Preston Brown to Monty and Marsha Brown.
8. Walter "Brownie" McGhee to Kip Lornell.
9. JAL to RTL, September 26, 1934, Briscoe. As biographer Nolan Porterfield noted, Lomax could be careless with specifics. He seems to have started the letter "Wednesday" and picked it up later in the week to continue.
10. JAL to RTL, September 28, 1934, Briscoe.
11. *NFS*, 36.
12. *NFS*, 36.
13. Stephen Wade, *The Beautiful Music All Around Us: Field Recordings and the American Experience*. Chicago: University of Illinois Press, 2012, 49.
14. Wade, 47.
15. "Rock Island Line." See music credits for details. Recording, AFC 1935/002; Lomax also recorded the song at Cummins in 1939.
16. American Folklife Center, AFS 995B2.
17. A more detailed discussion of "Rock Island Line" can be found in Wade, *The Beautiful Music All Around Us*.

18. JAL to Strunk, October 1, 1934, AFC 1933/001: Box 1, Folder 21. Lomax, John A. Correspondence, John A. Lomax, October, John A. Lomax and Alan Lomax papers. United States, 1934. Manuscript/Mixed Material. www.loc.gov/item/afc1933001_ms021.

19. JAL to RTL, October 2, 1934, Briscoe.

20. Colin Woodward, Center for Arkansas History and Culture, "Cummins Unit." *Encyclopedia of Arkansas*, https://encyclopediaofarkansas.net/entries/cummins-unit-7607.

21. Robert Perkinson, *Texas Tough: The Rise of America's Prison Empire.* New York: Picador, 2010, 152.

22. JAL to RTL, October 2, 1934, Briscoe.

23. *NFS*, 2.

24. *NFS*, 5.

25. *NFS*, 5.

26. *NFS*, 6.

27. *NFS*, 7.

28. *NFS*, 7–8.

29. Department of Commerce and Labor, Thirteenth Census of the United States Taken in the Year 1910, Statistics for Louisiana, Washington, D.C.: Government Printing Office, 1913, 569.

30. Moses Asch and Alan Lomax, *The Leadbelly Songbook.* New York: Oak Publications, 1962, 32.

31. Cheryl H. White, "The Red-Light District in Shreveport," in Bernadette J. Palombo, Gary D. Joiner, W. Chris Hale, and Cheryl H. White, *Wicked Shreveport.* Charleston, SC: The History Press, 2012, 59–70.

32. "Mister Tom Hughes's Town." See music credits for details. Recording AFC 1933/001: Box 14, Folder 443.

33. Mister Huddie blogspot, Chapter 2: "Sukey Jump: 1889–1909."

34. Marriage record 4329, July 20, 1908, "Miss Aletta Henderson" and "Juda Ledbetter." County of Kaufman, Texas. Certified copy sent June 17, 1991 by County Clerk's office to Kip Lornell, Box 4, folder 14, Killeen. Aletha's age: 1900 census, Aletha, b. September 1890 in Texas; 1910; Census Place: Leigh, Harrison, Texas; Roll: T624_1561; Page: 13B; Enumeration District: 0035; FHL microfilm: 1375574.

35. Married in December 1907, Allen Davis. Copy of license in Cornell file, File, "Lead Belly – relatives" 1878–1996; July 27 11.27. Copy of marriage record, Box 5, folder 9, Killeen.

36. 1910; Census Place: Leigh, Harrison, Texas; Roll: T624_1561; Page: 13B; Enumeration District: 0035; FHL microfilm: 1375574.

37. The evidence for these birth dates is inconsistent, but the dates given here seem most accurate. The daughters are not mentioned in the 1910 census of

Harrison County, Texas; "Margrete," two of her sisters, and two nieces (aged eleven and seven) are living with Coleman's widowed mother. In the 1920 census, enumerated in January, Margaret (now head of household) has relocated to Dallas and is sharing a home with daughters May A. [Arthur Mae], thirteen, and Irma [Erma], twelve, and her mother. In the 1930 census, "Arthur M. Ledbetter" is listed as twenty-two years old; in the 1940 census, she's listed as twenty-six. In other words, Arthur Mae is recorded as being thirteen in January 1920 (i.e., born 1907); she's twenty-two in April 1930 (i.e., born 1908); and somehow, she's only twenty-six (four years older) in 1940. Clearly, the last census is an outlier. There is other evidence: In the fall of 1951, sixty-two-year-old Margaret Coleman helped Arthur Mae secure a belated birth certificate. On it, Coleman said that she was seventeen (and Ledbetter eighteen) when Arthur Mae was born at 6:00 a.m. on January 28, 1906. (Texas Department of Health, Bureau of Vital Statistics, vol. 27, 65; reel 1403330.) This date seems early, given the census records of 1910 and 1920, and the birthdate of her sister, Erma. Later, on Arthur Mae's death certificate, her aunt Essie erroneously gave Arthur Mae's date of birth as January 28, 1915.

38. *NFS*, 5.
39. Margaret Coleman's father, James, died sometime between 1900 and 1910.
40. Dallas, Texas, City Directory, 1912, 164.
41. Texas Department of State Health Services; Austin, Texas, USA, Death Certificates 1903–1982. In her interview, Mary Patterson remembered that there were two children, "close together," and they'd moved to Dallas. She thought "the youngest one died," although she "was a big girl" by then. Box 5, folder 9, Killeen.
42. Queenie Davidson to Joni Haldeman.
43. Irene Batts Daniels to Monty and Marsha Brown.
44. "Ain't Goin' Down to De Well No Mo'." See music credits for details.
45. William Barlow, *Looking Up at Down: The Emergence of Blues Culture*. Philadelphia: Temple University Press, 2011, 230.
46. Alan B. Govenar and Jay F. Brakefield, *Deep Ellum and Central Track: Where the Black and White Worlds of Dallas Converged*. Denton, TX: University of North Texas Press, 1998.
47. Carpenter Park, "The History of Deep Ellum." Parks for Downtown Dallas, April 22, 2019, https://parksfordowntowndallas.org/the-history-of-deep-ellum.
48. Kip Lornell, "Blind Lemon Meets Leadbelly." *Black Music Research Journal* 20, no. 1 (2000), 25–26.
49. "Silver City Bound." See music credits for details.
50. Lornell, "Blind Lemon Meets Leadbelly," 26, citing *Leadbelly's Last Session*, Smithsonian Folkways SF CD 40068/71.

51. Charles Wolfe and Kip Lornell, *The Life and Legend of Leadbelly*. New York: Da Capo Press, 1992, 45–46.
52. *Leadbelly Live!*, a recording of this Austin 1949 concert, is available commercially, aired with some songs from New York in 1947.
53. Sean Killeen, *Lead Belly Letter*, Summer 1995. Box 5, file 3, Killeen.
54. William R. MacKaye, "Esther Mae Scott dies, D.C. Singer, Composer," *The Washington Post*, October 17, 1979.
55. *NFS*, 39.
56. JAL to RTL, October 5, 1934, Briscoe.
57. JAL to RTL, October 14, 1934, Briscoe.
58. RTL to JAL, October 15, 1934, Briscoe.
59. JAL to RTL, October 17, 1934, Briscoe.

Chapter 4 1915: *The State of Texas v. Huddie Ledbetter*

1. *NFS*, 7, 10.
2. Moses Asch and Alan Lomax, *The Leadbelly Songbook*. New York: Oak Publications, 1962, 29.
3. Viola Batts Daniels to Monty and Marsha Brown.
4. *NFS*, 6–7.
5. Brandon Jett, "'Let Us Be Law Abiding Citizens': Mob Violence and the Local Response in Harrison County, Texas, 1890–1925." *East Texas Historical Journal* 54, no. 2 (2016), article 4.
6. *NFS*, 7.
7. *NFS*, 10.
8. "Shooting at Leigh," *The Marshall Messenger*, June 15, 1915, 4.
9. "Grand Jury Is Called to Meet at Marshall," *The Shreveport Times*, June 17, 1915, 2.
10. US, World War I Draft Registration Cards, 1917–1918 (database on-line). Provo, UT, United States.
11. "Railway Litigation and Grand Jury," *The Marshall Messenger*, January 18, 1915, 2.
12. "Grand Jury Meets," *The Marshall Messenger*, June 17, 1915, 3.
13. "Grand Jury Recessed," *The Marshall Messenger*, June 22, 1915, 4.
14. There is a notice of this conveyance, Box 4, folder 24, Killeen. Deed conveyed June 21, 1915; filed August 18, 1915; Book 87, page 524. A copy of the document itself is in Box 4, folder 25, Killeen.
15. Year: 1910; Census Place: Justice Precinct 4, Harrison, Texas; Roll: T624_1562; Page: 13A; Enumeration District: 0054; FHL microfilm: 1375575.
16. "Vance & Lea, Lawyers," introduced in *The Marshall Messenger* on June 5, 1915, 3. A copy of this document is in Box 12, folder 12, Killeen.
17. "Grand Jury Report Made to the Court," *The Marshall Messenger*, June 24, 1915, 6.
18. "Grand Jury Indictments," *The Marshall Messenger*, June 26, 1915, 1.
19. "Furrh to Plead Self Defense." *The Houston Post*, June 7, 1915, 1.

20. "Surrenders after Hendrix Shooting," *Fort Worth Record-Telegram,* June 6, 1915, 6.
21. "Jury Acquits Junius Furrh," *The Marshall Messenger,* April 11, 1916, 1.
22. County Clerk's office, Harrison County, Texas, in Marshall. Poor-quality copies also available in Box 12, folder 12, Killeen.
23. 1910; Census Place: Leigh, Harrison, Texas; Roll: T624_1561; Page: 12B; Enumeration District: 0035; FHL microfilm: 1375574.
24. Official Records, The District Court, *The Marshall Messenger,* December 10, 1915, 5.
25. "G.L. Huffman Succumbs at Dallas Hospital," *The Marshall News Messenger,* February 27, 1944, 3.
26. Penal Code of the State of Texas, Adopted at the Regular Session of the Thirty-Second Legislature, 1911; Chapter 4, "Unlawfully Carrying Arms," Article 475 (388), 117. For updates to the penal code as of 1915, see Hans Peter Mareus Neilsen Gammel, *The Laws of Texas, 1915–1917* [Volume 17], book, 1917; Austin, Texas. University of North Texas Libraries, The Portal to Texas History, https://texashistory.unt.edu.
27. For a discussion of race and the Second Amendment, see Carol Anderson, *The Second: Race and Guns in a Fatally Unequal America.* New York: Bloomsbury Publishing, 2021.
28. *American Ballads,* xi. John A. Lomax: "When I went first to college in Texas I carried in my trunk, along with my pistol and other implements of personal warfare, a little manuscript roll of cowboy songs."
29. "Surrenders after Hendrix Shooting: Bond of Junius Furrh Is Fixed at $10,000 Which He Furnishes," *Fort Worth Record-Telegram,* June 6, 1915, 6.
30. "Pistol Toting Arrest," *The Marshall Messenger,* September 3, 1915, 7.
31. "Official Records, County Court," *The Marshall Messenger,* September 9, 1915, 1.
32. *The Shreveport Times,* September 10, 1915, 7.
33. "Official Records, County Court," *The Marshall Messenger,* September 10, 1915, 3.
34. Criminal Docket, Case 8455, County Clerk's Office, Marshall, Texas. Photocopy in the records of Monty and Marsha Brown.
35. Gammel, *The Laws of Texas, 1915–1917* [Volume 17], 143, 140.
36. "Leaves with Prisoners," *The Shreveport Times,* September 27, 1915, 10.
37. *NFS,* 2–3.
38. Walter F. Willcox, "The Negro Population." Summary of the 1900 census, online at https://www2.census.gov/prod2/decennial/documents/03322287 no8ch1.pdf, 11.
39. J. Morgan Kousser, *Colorblind Injustice: Minority Voting Rights and the Undoing of the Second Reconstruction.* Chapel Hill: The University of North Carolina Press, 1999.
40. "On this Day – May 12, 1898: Louisiana Officially Disenfranchises Black Voters and Jurors." Equal Justice Initiative, *A History of Racial Justice,* https://calendar.eji.org/racial-injustice/may/12.

41. Randolph B. Campbell, "Population Persistence and Social Change in Nineteenth-Century Texas: Harrison County, 1850–1880." *The Journal of Southern History* 48, no. 2 (May 1982), 188.
42. Box 4, folder 24, Killeen. There is a handwritten note, Tax roll 1405780, that, in 1900, "Wes votes GOP" – but there are other errors on this handwritten page, so the facts are uncertain.
43. Randolph B. "Mike" Campbell, "Harrison County," Texas State Historical Association, www.tshaonline.org/handbook/entries/harrison-county.
44. Pete Daniel, *Dispossession: Discrimination against African American Farmers in the Age of Civil Rights.* Chapel Hill: University of North Carolina Press, 2013, 5–6.
45. D.H. Bancroft, "Sketch of the History of Oil and Gas in Caddo Parish," in Maude Hearn O'Pry, *Chronicles of Shreveport and Caddo Parish.* Shreveport, LA: Journal Printing Company, 1928, 106.
46. Vol. 61, Page 212, Deed Records, Harrison County, Texas.
47. Vol. 66, Page 288, Deed Records, Harrison County, Texas.
48. Vol. 66, Page 450, Deed Records, Harrison County, Texas.
49. Vol. 71, Page 587, Deed Records, Harrison County, Texas. Copies of some of these contracts are available in Box 4, folder 25, Killeen.
50. "Offshore Drilling History," American Oil & Gas Historical Society, https://aoghs.org/offshore-history/offshore-oil-history.
51. "Caddo Lake (Cypress River Basin)." Texas Water Development Board, www.twdb.texas.gov/surfacewater/rivers/reservoirs/caddo/index.asp.
52. "The Historic Caddo Lake Drawbridge," Mooringsport, LA: The Historic Caddo Lake Drawbridge Perpetuation Committee, 2014, www.caddolakedrawbridge.com.
53. "Oil City, Louisiana," town website, www.townofoilcity.com/history.html.
54. "H.T. Lyttleton, Retired Jurist, Taken by Death," *The Marshall News Messenger*, July 18, 1944, 1.
55. "County Courthouses Many," *Longview News-Journal*, October 10, 1971, 19.
56. "Judge Lyttleton's Handsome Gift," *The Marshall Messenger*, March 12, 1909, 7.
57. "Lyttleton Is Judge," *The Marshall Messenger*, March 14, 1911, 1.
58. Jefferson Jimplecute, "Judge Lyttleton Inspects Oilfield," *The Marshall Messenger*, October 25, 1915. His initials are miswritten as "T.W.," but other materials, including the Harrison County Historical Museum, confirm his identity.
59. This seems to be William Hugh Lane, Jr., nephew of the Hon. Walter C. Lane, although it's not certain.
60. For example, "Club Share," *The Marshall Messenger*, May 5, 1914, 3.
61. Patricia Benoit, "Automobiles Come to Texas in 1899 – and Forever Change the Culture," *Killeen Daily Herald*, August 4, 2014.

62. "Harrison County – Amending Special Road Law." HB No. 231. In Gammel, *The Laws of Texas, 1915–1917* [Volume 17, p. 25]; HB No. 231, Chapter 7, "Became a law February 16, 1915."

63. "Robert A. Hope Dies at Motel," *The Marshall News Messenger*, August 23, 1950, 1.

64. "Huffman Goes to Austin," *The Marshall Messenger*, March 2, 1915, 1.

65. "Notice to Contractors," *The Marshall Messenger*, May 13, 1915, 4.

66. For a discussion of Black women forced to serve on road crews, see Sarah Haley, *No Mercy Here: Gender, Punishment, and the Making of Jim Crow Modernity*. Chapel Hill: The University of North Carolina Press, 2016.

67. Walter Wilson, "The Chain Gang and Profit," *Harper's*, April 1933, 539–540; Frank Tannenbaum, *Darker Phases of the South*, New York: G.P. Putnam's Sons, 1924, 94–95.

68. Daniel, *Dispossession*, 5–6.

69. Charles E. Hall, "The Negro Farmer in the United States," United States Bureau of the Census, Fifteenth Census of the United States: 1930. Washington, D.C.: US Government Printing Office, 1933. 5. https://catalog.hathitrust.org/Record/000339522.

70. Hall, "The Negro Farmer in the United States," 5. Hall notes that the acreage lost by Black farmers was "slightly larger than the combined land areas of Connecticut and Rhode Island."

71. Todd Lewan and Dolores Barclay, "Torn from the Land," Associated Press, part 1 of 3, December 2, 2001; National Agricultural Statistics Service, *1982 Census of Agriculture* (Washington, D.C.: US Department of Agriculture, 1984).

72. Dolores Barclay, Todd Lewan, and Allen G. Breed, "Torn from the Land," Associated Press, part 2 of 3, December 4, 2001.

73. Dania V. Francis, Grieve Chelwa, Darrick Hamilton, Thomas W. Mitchell, Nathan A. Rosenberg, and Bryce Wilson Stucki, "The Contemporary Relevance of Historic Black Land Loss." *Human Rights Magazine* 48, no. 2 (2023), 3.

74. Personal correspondence, Michael Warwick and the author.

75. The deed of this transaction is not in the records and might not have been recorded, according to Michael Warwick, but that wouldn't be unusual. "It would have been up to Wesley Ledbetter to record the deed, traveling about 18 miles into Marshall to submit it to the county clerk's office – and assuming the deed was actually delivered to him," Warwick wrote.

76. Viola Batts Daniels and Irene Batts Campbell to Monty and Marsha Brown. Wesley Ledbetter and his family, 1920; Census Place: Police Jury Ward 3, Caddo, Louisiana; Roll: T625_607; Page: 5B; Enumeration District: 39. The remaining 38.5 acres were possibly left to the care of relatives.

77. Walter C. Lane died of appendicitis on November 24, 1918. Texas, Death Certificates, 1903–1982. There are numerous real estate transactions in the

press involving his son and widow. The suit against Wesley Ledbetter is Cause No. 3066, District Court of Harrison County, Texas: Book V, Page 584, Civil Minutes.

78. Honorable district court of Harrison County, order of sale issued February 17, 1920, Case No. 3066, File 4625-L. *William Lane and Nannie W. Lane v. Wesley Ledbetter.* A copy of this document is in Box 4, folder 26, Killeen.
79. *The Marshall Messenger,* March 4, 1920, 3. Also March 18 and March 25.
80. The deed was recorded in Vol. 116, Page 466; see Box 4, folder 24, Killeen (which lists the date as May 4, not May 6).
81. Deaths: Charles Carney, *The Marshall Messenger,* March 5, 1923, 3.
82. "Hope–Carney," *The Marshall Messenger,* March 21, 1919, 2.

Chapter 5 Frayed Nerves

1. JAL to RTL, October 20, 1934, Briscoe.
2. JAL to RTL, October 21, 1934, Briscoe.
3. JAL to Strunk, October 23, 1934, AFC 1933/001: Box 1, Folder 21.
4. "About the MLA," Modern Language Association website, www.mla.org/About-Us/About-the-MLA.
5. Nolan Porterfield, *Last Cavalier: The Life and Times of John A. Lomax.* Chicago: University of Illinois Press, 1996, 143–144.
6. John Szwed, *Alan Lomax: The Man Who Recorded the World.* New York: Viking, Penguin Group, 2010, 54.
7. "Lecturer Seeks Old Folk-Songs," *The Crimson-White,* University, Alabama, November 2, 1934, 1.
8. *NFS,* 39.
9. JAL to RTL, October 26, 1934, Briscoe.
10. *NFS,* 39.
11. "Conyers Renamed Hotel Roosevelt," *The Montgomery Advertiser,* October 6, 1933.
12. "History," Dexter Avenue King Memorial Baptist Church, https://dexterkingmemorial.org/history.
13. The Martin Luther King, Jr. Research and Education Institute, Stanford University, https://kinginstitute.stanford.edu.
14. Richard Wright, "Huddie Ledbetter, Famous Negro Folk Artist, Sings the Songs of Scottsboro and His People," *Daily Worker,* August 12, 1937.
15. "Scottsboro Boys," Smithsonian Folkways 2015 release, Catalog no. SFW40201. Produced by Jeff Place and Robert Santelli.
16. JAL to RTL, October 27, 1934, Briscoe.
17. JAL to RTL, October 28, 1934, Briscoe.
18. *NFS,* 40.
19. HL to JAL, undated on Roosevelt Hotel stationery, in Briscoe. Written on Roosevelt Hotel stationery, but Ledbetter penciled in "14 S. Decator Street."

20. *NFS*, 40.
21. *NFS*, 40–41.
22. *NFS*, 41–42. Lomax did not mention this incident in his letter to Ruby dated Tuesday, October 30, 1934.
23. "Hard Rain Drenches City," *The Montgomery Advertiser*, October 31, 1934.
24. *NFS*, 42.

Chapter 6 1918: *The State of Texas v. Walter Boyd*

1. Criminal Docket, Case 8455, County Clerk's Office, Marshall, Texas. Photocopy in the records of Monty and Marsha Brown.
2. "Trusty Connived at the Escape of Road Prisoners," *The Marshall Messenger*, February 22, 1916, 1.
3. The name "Boyd" was common in the region; it was also Aletha's mother's maiden name (Laura Boyd Henderson).
4. According to probate records, John T. Cowan was born July 5, 1847, in Buncombe County, North Carolina. He may have fought with the 4th Regiment, North Carolina Infantry, as a private in company B – see film no. M230 roll 9, US Civil War.
5. The ledger was discovered at a yard sale by DeKalb Judge Joni Haldeman, who allowed the author to borrow it.
6. 1910; Census Place: Justice Precinct 3, Bowie, Texas; Roll: T624_1534; Page: 6a; Enumeration District: 0015; FHL microfilm: 1375547.
7. Joni Haldeman notes, shared with the author.
8. 1900; Census Place: Commissioner Precinct 3, Bowie, Texas; Roll: 1613; Page: 1; Enumeration District: 0009.
9. Viola Batts Daniels and Irene Batts Campbell to Monty and Marsha Brown.
10. Margaret Cornelious to Joni Haldeman, June 7, 1991, second session.
11. Zollie Jones, 1894–1970. 1900; Census Place: Commissioner Precinct 3, Bowie, Texas; Roll: 1613; Page: 17; Enumeration District: 0009; FHL microfilm: 12416138.
12. Notes, Joni Haldeman telephone conversation with the author, January 31, 2019.
13. *NFS*, 13–14.
14. Married in 1900; Louisiana, Marriages, 1718–1925.
15. Viola Batts Daniels to Kip Lornell.
16. The 1910 census finds Stafford, age twenty-seven, living with Mary (Pig), twenty-six and Mary's daughter, Willie K., ten, in the west half of Ward 3, Caddo Parish, Louisiana. (1910; Census Place: Police Jury Ward 3, Caddo, Louisiana; Roll: T624_510; Page: 10B; Enumeration District: 0033; FHL microfilm: 1374523.)
17. Clara Boyd was using this name when she died on November 30, 1973. Presley Stafford filled out the form and listed her as married and retired. Listed date of birth was April 6, 1900. Texas, Death Certificates, 1903–1982.

18. Presley Stafford, World War II draft card, National Archives at St. Louis; St. Louis, Missouri; World War II Draft Registration Cards for Texas, 10/16/1940–03/31/1947; Record Group: Records of the Selective Service System, 147; Box: 1430.

19. 1910 census, Millie Jones, forty-two, widow. Owns farm. Seven children born, five living: Chammie (twenty-three), Minnie (seventeen), Peter (nine), Jodie (five), Henrietta (Chammie's daughter, according to Zeola Vaughn) (two). (1910; Census Place: Justice Precinct 3, Bowie, Texas; Roll: T624_1534; Page: 9a; Enumeration District: 0016; FHL microfilm: 1375547.)

20. Margaret Cornelious to Joni Haldeman.

21. *NFS*, 15.

22. Viola Batts Daniels and Irene Batt Campbell to Kip Lornell.

23. Cornelious, born in 1903, was interviewed by Joni Haldeman in June 1991, when she was eighty-eight. Her mother had known Nick Boyd and Alex Griffin (Ms. Cornelious's uncle) before joining them in the Beaver Dam area. Margaret Cornelious was not only Alex Griffin's niece; in November 1919, she married Will Stafford's brother, Richard. His first wife, Willie Kate (the daughter of Pig Stafford) died a few days after giving birth to a second daughter, Willie Ruth (March 27, 1918), and Cornelious became stepmother to her and to Acie, Willie Kate's daughter with Will Stafford.

24. Charles Wolfe and Kip Lornell, *The Life and Legend of Leadbelly*. New York: Da Capo Press, 1992, 71.

25. "Local News," *The Paris Morning News*, December 14, 1917, 5; also "Drouth [sic] and Waterways," from the *Fort Worth Star-Telegram*, reprinted in *The Houston Post*, December 1, 1917, 6.

26. H.P. Briley, foreman; filed with L.C. Lynch, Clerk of the District Court. This is from the Harrison County records materials gathered by Michael Warwick.

27. A copy of the document in this case can be found in the Sean F. Killeen Lead Belly research collection, 1885–2002, Collection Number: 6789, marked as "copied from holdings of the Texas State Archives."

28. "Jail-House Blues." See music credits for details.

29. "Capital Cases Taken up in Bowie District Court," *Four States Press and Texarkana Courier*, February 21, 1918, 8.

30. "Texas Banker Who Died Here Will Be Buried in Atlanta," *The Shreveport Journal*, December 7, 1935, 13.

31. *The Marshall Messenger*, March 5, 1923, obituary for Charles Carney, "one of the best known railroad men in the state. He is survived by his wife and one daughter, Mrs. Robert Hope; two brothers, W.H. Carney, of Memphis, Tenn. and John Carney of San Antonio, and a nephew, Judge Hugh Carney of Atlanta, Texas."

32. The shuck is Case No. 14185, "State of Texas v. Huddie Ledbetter," a copy of which was obtained by Michael Warwick from the Harrison County records. The Killeen archive holds a twenty-one-page document "The State of Texas v. Walter Boyd No. 4890," which includes Presentment of Indictment; Indictment filed 1/29/1918; Court Charges filed 2/21/1918; Defendant's exceptions to Court's Charge, filed 2/21/1918; Defendant's Special charge No. 1, Filed 2/21/1918; Judgment of the Court 2/20/1918; Defendant's Amended Motion for a new trial Filed 3/11/1918. Also the court over-ruling defendant's motion for a new trial, 3/13/1918; Sentence, 3/13/1918; Affidavit of Deputy Sheriff as to Escape of Defendant after Conviction (Henry Brooks; says escape was April 1, 1918) – sworn and subscribed 4/22/1918. Certificate that "Boyd" is confined in County Jail, 4/25/1918. Bill of costs for transcript ($8.00) Clerk's certificate re: the transcript; shuck covers. Hugh Carney is the District Attorney, from Atlanta, Texas. Mahaffey, Keeny, & Dalby are in Texarkana, Texas.
33. Texas Code of Criminal Procedure – CRIM P Art. 38.14. Testimony of accomplice. "A conviction cannot be had upon the testimony of an accomplice unless corroborated by other evidence tending to connect the defendant with the offense committed; and the corroboration is not sufficient if it merely shows the commission of the offense."
34. *The Daily Texarkanian*, February 22, 1918, 4.
35. Incognito Forensic Foundation, "The History of Forensic Ballistics – Ballistic Fingerprinting," https://ifflab.org/the-history-of-forensic-ballistics-ballistic-fingerprinting.
36. Presley Stafford, born 1915, was the son of Will Stafford and Clara Boyd (Nick Boyd's daughter); Willie Richard, born 1918, was the daughter of Richard Stafford (Will's brother) and Margaret Cornelious. Information about Presley inheriting the gun comes from Joni Haldeman's notes of a telephone conversation, June 6, 1991, with Willie Richard Stafford Wilson (1918–1999), who was then in Idabel, Oklahoma.
37. Queenie Davidson to Joni Haldeman.
38. "Jailor Brooks Overpowered: Desperate Attempt to Get Away Made by Boston Prisoners . . .," *Four States Press and Texarkana Courier*, April 2, 1918, 1; "James Mosley Is Shot; Another Negro Escapes; Two Other Negroes Caught after Breaking from County Jail," *Four States Press and Texarkana Courier*, April 2, 1918, 1.
39. Bill Kroger, "The Turning Point in Lead Belly's Life," *Texas Bar Journal*, State Bar of Texas, March 2012, 208.
40. *Southwestern Reporter*, June 5–July 10, 1918, 900. There are also references to this case in two letters from attorney A.L. Burford, in Texarkana, to John A. Lomax, February 20 and 22, 1935. The case is *Boyd v. State*, no. 5040,

reported in 203 S.W. 900. P. 28–9. Also AFC 1933/001, Writings, books, "Notes on the Songs of Huddie Ledbetter," 4/7, John A. Lomax and Alan Lomax papers. United States, 1907–1969. Manuscript/Mixed Material. www.loc.gov/item/afc1933001_ms440.

41. Sometime in the early 1990s, according to her notes, Joni Haldeman spoke with John Q. Mahaffey's son, John Q. Mahaffey, Jr. (1907–2000), a Texarkana journalist, who told her that the case had really stayed with his father, and that nobody believed Ledbetter had done it, and that someone had perhaps set him up.

42. 1920; Census Place: Justice Precinct 3, Bowie, Texas; Roll: T625_1775; Page: 10B; Enumeration District: 16. A copy of her death certificate, state file 35171, is available in Box 5, folder 41, Killeen.

43. Interviewed by Joni Haldeman, June 21, 1991.

44. Iola Boyd married Haywood Johnson (1899–1967) on March 12, 1919 (Red River County Clerk's Office; Clarksville, Texas; Red River County Marriage Records; The Book Series: MR; Volumes: P; Pages: 546).

45. Mary Patterson, interviewed by Wyatt Moore, says the same: that Aletha moved on to Kansas City.

46. Married January 1, 1922, Hardy Clemmons and Narcissa Boyd. Texas County Marriages, 1817–1965, film number 001839953.

47. Texas State Library and Archives Commission; Convict Record Ledgers; Convict Number Range: B 042021–047020; Volume Number: 1998/038–160.

48. "Texas State Penitentiaries, Description of Convict When Received," also dated June 7, 1918. Box 12, folder 13, Killeen.

49. *Annual Report, Texas State Prison System, Fiscal Year Ending December Thirty-first, Nineteen Hundred Twenty One.* By the Board of Prison Commissioners, Huntsville.

50. "N.A. Shaw Dies at Texarkana," *The Marshall News Messenger,* January 6, 1924, 1.

51. "Members of Pardon Board Have Returned after a Busy Trip," *The Austin American,* July 6, 1918, 5.

52. "The Penitentiary System," *The Houston Post,* February 3, 1918, 15.

53. *NFS*, 15.

54. Box 12, folder 11, Killeen. "Escape Record" (stamped as "reproduced from the holdings of the Texas State Archives").

55. "Goodnight, Irene." See music credits for details.

56. 1920; Census Place: Justice Precinct 3, Bowie, Texas; Roll: T625_1775; Page: 14A; Enumeration District: 15. "Walter Boyd" can also be found on this page.

57. *NFS*, 17.

58. Conduct Register, page 536, Walter Boyd; also Escape Record. Both stamped "Reproduced from the holdings of the Texas State Archives." Box 12, folder 11, Killeen.

59. Porterfield, *Last Cavalier*, 256.
60. *NFS*, 19.
61. Robert Perkinson, *Texas Tough: The Rise of America's Prison Empire*. New York: Picador, 2010, 179.
62. "Bud Russell, Who Shepherded Over 115,000 to Prison, Dies at Ranch Home," *Fort Worth Star-Telegram*, February 1, 1955, 1.
63. "The Midnight Special." See music credits for details. Each state had its own transfer man. In Tennessee, for a time, it was Joseph W. Turney, brother of Pete Turney, governor from 1893 until 1897. Turney is immortalized in songs as "Joe Turner."
64. Perkinson, *Texas Tough*, 99.
65. Perkinson, *Texas Tough*, 127.
66. "Go Down, Ol' Hannah." See music credits for details.
67. Paul M. Lucko, "Prison System," *Handbook of Texas*, Texas State Historical Association, www.tshaonline.org/handbook/entries/prison-system.
68. George W. Dixon, "The Texas Prison Camps," *The Prison Journal*, The Pennsylvania Prison Society, April 1921, 12–14.
69. Paul M. Lucko, "Texas Committee on Prisons and Prison Labor," *Handbook of Texas*, Texas State Historical Association, www.tshaonline.org/handbook/entries/texas-committee-on-prisons-and-prison-labor; Perkinson, *Texas Tough*, 181.
70. *A Summary of the Texas Prison Survey*, Vol. 1, Texas Committee on Prisons and Prison Labor, 1924.
71. Department of Commerce, Bureau of the Census, *Fourteenth Census of the United States Taken in the Year 1920*. Vol. 2, Population, General Report and Analytical Tables, Chapter 1, "Color or Race, Nativity, and Parentage"; "Table 24. – Color or Race, Nativity, and Parentage."
72. *A Summary of the Texas Prison Survey*, 11, 13.
73. Quoted in Wolfe and Lornell, *The Life and Legend of Leadbelly*, 85–86. Original not found.
74. This story is corroborated by Dorothy Scarborough, *On the Trail of Negro Folk Songs*. Cambridge, MA: Harvard University Press, 1925.
75. "Governor Pat Neff." See music credits for details.
76. Thomas E. Turner, "Pat M. Neff." The Texas Prison Politics Project at the University of Texas at Austin. https://texaspolitics.utexas.edu/educational-resources/pat-neff.
77. Perkinson, *Texas Tough*, 183–184.
78. "Negro with Foghorn Voice Sings His Way to Official Pardon," *The Marshall News Messenger*, January 24, 1925, 7. Other versions of the story can be found, including "Negro's Song Wins Pardon by Gov. Neff," *The Austin American*, January 22, 1925, 5.

NOTES TO PAGES 104–109

79. Pat Morris Neff, *The Battles of Peace.* Fort Worth: Bunker Printing and Book Company, 1925, 176–177; punctuation as in the original. A copy of the official pardon can be viewed in Box 12, folder 11, Killeen (reproduced from the Texas State Library and Archives Commission).

Chapter 7 Northern Debut

1. *NFS*, 43; letter from Scudder to JAL, October 31, 1934.
2. Martha Ledbetter to JAL, November 7, 1934, Briscoe. In the letter, she references money that Lomax sent to her from Montgomery, although not the amount.
3. HL to JAL, November 7, 1934, Briscoe.
4. *American Ballads*, xxix.
5. *American Ballads*, xxxv.
6. *American Ballads*, xxxiv.
7. Alan Calmer, "A Part of Our Folk Literature," review of *American Ballads and Folk Songs. New Masses* 13, no. 6 (November 6, 1934), 23–24. All of the 1934 volumes of *New Masses* are available online, www.marxists.org/history/usa/pubs/new-masses/1934/index.htm.
8. Lawrence Gellert, "Correspondence: Entertain Your Crowd." *New Masses* 13, no. 8 (November 20, 1934), 19.
9. Lew Ney, "Correspondence: 'A Southerner's Prejudices'" and Lawrence Gellert, "Lawrence Gellert's Reply." *New Masses* 13, no. 11 (December 11, 1934), 21–22.
10. Lew Ney to "Leadbelly," November 8, 1934, Briscoe.
11. Widen, "Leadbelly Carries On," typed manuscript, hand-dated 1942, in files shared with the author by John Reynolds, and reprinted in Tiny Robinson and John Reynolds (eds.), *Lead Belly: A Life in Pictures.* Göttingen: Steidl, 2008, 164–165.
12. "Atlanta Hotels Drop Color Line: 14 Leading Establishments Agree to Admit Negroes in Bid to Avert Protests," *The New York Times*, January 12, 1964, 1.
13. JAL to RTL, Monday, 1 p.m. (probably December 10, 1934), Briscoe.
14. JAL to RTL, December 12, 1934, Briscoe.
15. Alex Lichtenstein, "Chain Gangs, Communism, and the 'Negro Question': John L. Spivak's *Georgia N[–]*." *The Georgia Historical Quarterly* 79, no. 3 (Fall 1995), 635.
16. John L. Spivak, *Georgia N[–]*. New York: Brewer, Warren & Putnam, 192. The book was reissued with a new title, *Hard Times on a Southern Chain Gang.* Columbia, SC: University of South Carolina Press, 2012.
17. Lichtenstein, "Chain Gangs," 642.
18. JAL to RTL, December 14, 1934, Briscoe.
19. JAL to RTL, "Sunday night," December 15, 1934, Briscoe.

20. *Ballad Hunter*, 155–156.
21. JAL to RTL, December 14, 1934, Briscoe.
22. Some Texas "cedars" are actually members of the juniper family.
23. Alan Lomax Recordings of Huddie "Lead Belly" Ledbetter, 1940 (AFC 1941/ 024), Archive of Folk Culture, American Folklife Center, Library of Congress, Washington, D.C., https://lccn.loc.gov/2008700335.
24. JAL to RTL, December 26, 1934, Briscoe.
25. David and Brittany Witoslawski, Interesting Pennsylvania and Beyond (website), www.interestingpennsylvania.com/2015/06/benjamin-franklin-hotel-p hiladelphia-pa.html.
26. Kenton Jackson, "Two Time Dixie Murderer Sings Way to Freedom," *Philadelphia Independent*, January 6, 1935. The interview was conducted on December 28, 1934.
27. Nolan Porterfield, *Last Cavalier: The Life and Times of John A. Lomax*. Chicago: University of Illinois Press, 1996, 343.
28. *NFS*, 45.
29. "Murderous Minstrel," *Time*, January 14, 1935, 50.
30. JAL to RTL, December 29, 1934, Briscoe.
31. "Proceedings of the Modern Language Association of America." *PMLA* 49, Supplement (1934), 1323–1324.
32. *NFS*, 45.
33. *NFS*, 52.
34. *NFS*, 52.
35. JAL to RTL, December 29, 1934, Briscoe.
36. Porterfield, *Last Cavalier*, 347.
37. JAL to RTL, January 26, 1935, Briscoe.
38. *NFS*, 47; also JAL to RTL, January 8, 1935, Briscoe.
39. Sandra E. Garcia, "The Visionary Community of the Harlem Y.M.C.A.," *The New York Times*, October 15, 2021.
40. JAL to RTL, January 8, 1935, Briscoe.
41. Charles Wolfe and Kip Lornell, *The Life and Legend of Leadbelly*. New York: Da Capo Press, 1992, 138.
42. Advertisement, *The New York Age*, December 29, 1934, 5.
43. "Lomax Arrives with Leadbelly, Negro Minstrel," *New York Herald Tribune*, January 3, 1935.
44. *NFS*, 49.
45. JAL to RTL, January 3, 1935. Underlining in the original. Briscoe.
46. "Murderous Minstrel," *Time*, January 14, 1935, 50.
47. "Songs Win Cash and Stage Bids for Lead Belly: Lomax Protégé Heard Here in Original Compositions That Brought 2 Pardons," *New York Herald Tribune*, January 5, 1935, 8.

48. JAL to RTL, January 6, 1935, Briscoe.
49. For example, "Swamp Negro's Songs Make Hit: Broadway Wants 'Lead Belly' Who Twice Has Sung His Way Out of Prison," *The Charlotte Observer*, January 6, 1935, 16; this story or a version of it appears in the *Fort Worth Star Telegram*, January 6, 1935, 1; *The Paris News*, January 6, 1935, 1; and *The Tennessean*, January 7, 1935, 1.
50. "Lead Belly Coming to Strum at Harvard: His Guitar Gets Him In and Out of Prison and He's Not Modest," *The Boston Globe*, January 7, 1935, 5.
51. JAL to RTL, January 6, 1935, Briscoe.
52. Winston Burdett, "Lead Belly a Virtuoso of Knife and Guitar: Louisiana 'Natural' to Submit to Refining Influences of Brooklyn and Harvard," *The Brooklyn Daily Eagle*, January 17, 15.

Chapter 8 Contracts

1. "Wilton Town History," The Town of Wilton, Connecticut website, www.wilt onct.org/welcome-wilton-ct/pages/wilton-town-history.
2. Greg Bartlett, "Musicologist's 'Most Important Work' Happened Here," *The Wilton Bulletin*, July 25, 2002, 1.
3. No telephone line, according to Charles Wolfe and Kip Lornell, *The Life and Legend of Leadbelly*. New York: Da Capo Press, 1992, 148.
4. JAL to RTL, January 6, 1935, Briscoe.
5. With a controversial history of interpretation and enforcement, it was an act "to further regulate interstate commerce and foreign commerce by prohibiting the transportation therein for immoral purposes of women and girls, and for other purposes." For information on the history of the Mann Act, see David J. Langum, *Crossing over the Line*. Chicago: The University of Chicago Press, 1994.
6. JAL to RTL, January 6, 1935, Briscoe.
7. JAL to RTL, January 8, 1935, Briscoe.
8. There is a letter dated January 16, 1935 from George P. Brett at Macmillan to Mr. C.M. Leman, thanking him for his assistance. John Lomax, Brett wrote, "was afraid to send the woman [Martha Promise] the money direct, and asked whether there wasn't someone who might be persuaded to buy the ticket and give her just a little cash." George P. Brett to C.M. Leman, January 16, 1935, Macmillan Company records, New York Public Library.
9. Hirsch and Leman Company to JAL via Western Union, January 9, 1935, 11:55 p.m., Briscoe.
10. There are conflicting dates given for Martha Promise's birth, including 1904 and 1906. But the 1900 census clearly notes the presence of twin daughters, Martha and Mary, born in May 1900 to Sandy and "Dizzy" (Daisy) Primus. Source: 1900; Census Place: Police Jury Ward 3, Caddo, Louisiana; Roll: 559; Page: 7; Enumeration District: 0030; FHL microfilm: 1240559. (Her birthdate is given as June 19, 1899 in the United States Social Security Death Index.)

11. Martha Promise Ledbetter to Elizabeth Lomax.
12. Martha Promise Ledbetter to Elizabeth Lomax.
13. HL to Martha Promise, quoted in Wolfe and Lornell, *The Life and Legend of Leadbelly*, 149, citing the *New York Herald Tribune*, January 10, 1935.
14. "Marriage 'Cure' for Lead Belly: Advisor Seeks to Wean Pardoned Negro Tenor from Harlem Night Life," *Springfield* (Missouri) *Daily News*, January 10, 1935, 4.
15. Margaret Conklin to Richard Hall (for delivery to JAL), via Postal Telegraph, January 12, 1935, Briscoe.
16. *The March of Time* radio scripts 1931–1945; written on January 10, 1935 for broadcast on January 11, 1935, New-York Historical Society Digital Collections, Time, Inc. Can be viewed online: https://digitalcollections.nyhistory.org/isl andora/object/nyhs%3A208640#page/29/mode/1up. See also Raymond Fielding, *The March of Time, 1935–1951*. New York: Oxford University Press, 1978.
17. JAL to RTL, "Thursday," January 10, 1935, Briscoe.
18. "Lead Belly Sings the Blues When Bride-to-Be Misses Cue," *The Brooklyn Daily Eagle*, January 14, 1935, 16.
19. "Lead Belly Gets a Bad Scare as Fiancée Rolls In," *New York Herald Tribune*, January 14, 1935, 30.
20. Martha Promise Ledbetter to Elizabeth Lomax.
21. JAL to RTL, January 13, 1935, Briscoe. Cited in Nolan Porterfield, *Last Cavalier: The Life and Times of John A. Lomax*. Chicago: University of Illinois Press, 1996, 351.
22. "Lead Belly Sings the Blues When Bride-to-Be Misses Cue," *The Brooklyn Daily Eagle*, January 14, 1935, 16.
23. "Murderous Minstrel," *Time*, January 14, 1935.
24. William Rose Benet, "Ballad of a Ballad Singer," *The New Yorker*, January 19, 1935, 40.
25. Winston Burnett, "Lead Belly a Virtuoso of Knife and Guitar: Louisiana 'Natural' to Submit to Refining Influences of Brooklyn and Harvard," *The Daily Brooklyn Eagle*, January 17, 1935, 15.
26. Marriage license, Box 4, folder 14, Killeen.
27. The church, Norwalk's oldest African American church, was then located on Knight Street. See www.bethel-norwalkamechurch.com.
28. Martha Promise Ledbetter to Elizabeth Lomax.
29. "Lead Belly Plays at Own Wedding" (dispatch to *New York Herald Tribune*), *The Baltimore Sun*, January 22, 1935, 12.
30. "Gay Lead Belly Sings Own Wedding Tune: Resplendent in Red-Checked Suit, Minstrel of Bayous Starts Honeymoon with Recital at Tea Given Here," *The Brooklyn Daily Eagle*, January 21, 1935, 5.

31. Wolfe and Lornell, *The Life and Legend of Leadbelly*, 279. A copy of pages from Lomax's ledger are in the files of Monty and Marsha Brown.
32. "Lead Belly Plays at Own Wedding."
33. "Honey," words and music by Seymour Simons, Haven Gillespie, and Richard A. Whiting, 1928.
34. "Lead Belly Plays at Own Wedding.".
35. *The Brooklyn Daily Eagle*, January 21, 1935, 5.
36. John Szwed, *Alan Lomax: The Man Who Recorded the World*. New York: Viking, Penguin Group, 2010, 69. At various times it was also called the American Recording Company.
37. Nolan Porterfield, *Last Cavalier: The Life and Times of John A. Lomax*. Chicago: University of Illinois Press, 1996, 348.
38. JAL to RTL, January 22, 1935, Briscoe.
39. For example, a 1937 royalty agreement between ARC and The Mitchell Brothers, a trio of young white singers from rural Alabama, involved recording four songs for "ONE HALF CENT per selection." This contract, certainly like Ledbetter's, included a notice: "It is agreed and understood that the American Record Corporation shall be the sole judge as to whether or not the above named songs shall be released as recorded by Mitchell Brothers." www.themitch ellbros.com/Default.asp?ID=59&pg=ARC+Royalties+contract.
40. JAL to Edward Crane, September 5, 1935, Briscoe.
41. Biography on the website of the Country Music Hall of Fame, into which Satherly was inducted in 1971. The biography was adapted from the Country Music Hall of Fame® and Museum's *Encyclopedia of Country Music*, published by Oxford University Press.
42. Confirmed in Ed Sullivan, "Looking at Hollywood: One Man on a Movie Horse," *Chicago Tribune*, June 11, 1939, 114.
43. Wolfe and Lornell, *The Life and Legend of Leadbelly*, 157–159.
44. *NFS*, 53–54.
45. *NFS*, 54.
46. JAL to RTL, January 27, 1935, Briscoe.
47. JAL to RTL, January 26, 1935, Briscoe.
48. *NFS*, 55.
49. JAL to RTL, February 5, 1935, Briscoe.
50. JAL to RTL, February 6, 1935, Briscoe.
51. Martha Ledbetter to RTL, January 27, 1935, Briscoe.
52. HL to JAL, January 27, 1935, Briscoe.
53. A copy of the "Cameraman's Dope Sheet" can be found in Box 5, folder 24, Killeen.
54. Wolfe and Lornell, *The Life and Legend of Leadbelly*, 163.
55. JAL to RTL, January 10, 1935, Briscoe.

56. JAL to RTL, February 11, 1935, Briscoe.
57. The final filmed segment as released is *The March of Time*, vol. 1, episode 2. The series is now owned by HBO. Outtakes were viewed through Green Mountain Post Films.
58. JAL to RTL, February 11, 1935 (this may be mis-dated by Lomax; it's more likely the night of the 10th), Briscoe.

Chapter 9   1930: *The State of Louisiana v. Huddie Ledbetter*
1. See JAL to "Hymes," February 12, 1935, requesting Ledbetter's records and identifying him as "pardoned last August" and seeking "the reason for his pardon." Himes to JAL, February 15, 1935, Box 12, folder 4, Killeen.
2. Liz and Leonard Choyce to Monty Brown.
3. Max S. Lale, "Good Storytelling Prevails over Flawed Geography" (review of Frank X. Tolbert's *Tolbert's Texas*), *Fort Worth Star-Telegram*, September 18, 1983, 88. "Mrs. Winner [Mae Davis] Lane" in Caddo Lake country (born April 13, 1914, Leigh, Harrison County; died January 29, 2002, Dallas County).
4. John Ridge, "Kool Point, A 'Cool' Place on Caddo Lake," blog "Notable People, Lost Tales, and Forgotten Facts of Oil City, Louisiana," October 25, 2016. http://people-tales-facts-of-ocla.blogspot.com.
5. Born 1904, died 1995, Mary E. Pugh Carey was the daughter of Azzie Pugh and Lucy Davis Pugh. 1920; Census Place: Marshall, Harrison, Texas; Roll: T625_1815; Page: 9A; Enumeration District: 56.
6. In February 1991, Kip Lornell spoke with Lizzie Pugh Carey in Houston.
7. Azzie Pugh was the son of Kemp Pugh (Sallie's half-brother) and Mary Ledbetter Pugh (Wesley Ledbetter's sister).
8. Jessie Mae Ledbetter Bailey, born in 1927, died in California in 1990. Her death certificate listed her father as Huddie Ledbetter and her mother as Mary Elizabeth Pugh (Box 5, folder 9, Killeen). According to her daughter (Ledbetter's granddaughter), Betty Baisley-Sorrell, interviewed by Kip Lornell in 1991, Lizzie Pugh Carey was notified when Ledbetter died in 1949, and both she and Jessie Mae Ledbetter may have attended the funeral.
9. These notes, in Alan's handwriting, AFC 1933/001, Writings, books, "Notes on the Songs of Huddie Ledbetter," 4/7.
10. Adam Gussow, "'Shoot Myself a Cop': Mamie Smith's 'Crazy Blues' as Social Text." *Callaloo* 25, no. 1 (2002), 9.
11. Paige A. McGinley, *Staging the Blues: From Tent Shows to Tourism*. Durham, NC: Duke University Press Books, 2014, 33.
12. Confirmed by Moe Asch, in Israel Young, "Moses Asch: Twentieth Century Man," *Sing Out!* 26, no. 1 (1977), 3.
13. US Department of Commerce, *Abstract of the Fifteenth Census of the United States (1930)*. Washington, D.C.: United States Government Printing Office, 1933, 414.

14. Although there is no (or no longer a) marker, Wesley Ledbetter, Jr. is reportedly buried at the Shiloh Baptist Church cemetery in Mooringsport, where his parents and wife, Sallie, are also buried. Queenie Davidson to Joni Haldeman, February 22, 1991.

15. Carr was not interested in farming, but in real estate; she also managed property in Dallas owned by her father. Carr's niece, Mattie Carr Davis (1911–1999), spoke with Sean Killeen about her aunt in 1995. She remembered Australia as being enterprising and independent. Box 13, folder 40, Killeen.

16. June 21, 1915: Thirty acres to Lane & Lane (vol. 87, p. 524); December 13, 1924: Sallie Ledbetter, 9.6 acres to her daughter, Australia Carr, for $5 (vol. 134, p. 494); March 16, 1927: Australia Carr [a widow], 9.6 acres to J.J. Fugler for $100 cash; June 26, 1928, J.J. Fugler, 9.6 acres to Early and Queenie Davidson for $175 cash (vol. 152, p. 611); December 3, 1928: "Sallie Ledbetter a feme sole and Huddie Ledbetter the sole and only heirs of Wesley Ledbetter deceased," 12 acres to Early and Queenie Davidson for $228 (vol. 157, p. 198); October 26, 1929: Sallie Ledbetter, 9 acres to Australia Carr for $10 "and the further consideration of the love and affection I have for my daughter Australia Carr" (vol. 162, p. 27); November 21, 1929: Sallie Ledbetter and Huddie Ledbetter, 17.5 acres "more or less" to Australia Carr for $10 (vol. 161, p. 278); January 13, 1930: Australia Carr, 17 acres to T.J. Taylor (Lady Bird Johnson's father) and N.L. Howard for $212.50 (vol. 161, p. 279). For reasons that are not clear, these numbers add up to about 9.6 acres in excess of the 68.5-acre total. Documents via Harrison County records; copies of some of these documents are also in Box 4, folder 25, Killeen.

17. *NFS*, 23.

18. "To Enter College," *The Shreveport Journal*, September 10, 1929, 8.

19. Handwritten note, Monty thesis file – Ellet was a private, Medical Department, World War I.

20. Ellett passport application, June 1920: National Archives and Records Administration (NARA); Washington D.C.; Roll #: 1257; Volume #: Roll 1257 – Certificates: 52876–53249, 14 June 1920–15 June 1920.

21. Ellett, Year: 1900; Census Place: Police Jury Ward 3, Caddo, Louisiana; Roll: 559; Page: 11B; Enumeration District: 0030; FHL microfilm: 1240559; Ledbetter, page 11A.

22. "Charge Negro with Stabbing White Man in an Altercation: Alleged Drink-Crazed Black Starts Trouble by Dancing during Religious Service," *The Shreveport Journal*, January 16, 1930, 1. A decade later, in 1940, Dick Ellett was still working as a laborer in the oil industry and still living with his sister. He eventually moved to Waco, Texas, where he died in 1961, at the age of sixty-eight. 1940; Census Place: Mooringsport, Caddo, Louisiana; Roll: m-t0627-01385; Page: 3A; Enumeration District: 9–11.

23. "Deputies Rescue Negro from Mob at Mooringsport," *The Shreveport Times*, January 16, 1930, 1.
24. "Charge Negro with Stabbing White Man in an Altercation."
25. *NFS*, 24.
26. Frederic Ramsey, Jr., "Leadbelly, a Great Long Time," *Sing Out!* (January 1965).
27. Racial Justice Initiative, *Lynching in America: Confronting the Legacy of Racial Terror*, third edition, 2007. https://lynchinginamerica.eji.org. See pages 40–41 for county statistics.
28. "Deputies Rescue Negro From Mob at Mooringsport."
29. Maude Hearn O'Pry, *Chronicles of Shreveport and Caddo Parish*. Shreveport, LA: Journal Printing Company, 1928, 358.
30. Ambush, "Services Set," obituary, *The Monroe News-Star*, August 3, 1965, 6; glasses, http://texashideout.tripod.com/glasses.html.
31. The Caddo Parish courthouse opened in 1926; the large oaks on its grounds were donated by Judge Thomas Fletcher Bell in the 1800s. www.caddo.org/209/Historic-Courthouse. For more on Bell, see Lilla McLure and J. Ed Howe, *History of Shreveport and Shreveport Builders*. Self-published: J. Ed Howe, 1937, 245.
32. "Lal C. Blanchard Rites Thursday," *The Shreveport Journal*, 13 February 1946, 2.
33. Misspellings in the original document. Box 12, folder 4, Killeen. This document seems to be in this file because it was sent to New York City as evidence in the 1939 trial.
34. O'Pry, *Chronicles of Shreveport and Caddo Parish*, 152.
35. John E. Deacon, Attorney and Courthouse Historian, website, www.courthouses.co/us-states/h-l/louisiana/caddo-parish.
36. The monument was relocated in 2022. Alex Onken, "Preliminary Work Begins on Caddo Confederate Monument Removal," *KSLA News*, Shreveport, Louisiana, May 25, 2022.
37. Shiloh Baptist Church, est. 1871; 10395 Blanchard-Latex Road, Mooringsport 71060.
38. Docket 28640, *State of Louisiana v. Huddie Ledbetter*, assault to murder, handwritten note, Shreveport, LA. "We, the jury, find the defendant guilty as charged." Box 12, folder 4, Killeen.
39. "Judge T.F. Bell Dies; Funeral Today," *The Shreveport Times*, October 29, 1938, 1, 3.
40. Thomas Aiello, *Jim Crow's Last Stand: Nonunanimous Criminal Jury Verdicts in Louisiana*. Updated edition. Baton Rouge: Louisiana University Press, 2019, 85–86.
41. "Jurors Named for Criminal District Court," *The Shreveport Times*, February 5, 1930, 15. "The names of the following 30 veniremen were drawn by the commission and notified to appear for duty two weeks hence …."

42. "Death Takes Lawyer Here for 60 Years," *The Shreveport Times*, September 4, 1930, 1, 18.

43. "Final Rites for Attorney," *The Shreveport Times*, September 5, 1930, 11.

44. "Negro Guilty of Assault to Kill Mooringsport Man," *The Shreveport Times*, February 19, 1930, 2.

45. AFC 1933/001, Writings, books, "Notes on the Songs of Huddie Ledbetter," 7/7, John A. Lomax and Alan Lomax papers. United States, 1907–1969. Manuscript/Mixed Material. www.loc.gov/item/afc1933001_ms443.

46. 1900; Census Place: Police Jury Ward 3, Caddo, Louisiana; Roll: 559; Page: 4; Enumeration District: 0029.

47. US, World War I Draft Registration Cards, 1917–1918.

48. "Edwin T. Currie, 67, Dies in Mooringsport," *The Shreveport Journal*, September 16, 1957, 7. (There is a park in Mooringsport named for his son, Edwin Tuttle Currie.)

49. 1930; Census Place: Mooringsport, Caddo, Louisiana; Page: 7A; Enumeration District: 0007; FHL microfilm: 2340521.

50. AFC 1933/001, Writings, books, "Notes on the Songs of Huddie Ledbetter," 4/7.

51. Box 5, folder 10, Killeen.

52. AFC 1933/001, Writings, books, "Notes on the Songs of Huddie Ledbetter," 4/7.

53. "Negro Guilty of Assault to Kill Mooringsport Man."

54. AFC 1933/001, Writings, books, "Notes on the Songs of Huddie Ledbetter," 4/7.

55. Martha Promise Ledbetter to Elizabeth Lomax.

56. Box 12, folder 4, Killeen.

57. "The Shreveport Jail." See music credits for details.

Chapter 10 The End of the Road

1. John F. Worley Directory Co. Dallas City Directory, 1934–1935, book, 1934, University of North Texas Libraries, The Portal to Texas History.

2. Nolan Porterfield, *Last Cavalier: The Life and Times of John A. Lomax*. Chicago: University of Illinois Press, 1996, 356.

3. The title is actually "'Fo' Day Worry Blues," as in "before day," but "Four Day Worry Blues" is how it was released.

4. Charles Wolfe and Kip Lornell, *The Life and Legend of Leadbelly*. New York: Da Capo Press, 1992, 159.

5. JAL to RTL, March 5, 1935, Briscoe.

6. JAL to RTL, March 5, 1935, Briscoe.

7. *NFS*, 57. Police records from this date could not be located.

8. "A History of the Rochester, NY Police Department," City of Rochester website, www.cityofrochester.gov/article.aspx?id=8589935691.

9. JAL to RTL, March 6, 1935, Briscoe.

10. JAL to RTL, March 5, 1935, Briscoe.

11. *NFS*, 57.
12. JAL to RTL, October 26, 1934, Briscoe.
13. John A. Lomax, "Lead Belly and the Gulf," unpublished. Briscoe.
14. "'Lead Belly,' Sweet Singing Savage of South, Weaves Spell of Rhythm at U. of R. Concert," *Democrat and Chronicle*, March 6, 1935, 19.
15. Reed McBane, "Leadbelly Lingers in Wicked City as Lomax Leads Desperate Hunt." *The Campus* 60, no. 19 (March 8, 1935), 1.
16. JAL to RTL, March 5, 1935, Briscoe.
17. JAL to RTL, March 5, 1935, Briscoe.
18. *NFS*, 58.
19. JAL to RTL, March 6, 1935, Briscoe.
20. Wolfe and Lornell, *The Life and Legend of Leadbelly*, 172.
21. Rick Falkowski, "The Historic Colored Musicians Club," *Buffalo Spree*, November 30, 2020.
22. Wolfe and Lornell, *The Life and Legend of Leadbelly*, 172.
23. JAL to RTL, March 7, 1935, Briscoe.
24. *NFS*, 59.
25. JAL to RTL, March 7, 1935, Briscoe.
26. *NFS*, 60.
27. "City Briefs," *The Buffalo News*, March 6, 1935, 19.
28. JAL to RTL, "Monday morning," March 11, 1935, Briscoe.
29. JAL to RTL, March 17, 1935, Briscoe. Evidence that this might be true, at least partially, is that the 1930 census for Rochester includes Lewis "Lew" Stegman, a "confidential investigator." (1930; Census Place: Buffalo, Erie, New York; Page: 10A; Enumeration District: 0204; FHL microfilm: 2341166.)
30. JAL to RTL, March 17, 1935, Briscoe.
31. Rollin Palmer, "Shirley Temple in New Conquest," *Buffalo Evening News*, March 11, 1935, 7.
32. JAL to RTL, March 11, 1935, Briscoe.
33. JAL to RTL, March 6, 1935, Briscoe.
34. Lomax forbade Ledbetter to stay at the Thompson home on the return stop in Albany, but his letter to Ruby on March 6, 1935 suggests that Ledbetter had also not stayed with them on their first stop there: "Sunday night Lead Belly and I 'lay' at Albany, I in the hospitable home of Professor Thompson where after dinner Lead Belly gave us a concert . . . ."
35. Katy Thompson DePorte to Kip Lornell.
36. Katy Thompson DePorte to Kip Lornell.
37. JAL to RTL, March 12, 1935, Briscoe.
38. "Negro Who Sung Way Out of Southern Prisons Wins Two Harvard Audiences," *The Boston Globe*, March 14, 1935, 12.

39. "Lead Belly Gives Program of Songs from Negro Prisons; Songs Depict Negro as Man Apart from Religion, Simple and Natural," *Harvard Crimson*, March 14, 1935, 1, 4.

40. JAL to RTL, "Thursday morning," March 14, 1935, Briscoe.

41. JAL to RTL, March 14, 1935, Briscoe.

42. JAL to RTL, March 17, 1935, Briscoe.

43. Porterfield, *Last Cavalier*, 365.

44. Wolfe and Lornell, *The Life and Legend of Leadbelly*, 178.

45. HL to JAL, typed copy from original, 3D157, p. 68 of scan. Undated.

46. Website of the Strand Theatre, Shreveport, Louisiana, www.thestrandtheatre.com/about.

47. HL to JAL, c. March 29–30, 1935, undated typed copy of original, Briscoe.

48. Huddie and Martha Ledbetter to JAL via Western Union, April 4, 1935, Briscoe.

49. Himes to JAL, February 15, 1935, Box 12, folder 3, Killeen.

50. Handwritten draft of telegram, JAL to Sheriff Hughes, April 5, 1935. AFC 1933/001, Writings, books, "Notes on the Songs of Huddie Ledbetter," 4/7.

51. Himes to Hughes, September 28, 1934, Box 16, folder 5, Killeen.

52. W.S. Johnson to JAL, April 6, 1935, Briscoe.

53. T.R. Hughes to JAL c/o Macmillan via Western Union, April 8, 1935, Briscoe. Copies of the three checks, made out to "Huddie Ledbetter & Martha Ledbetter," are also in the file, along with a copy of the $150 replacement check.

54. W.S. Johnson to American Record Corporation, April 16, 1935, Briscoe.

55. Art Satherly to JAL, April 19, 1935, Briscoe.

56. Art Satherly to Alan Lomax, May 3, 1935, Briscoe.

57. Martha Promise Ledbetter to Elizabeth Lomax.

58. E.S. Pearce to JAL, May 7, 1935, Briscoe.

59. Brett to JAL, May 13, 1935, Briscoe.

60. JAL to George P. Brett, May 16, 1935. Lomax John (3) Part 1. Macmillan Company records, New York Public Library.

61. Martha and Huddie Ledbetter to JAL, May 22, 1935, Briscoe.

62. Huddie Ledbetter to JAL, from Dallas, June 3, 1935, Briscoe. (Martha's handwriting.)

63. Porterfield, *Last Cavalier*, 365.

64. Joseph Utay to JAL, June 11, 1935. AFC 1933/001, Writings, books, "Notes on the Songs of Huddie Ledbetter," 4/7.

65. Joseph Utay to JAL, July 8, 1935, Briscoe.

66. JAL to Edward Crane, August 28, 1935, Briscoe.

67. Edward Crane to JAL, September 12, 1935, Briscoe.

68. Dallas, Texas, September 12, 1935, Briscoe.

69. Huddie Ledbetter, John Lomax, Alan Lomax, and The Macmillan Company, agreement dated October 20, 1937. Macmillan Company records, New York Public Library.

70. It seems likely that witness Elnora Leavison, described in census records as a Black woman about forty-five years old, was the Elnora who worked as a live-out domestic in the Lomaxes' Austin home. Eckert, a white woman, was a 1934 graduate of the University of Texas at Austin and likely a friend of Alan's. (1940; Census Place: Austin, Travis, Texas; Roll: m-t0627-04148; Page: 8A; Enumeration District: 227–24.)

71. HL to JAL, December 18, 1935, Briscoe. The letter ends with a confusing reference to ten acres of land that Ledbetter might help Lomax lease, presumably as an investment.

72. HL and MPL to JAL, December 23, 1935, Briscoe.

73. Publicity photo by Otto F. Hesse (1906–1968), who immigrated to the United States in 1930 from Germany. His work and more information are available in the Archives & Manuscripts Division of the New York Public Library, https://archives.nypl.org/mus/24542.

74. "To Publish 'Lead Belly's' Songs," *The Arizona Gleam*, September 4, 1936, 5 (typos in the original).

75. John Selby, "Reading and Writing," *Big Spring* (Texas) *Daily Herald*, November 27, 1936, 9.

76. "The First Reader," *Greensboro Daily News*, November 28, 1936, 7.

77. *NFS*, x.

78. James Weldon Johnson, "'Lead Belly,' Who Sang His Way Out of Jail: The Amazing Story of a Strutting Genius of American Folk-Song," *New York Herald Tribune*, February 21, 1937.

79. Floyd J. Calvin, "Around the World," *New York Amsterdam News*, February 27, 1937, 15.

80. Letter dated May 22, 1947. Correspondence, Moses and Frances Asch Collection, 1926–1986, Series 1: Correspondence: Ledbetter, Huddie (Lead Belly), 1944–1952, Ralph Rinzler Folklife Archives and Collections, Smithsonian Institution, https://edan.si.edu/slideshow/viewer/?eadrefid=CFCH.ASCH_ref1933.

81. Box 5, folder 11, Killeen.

82. George P. Brett to JAL, March 4, 1937. Macmillan Company records, New York Public Library.

83. AFC 1933/001, Writings, books, "Notes on the Songs of Huddie Ledbetter," 1/7, John A. Lomax and Alan Lomax papers. United States, 1907–1969. Manuscript/Mixed Material. www.loc.gov/item/afc1933001_ms437.

Epilogue

1. "'Lead Belly,' Who Won International Fame as Interpreter of Negro Folk Songs, Is Dead," *The New York Times*, December 7, 1949, 36.
2. Lomax, Alan. Alan Lomax Collection, Manuscripts, Lead Belly Memorial Concert. 1950. Manuscript/Mixed Material. www.loc.gov/item/afc2004004 .ms030113.
3. Walter "Brownie" McGhee to Kip Lornell. The bracketed word "folk" is in the printed transcript.
4. AFC 1933/001, Writings, books, "Notes on the Songs of Huddie Ledbetter," 3/7.
5. Martha Promise Ledbetter to Elizabeth Lomax.
6. John Reynolds, "Cousin Edmon," edited typescript for undated 1990s contribution to the *Lead Belly Letter*, describing 1955 visit to Louisiana. Box 5, folder 10, Killeen. Also in Tiny Robinson and John Reynolds (eds.), *Lead Belly: A Life in Pictures*. Göttingen: Steidl, 2008, 27–28.
7. Lincoln Barnett, "'Ain't It a Pity?' But Lead Belly Jingles into the City," *New York Herald Tribune*, March 2, 1936.
8. "Apollo History," www.apollotheater.org/about/history.
9. "Ex-Convict Is Apollo's Star," *New York Amsterdam News*, April 4, 1936, 8.
10. "Seeing the Show with Joe Bostic," *The New York Age*, April 11, 1936, 8.
11. "Ex-Convict Is Apollo's Star," *New York Amsterdam News*, April 4, 1936, 8.
12. "After Lead Belly, Ironhead," *Time*, April 6, 1936, 42.
13. Nolan Porterfield, *Last Cavalier: The Life and Times of John A. Lomax*. Chicago: University of Illinois Press, 1996, 375.
14. Texas State Library and Archives Commission; Convict Record Ledgers; Convict Number Range: B 057101–062200; Volume Number: 1998/038–163; convict number 57469.
15. Porterfield, *Last Cavalier*, 375.
16. Porterfield, *Last Cavalier*, 535.
17. Porterfield, *Last Cavalier*, 379.
18. "Negro Loses Reprieve Won by Singing," *Sun Herald* (Mississippi), August 4, 1937, 10.
19. James Baker's death certificate (prisoner number #57469) states that his true name was Tom Barkley, the son of Tom and Ise Barkley. Texas Department of State Health Services; Austin, Texas; Texas Death Certificates, 1903–1982.
20. Box 12, folder 9, Killeen. See also Box 4, folder 2 (FBI records and correspondence, 1939–1998), Killeen.
21. Box 12, folder 9, Killeen.
22. Box 4, folder 2, Killeen. Specifies the weapon as a "Pocket knife."
23. See, for example, May 10, 1939, letter from I.W. Halpern, Court of General Sessions, Probation Department, New York, to W.H. Long, Warden, Louisiana State Penitentiary, seeking "information ... regarding the details and nature

of [Ledbetter's] offense, conduct in your institution, the date and circumstances of his release." Reply follows, "He is not wanted here" and noting the false story of the Angola pardon. Box 12, folder 4, Killeen.

24. Box 12, folder 9, Killeen. *The People of the State of New York against Huddie Ledbetter*, Thomas E. Dewey, district attorney.

25. Box 12, folder 8, Killeen. Handwritten receipt from Alex J. Reuben, "Bail and Surety Bonds": "Received from Alan Lomax . . . fifty dollars ($50.00) premium, bond of $1000. for Huddie Ledbetter, Gen. Sess., NY."

26. Charles Wolfe and Kip Lornell, *The Life and Legend of Leadbelly*. New York: Da Capo Press, 1992, 212–213.

27. Wolfe and Lornell, *The Life and Legend of Leadbelly*, 212–214.

28. Box 12, folder 9, Killeen.

29. "Jack Buitenkant, a Criminal Lawyer and Union Counsel," *The New York Times*, January 26, 1978, 22.

30. M.R. Werner, "A Reporter at Large: Ordeal by Jury," *The New Yorker*, June 10, 1939, 42–53.

31. Box 12, folder 9, Killeen.

32. "Lead Belly Takes Guitar to Jail," *The Courier Journal* (Louisville, Kentucky), May 20, 1939, 2.

33. Box 12, folder 8, Killeen.

34. Wolfe and Lornell, *The Life and Legend of Leadbelly*, 217. For more on Guthrie and Ledbetter, see Moses Asch (ed.), *American Folk Song: Woody Guthrie*. New York: Oak Publications, Inc. 1947. The Woody Guthrie material, they report, is "drawn from a pamphlet, Woody Guthrie/American Folksong, in an essay entitled 'Leadbelly Is a Hard Name,' published by Folkways owner Moe Asch and DISC company, New York, 1947, p. 9 ff."

35. New York City Municipal Archives; New York, New York; Borough: Manhattan; Indexed Number: 16.

36. Handwritten notes from Robinson, Box 5, folder 11, Killeen. Arthur Mae Ledbetter Richardson died in 1974, having been diagnosed, like her father, with ALS (Texas, Death Certificates, 1903–1982).

37. A copy of his passport lists his birthdate as January 20, 1889 and his occupation as "Concert Singer." Box 4, folder 14, Killeen.

38. See also Wolfe and Lornell, *The Life and Legend of Leadbelly*, 254.

39. United States of America, Bureau of the Census; Washington, D.C.; Seventeenth Census of the United States, 1950; Record Group: Records of the Bureau of the Census, 1790–2007; Record Group Number: 29; Residence Date: 1950; Home in 1950: New York, New York.

40. Wolfe and Lornell, *The Life and Legend of Leadbelly*, 257; Harry MacArthur, "After Dark." *The Evening Star*, Washington, D.C., August 15, 1950, B-16.

41. "About the Lomax Family Collections," The American Folklife Center website, www.loc.gov/research-centers/american-folklife-center/about-this-research-center.

42. See Lizzy Cooper Davis, "All Rights Reserved: Behind the Strategic Copyright of 'We Shall Overcome.'" *Journal of the Society for American Music* 16 (2022), 259. Additional information on efforts to ensure that Martha Ledbetter was fairly compensated can be found in Box 13, folder 5, Killeen.

Selected Sources

ARCHIVAL COLLECTIONS

American Folklife Center, Library of Congress, Washington, D.C.
Lomax Family Collections
- John A. Lomax and Alan Lomax papers, 1932–1968, AFC 1933/001
- 1933 recordings, June–July, AFC 116 and 119–121a
- 1934 recordings, June–December, AFC 1935/002
- 1935 recordings, February–March, AFC 1935/002
- John A. Lomax southern states collection, 1933–1937, AFC 1935/002
- John A. Lomax southern states collection, 1937, AFC 1937/007
- Alan Lomax recordings of Leadbelly, 1937, AFC 1937/011
- Alan Lomax miscellaneous photographs, 1935–1950, AFC 1939/021
- Alan Lomax recordings of Huddie "Lead Belly" Ledbetter, 1938, AFC 1939/023
- Writings, books, "Notes on the Songs of Huddie Ledbetter," Manuscript/Mixed Material, AFC 1933/001, MS 437–443.

Dolph Briscoe Center for American History, University of Texas, Austin
John Avery Lomax Family Papers, 1842 and 1853–1986
- John A. Lomax, Sr., Personal Family Correspondence, 3D150:
  - Ruby Terrill Lomax, September–October 1934
  - Ruby Terrill Lomax, November–December 1934
  - Ruby Terrill Lomax, January–February 1935
  - Ruby Terrill Lomax, February–March 1935
- Personal, Friends and Colleagues, Correspondence and other Materials, 3D157
  - Huddie Ledbetter, Leadbelly, 1934–1944 and undated
  - George Hertzog, 1934–1936

Cornell University Library, Cornell University, Ithaca, New York
Sean F. Killeen Lead Belly research collection, #6789, 1885–2002.

Division of Rare and Manuscript Collections
Boxes 1, 4, 5, 6, 12, 13, 16, 17, 18, 20, 24, 26
Noel Memorial Library, Louisiana State University, Shreveport
    Northwest Louisiana Archives
    • Huddie Ledbetter Collection, 1930–1995, Collection 367 (John Reynolds)
    • Kip Lornell's Research on Leadbelly, 1908–1998, Collection 520
Louisiana State Archives and Libraries, Baton Rouge
    Records of the State of Louisiana Board of Pardons and Parole
    • Louisiana State Penitentiary Records: 1866–1998; (P1980-353, vol. 32), convict #19469 (Walter Boyd) prison record
    • Pardons: 1879–1940 (P1975-21), box 11, Gov. Allen letter of commutation, July 25, 1934; (P1988-1433), box 51 location 9851, Working Papers; (P1981-451) location 12967, Louisiana State Penitentiary Disbursement Records
Texas State Library and Archives Commission, Austin
The New York Public Library, New York
    The Macmillan Company records, Manuscripts and Archives Division
    • Box 62; 3 folders, Lomax, John and Alan – *Cowboy Songs*; suit by Ledbetter against Lomax 1937
University at Albany, State University of New York, Albany
    M.E. Grenander Department of Special Collections & Archives
    • Alumni Association Records, Series 1
University of North Texas Libraries, The Portal to Texas History
Primary source materials were also accessed via Archive.org, Ancestry.com, FamilySearch.com, HathiTrust.org, and Newspapers.com.

PRIVATE COLLECTIONS

Research files, Monty and Marsha Brown, shared with the author.
Research files, Joni T. Haldeman, shared with the author.
Research files, John Reynolds, shared with the author. See also the John Reynolds Collection, Smithsonian Center for Folklife & American Culture, Washington, D.C.

INTERVIEWS AND ORAL HISTORIES

Transcripts of the interviews conducted by Kip Lornell are in the archives at Louisiana State University, Shreveport; copies of some of these interviews are also available at the Sean F. Killeen Lead Belly research collection, Cornell.

Transcripts of the interviews conducted by Monty and Marsha Brown were shared with the author; copies of some of these interviews are also available in the Killeen archive at Cornell.

Transcripts and in some cases audio of the interviews conducted by Joni Haldeman were shared with the author and will be donated to The Portal to Texas History, University of North Texas Libraries (https://texashistory.unt.edu), in a project supported by the Summerlee Foundation.

Addeo, Edmond (Interviewed by Kip Lornell), Mill Valley, California, July 4, 1990.

Baisley-Sorrell, Betty (Interviewed by Kip Lornell), Sugar Land, Texas, February 12, 1991. A copy in Killeen, Box 13, folder 14.

Brown, Preston (1896–1994) and Brown, Mary Jenkins Hayward (1909–2007) (Interviewed by Monty and Marsha Brown), March 20, 1990; (Interviewed by Monty and Marsha Brown), March 1991 – in Box 5, folder 9, Killeen (p. 112, 7/27; 11.27).

Campbell, Irene Batts (1904–2004) and Daniels, Viola Batts (1902–2001) (Interviewed by Wyatt Moore), Karnack, Texas, 1972. Box 5, folder 9, Killeen – Irene alone; (Interviewed by Monty and Marsha Brown), Marshall, Texas, March 14, 1991; (Interviewed by Kip Lornell), Marshall, Texas, November 25, 1989.

Carey, Mary E. (Lizzie) Pugh (1904–1995) (Interviewed by Kip Lornell), Houston, Texas, February 12, 1991.

Choyce, Leonard (1911–1997) and Choyce, Liz Moore (1911–2000) (Interviewed by Monty Brown), Mooringsport, Louisiana, January 8, 1991.

Cornelious, Margaret Stafford (1903–1996) (Interviewed by Joni Haldeman), June 6, 1991.

Davidson, Queen Esther Pugh (1893–1996) (Interviewed by Marsha Brown), June 7, 1990; Davidson's daughter Mary present; (Interviewed by phone by Joni Haldeman), handwritten notes, January 15, 1992.

DePorte, Katy Thompson (1921–2012) (Interviewed by Kip Lornell), Delmar, New York, December 20, 1989.

King, Taleta (Panthy) Boyd (1918–1991) (Interviewed by Joni Haldeman), June 21, 1991.

Ledbetter, Edmon (1886–1975) (Interviewed by Wyatt Moore), Longwood, Louisiana, 1971 (from Kip Lornell files).

Ledbetter, Martha Promise (1900–1968) (Interviewed by Elizabeth Goodman Lomax [Sturtz]), New York, New York, 1950s.

McGhee, Walter "Brownie" (1915–1996)
  (Interviewed by Kip Lornell), Oakland, California, October 14, 1989.
Patterson, Mary (1887–1973)
  (Interviewed by Wyatt Moore), Karnack, Texas, 1972. Box 5, folder 9, Killeen.
Vaughn, Zeola Jones (1912–2003)
  (Interviewed by Joni Haldeman), Beaver Dam, Texas, June 18, 1991.
Washington, Booker T. (born around 1903; specifics unknown)
  (Interviewed by Kip Lornell), Mooringsport, Louisiana, March 5, 1990.
Williams, Pinkie Ledbetter (1917–2000)
  (Interviewed by Monty Brown), June 8, 1990 – is in Box 5, folder 9, Killeen;
  (Interviewed by Kip Lornell), Shreveport, Louisiana, March 4, 1990.

MUSIC CREDITS

AIN'T GOIN' DOWN TO DE WELL NO MO'
Words and Music by Huddie Ledbetter
Collected and Adapted by John A. Lomax and Alan Lomax
© Copyright 1936; 1964 (Renewed) TRO/Folkways Music Publishers, Inc.,
New York and Global Jukebox Publishing
International Copyright Secured Made in U.S.A.
All Rights Reserved Including Public Performance For Profit
Used by Permission

ANGOLA BLUES (So Doggone Soon)
Words and Music by Huddie Ledbetter
Collected and Adapted by John A. Lomax and Alan Lomax
© Copyright 1936; 1964 (Renewed) TRO/Folkways Music
Publishers, Inc.,
New York and Global Jukebox Publishing
International Copyright Secured Made in U.S.A.
All Rights Reserved Including Public Performance For Profit
Used by Permission

GO DOWN, OL' HANNAH
Words and Music by Huddie Ledbetter
Collected and Adapted by John A. Lomax and Alan Lomax
© Copyright 1936; 1964 (Renewed) TRO/Folkways Music Publishers, Inc.,
New York and Global Jukebox Publishing
International Copyright Secured Made in U.S.A.
All Rights Reserved Including Public Performance For Profit
Used by Permission

GOODNIGHT, IRENE
Words and Music by Huddie Ledbetter and John A. Lomax
© Copyright 1936 (Renewed) 1950 (Renewed) Ludlow Music, Inc., New York,
NY
International Copyright Secured Made in U.S.A.
All Rights Reserved Including Public Performance For Profit
Used by Permission

GOVERNOR O.K. ALLEN
Words and Music by Huddie Ledbetter
Collected and Adapted by John A. Lomax and Alan Lomax
© Copyright 1936; 1964 (Renewed) TRO/Folkways Music Publishers, Inc.,
New York and Global Jukebox Publishing
International Copyright Secured Made in U.S.A.
All Rights Reserved Including Public Performance For Profit
Used by Permission

GOVERNOR PAT NEFF
Words and Music by Huddie Ledbetter
Collected and Adapted by John A. Lomax and Alan Lomax
© Copyright 1936; 1964 (Renewed) TRO/Folkways Music Publishers, Inc.,
New York and Global Jukebox Publishing
International Copyright Secured Made in U.S.A.
All Rights Reserved Including Public Performance For Profit
Used by Permission

JAIL-HOUSE BLUES
Words and Music by Huddie Ledbetter
Collected and Adapted by John A. Lomax and Alan Lomax
© Copyright 1936; 1964 (Renewed) TRO/Folkways Music
Publishers, Inc.,
New York and Global Jukebox Publishing
International Copyright Secured Made in U.S.A.
All Rights Reserved Including Public Performance For Profit
Used by Permission

THE MIDNIGHT SPECIAL
New Words and New Music Adaptation by Huddie Ledbetter
Collected and Adapted by John A. Lomax and Alan Lomax
© Copyright 1936; 1964 (Renewed) TRO/Folkways Music Publishers, Inc.,

Index

Acuff, Roy, 133
Addeo, Edmond, 4
Adventures of a Ballad Hunter (J. Lomax),
   10, 39, 42, 110
Aiello, Thomas, 149
"Ain't Goin' Down to de Well No Mo'," 56
"Ain't No More Cane on the Brazos," 99
Alabama, 80–85, 105
*Alan Lomax: The Man Who Recorded the
   World* (Szwed), 3
Albany, New York, 154, 158,
Allen, O.K., 22, 26, 50
American Ballads and Folk Songs (J. Lomax
   and A. Lomax), 8, 20, 42, 82, 117
   composite ballads, 107
   criticism of, 107–108
   criticism of "Negro folk songs,"
      107–108
   discussion of in *New Masses*, 107–108
   proposal to Macmillan, 42
   recording for, 1933, 42
   research travel, 20
American Bar Association, 77
American Record Corporation, 131, 141,
   153, 159, 162, 166
Angola, 8, *See* Louisiana State Penitentiary
Angola plantation, 11, 14–15
Apollo Theatre, 171
Asch, Moses, 39, 168
Associated Press, 77, 119

Association for Cultural Equity, 3
Atmore State Prison Farm, Alabama, 105
Austin, Texas, 42, 51, 105
Autry, Gene, 133–134, 144

"Backwater Blues," 59
Badger, Anthony J., 16
Baker, James, 172, 173
Baker, Jim "J.D.," 91
Baltimore Sun, The, 130, 131
Barnicle, Mary Elizabeth, 115, 130, 173
Basie, Count, 170
Baton Rouge, Louisiana, 26, 50
Battles of Peace, The (Neff), 104
Batts, Alonzo III, 88
Batts, Alonzo, Jr., 31, 34, 35, 54, 144
Batts, Joseph, 31
Batts, Queen Victoria, 34
Beals, Carlton, 147
Beaver Dam, Texas, 87, 90
   Huddie and Aletha bring Alonzo, Jr.'s
      children to live with them, 88
"Becky Dean," 38
Bell, Thomas Fletcher, 149
Bell, Thornton Fletcher, 148
Bellwood Prison Farm, Georgia, 109
Benet, William Rose, 129
"Billy in De Lowlands," 99
Birch, Louise, 32
Black Codes, 13

Black landowners, 70, 76–78
Blackmon, Douglas A., 1
Blanchard, Frank, 149
Blight, David, 14
Book of Texas, The (J. Lomax and H.Y.
   Benedict), 41
Bosque County, Texas, 40
Boston Globe, The, 119, 158–159
Bowie County, Texas, 86, 87, 88–89, 92
Boyd, Clara, 96
Boyd, Iola, 96
Boyd, Nick, 87, 90, 93, 96
Boyd, Walter (alias). *See* Ledbetter,
   Huddie
Boyd King, Taleta "Panthy," 96
Boykin, South Carolina, 110
Bradford, Perry, 143
Brakefield, Jay, 58
Brett, George P., Jr., 163, 165
Brooklyn Daily Eagle, The, 120, 129
Brown, Monty and Marsha, 32, 142, 151
Brown, Preston, 38, 47
Buffalo, New York, 156–157
Buffalo News, The, 157
"Bull Cow," 159
Bullock Museum, 5
Burnett, Winston, 129
Burns, Robert E., 109

Caddo Lake, 31, 32–33, 34, 35, 36, 70, 71,
   79, 90, 125, 142, 155
Caddo Parish, Louisiana, 31, 33, 70, 78,
   147, 151
Calloway, Cab, 115–116, 120
Calvin, Floyd J., 167
Campbell, Irene Batts, 34, 37, 38, 55, 88,
   96
   on Aletha Ledbetter's move to Kansas
   City, 96
Carby, Hazel, 6
Carleton, Mark, 15, 17

Carnegie Corporation, 20–21, 42
Carney, Charles, 79, 92
Carney, Christine, 79
Carney, Hugh, 92, 93
Carr, Australia, 32, 38, 54, 144, 162
Central State Prison Farm. *See* Imperial
   State Prison Farm
Choyce, Leonard, 142
Choyce, Liz, 142, 151
Cobain, Kurt, 1
Coleman, Bud, 37
Coleman, Margaret, 34, 36, 37, 52, 55,
   153, 171
Columbia Records, 144
Columbia University, 115
Conklin, Margaret, 115, 121, 130
Convict leasing, 1, 12–13
   in Louisiana in 1930, 15–16
   outlawed, 15
   under Samuel L. James, 15
Cooper, Alonzo (Lon), 40
"Corn Bread Rough," 61
Cornelious, Margaret, 88, 90, 91, 92, 94
Cornell University, 174
Cowan, John, 87, 88, 93
Cowboy Songs and Other Frontier Ballads (J.
   Lomax), 41, 98, 131
Cowley, John, 37
"Crazy Blues," 143
Cummins State Prison Farm, Arkansas,
   48, 51, 59
Cunningham, Edward H., 99
Currie, Edwin Tillinghast, 150

Daily Texarkanian, The, 94
Dalby, Norman L., 93
Dallas, Texas, 55, 56, 57, 162
Daniel, Pete, 20, 70, 76
Daniels, Irene Batts, 55
Daniels, Viola Batts, 34, 35, 36, 38, 47, 55,
   88, 90

Shreveport, Louisiana, 26, 29, 44, 53, 60,
105, 158, 160
Shreveport jail, 146
"Shreveport Jail" (song), 148, 149,
152
Shreveport Times, The, 64, 68, 69, 147
"Silver City Bound," 58
Sims, Henry, 33
sale of land to Ledbetters, 33–34
Sinatra, Frank, 1, 176
Slavery by Another Name (Blackmon), 1
Smith, Bessie, 59, 143
Songs of the Cattle Trail and Cow Camp (J.
Lomax), 41
South Carolina, 109–110
Spivak, John L., 109
Stafford, Mary "Pig" Walker, 90, 93
Stafford, Presley, 94
Stafford, Richard, 87
Stafford, Will, 87, 89, 90–91
Stafford, Willie Richard, 94
"Stagolee," 20
Strunk, Oliver, 50, 81, 139
Sullivan, Ed, 133
Sypert, R.L., 65, 66
Szwed, John, 3, 18, 176

"T.B. Woman Blues," 159
"Take a Whiff on Me," 9, 37
Tannenbaum, Frank, 73
Taylor, Thomas "T.J." Jefferson, 35
Texas Agricultural & Mechanical College,
41, 164
Texas Committee on Prisons and Prison
Labor "CPPL" 1924 report, 101
Texas State Penitentiary, 23
Texas v. Haddie (sic) *Ledbetter,* 67–68
Texas v. Huddie Ledbetter, case 14185, 63,
66–67
Texas v. Huddie Ledbetter, case 8455, 63,
67–68

Texas v. Walter Boyd, case 4890, 92–96
Texas v. Walter Boyd, case 4945, 95–96
Thompson, Harold, 158, 170
Time magazine, 119, 129, 172
Times-Picayune, The, 16, 22
Tucker, Arkansas, 48
Turner, R.K., 79
Tuscaloosa, Alabama, 81, 82

United Press, 119, 127, 174
University of Alabama, 80, 82
Ledbetter and Lomax perform at,
82
University of Buffalo, 156
University of Rochester, 155
University of Tennessee, 80
University of Texas, 30, 59, 67
Alan Lomax at, 42
Bess Brown Lomax at, 41
John Lomax at, 41
John Lomax employed by, 41
Ruby Terrill Lomax at, 11
Texas-Exes, 117, 131, 165
US Civil War, 1, 5, 31, 39, 157
US Constitution
13th Amendment, 12
14th Amendment, 13
15th Amendment, 13
US Department of Agriculture, 77
US Geological Survey, 72
Utay, Joseph, 164, 165, 166

Van Voorhis, Westbrook, 137
Vance, E.L., 65
Vaughn, Zeola Jones, 89, 96
Voting rights
Post Reconstruction disenfranchise-
ment, Texas and Louisiana, 70

Wade, Stephen, 48, 49
Walker, Donald, 100

239

Walker, Willie Kate, 90
Warwick, Michael, 78
Washington, Booker T., 142
Washington, D.C., 50, 110–111
Washington, Era, 143
Waskom, Asbery "Doc" and Sue Swanson, 34
Weavers, The, 176
  recording of "Goodnight, Irene," 176–177
"Western Cowboy, The," 9, 134
White, Cheryl H., 54
White, Josh, 133, 175
Widen, Luther. *See* Ney, Lew

Wilson, Clarence, 48
Wilson, E.B., 71
Wilson, Walter, 74
  description of steel cage wagon, 74
Wilton, Connecticut, 121, 153
Wolfe, Charles, 3, 10, 37, 50, 91, 134, 159, 174, 175
World War I, 66, 115, 133
World War II, 1

"Yellow Jacket," 159
YMCA, 115
"You Can't Lose-a-Me, Cholly," 9

About the Author

Sheila Curran Bernard is an associate professor in the Department of History at the University at Albany, State University of New York, and a director of its Graduate Program in Public History. An Emmy and Peabody Award-winning filmmaker, she is credited on numerous films and series, most of them carried nationally on PBS. She is the author of *Documentary Storytelling* (Focal Press/Routledge), now in its fifth edition and widely translated, and, with Kenn Rabin, *Archival Storytelling* (Focal Press/Routledge), now in its second edition. She has been honored with fellowships from MacDowell, the Virginia Center for the Creative Arts, and the New York Foundation for the Arts, and in 2021 received a Public Scholars Award from the National Endowment for the Humanities. She holds an MFA in Creative Writing from Goddard College. Please visit www.sheilacurranbernard.com.